What Every Principal Should Know About Transforming Schools

The Mandate For New School Leadership

Volume One

What Every Principal Should Know About Transforming Schools

The Mandate For New School Leadership

James Lewis, Jr., Ph.D.

Volume One

National Center to Save Our Schools
Westbury, NY 11590

Library of Congress Cataloging-ln-Publlcation Data
Lewis, James, 1930-
  What every principal should know about transforming schools :
  the mandate for new school leadership / James Lewis, Jr.
     p. cm.
     Includes bibilographIcal references (p.   ) and index.
     ISBN 0-915253-49-6
     1. School Improvement programs-Unlted States. 2. Educa-
  tional leadership-United States. 3. School principals-United
  States.
  I. Title.
LB2822.82.L48 1996
371.2 ' 00973—dc20   95-26510
                                                           CIP
  Printed in Canada

Copyright © 1996 by James Lewis Jr. PhD.

All rights reserved. No part of this publication may be reproduced or transmitted in any form or by any means, electronic or mechanical, including photocopy, recording, or any information storage or retrieval system, without permission in writing from the publisher except in the case of brief quotations embodied in critical articles and reviews. For information address The National Center To Save Our Schools, P.O. Box 948, Westbury, New York 11590.

*Dedicated to
Kelsy
Our Granddaughter
Who We love Very Dearly*

PREFACE

School transformation is a process upon which everyone within the school, meaning administrators, teachers, supervisors, directors, secretaries, clerks, maintenance and custodial people, etc., must willingly embark, knowing that the transformation is a journey requiring commitment, risk-taking, intention, and full participation.

When I speak of transformation, I am referring to direction change on all levels within the school; a change not only of how the administration within and without the school and teacher works, but also how they think, interact, participate, and perform.

When true transformation takes place, the process is not only possible but tremendously rewarding. The rewards don't only reflect higher level achievement by students, but the quality of work, the excitement of teachers and other school people, as well as a general feeling that they are not simply doing a job, but that their job and their life has more meaning. In transformational schools, teachers know they are adding value not only to their school, but to the community as well.

Principals who deeply recognize the creative potential of their teachers, who connect themselves to a vision of the future rather than to the fears from the past, and who also feel an expanded responsibility to students, teachers, and communities will stand out as the pioneers of creating transformational schools.

When change is mandated for the principal of the school and when he or she is largely inaccessible to teachers, movement in a new direction is highly unlikely. Schools don't change; teachers do. However, teachers don't change by demand regardless of who gives the orders. Teachers must be involved in the new philosophy and their participation must come originally and willingly for real transformation to take place.

What Every Principal Should Know About Transforming Schools is an exciting book because it offers tremendous insights into how principals and other school people within the school can integrate the information contained herein with effective decision-making, improved culture and climate, idea generation, and many other daily activities in school life. The processes and approaches mentioned in this book offer the transformational techniques necessary to bringing teachers and other school people together behind a common vision for connecting everyone within the school, as well as bridging any gap that may currently exist between the school and the community. It is essential in this era of expanding information that teachers not only be productive, but that they know how to ask the right questions and how to generate ideas that will lead to the transformation. Growth and diligence can only be accomplished if everyone is involved and entrusted to make creative decisions.

In these books, I have gone to great lengths to offer many new methods, practices, programs, and techniques that bring forth the creativity of everyone involved. Perhaps more important, I have explained at some depth the role the principal must take to encourage school people to grow and to explore new possibilities in transforming while the pursuit of the transformation is being made.

What Every Principal Should Know About Transforming Schools contains two volumes with six major parts and forty-two chapters of fact filled information to assist in the transformation. An outline of the content follows:

VOLUME ONE

In Part I, I discuss the characteristics of the transformational principal. This will help to differentiate the traditional principal from the transformational principal. I also cite a set of requirements to guide the efforts of the principal. Explanations are also given to change management skills necessary to create the transformational school. Finally, I describe the role of the principal as a social architect to motivate teachers and others within the school.

In Part II, I describe how to create a philosophy to guide the transformational process. I explain each component of the school philosophy. In addition, I discuss techniques to build and assess a strong and healthy school environment in order to continually improve the transformational school.

In Part III, I outline several innovative and creative practices that help to enhance the transformational school, such as empowering teachers, practicing visible management, creating an egalitarian school environment, using success emulation, and arriving at consensus.

VOLUME TWO

In Part IV, I identify how to produce creative school improvement plans in order to transform schools. I explain all of the components necessary to do so, with examples.

In Part V, I describe transformational tools to use to solve school-related problems. Some of these tools are brainstorming, nominal group progress, force-field analysis, causes-and-effect analysis, flow chart, and run chart. Some attention is also given to conducting problem-solving meetings and using design teams.

In Part VI, I highlight how the principal can improve human relations in school to make the transformation. I emphasize the appropriate communication styles, conflict resolution, motivational theories that work, team dynamics, as well as how to conduct the decision-making process.

SIX COMPELLING OBJECTIVES

My overall approach of this two-volume book is guided by six interlocking objectives:

1. To offer principals (as well as other school administrators) practical advice about how to change a traditional school to a transformational one by making comprehensive changes, not only

in the structure and environment, but also in the leadership style of the principal and the empowerment of teachers.
2. To recognize changing times and conditions necessitating school transformation.
3. To provide useful insights based upon my on-the-job experiences.
4. To cover all essential concepts for transforming schools.
5. To reflect the latest professional concepts and practices of supervisory and organizational behavior.
6. To employ the most effective principles, practices, concepts, and techniques for assisting principals to enjoy and assimilate the wealth of materials contained in these volumes.

With these six objectives serving as a foundation, What Every Principal Should Know About Transforming Schools provides an invaluable guide to a wide and diverse readership that includes:

- Practicing principals who are serious about making major improvements in their schools;
- Students training to become principals, who can profit from my forty years of experience as a teacher, principal, superintendent of schools, and professor of educational administration;
- Superintendents who will find it to be a complete reference guide for dealing with change, exploring appropriate supervisory skills, solving problems, understanding transformational practices, and handling teachers, as well as other school people; and
- Staff development directors and other human resource development professionals who can use these volumes for training purposes.

LEARNING COMPONENTS

To make this two-volume set user friendly, each chapter is arranged as follows:

1. A set of learning objectives, that illustrates and highlights major sections of each chapter and alerts you to what you should know or be able to do as a result of reading the chapter;
2. A brief discussion of the major points of the chapter in terms of what every principal should know about transforming schools;
3. A review of key points at the end of each chapter; and
4. A practical applications section is cited to enable the reader to gain some practical experience in applying the substance of the chapter in a school.

Throughout my thirty years in public education, I have written 30 books; trained nearly a million administrators, principals, teachers, other school people and parents; traveled and "creatively swiped" numerous programs and practices and improved on them; and have visited thousands of schools. My desire in this two-volume book is to share this knowledge and experience with you to help you to facilitate the transformation of your district or school

CONTENTS

Preface vii

Volume One

Part I - Managing and Supervising Teachers With a Human Touch

Chapter 1: Understanding the Requirements
for Transformational Leadership 3

Chapter 2: Changing the Role of the Principal
to Effect the Transformation 15

Chapter 3: Identifying Change-Management
Skills To Transform Schools 31

Chapter 4: Understanding the New Role of
Principal as Social Architect 51

Part II - Creating a Philosophy to Guide the Transformation Process

Chapter 5: Developing the School Mission 67

Chapter 6: Creating a School Vision 77

Chapter 7: Identifying the Shared Values of the School ... 97

Chapter 8: Building a Strong and Healthy School Culture 113

Part III - Identifying Practices That are Designed to Assist in Transforming Schools

Chapter 9: Empowering Teachers in Schools 135
Chapter 10: Managing by Walking Around 155
Chapter 11: Practicing Egalitarianism in the Schools 163
Chapter 12: Arriving at a Consensus 173
Chapter 13: Transforming Schools Through
    Success Emulation 195
Chapter 14: Transforming Schools Through
    Participative Management 217
Chapter 15: Implementing Total Quality in Schools 233
Chapter 16: Installing School-Based Management 253
Chapter 17: Inculcating Total Quality in the Classroom . . 267
Chapter 18: Implementing Outcomes-Based Education . . 297
References 317
Bibliography 323
Index 331

PART

1
Managing and Supervising the School With a Human Touch

This section of the book focuses on the management and supervisory role of the principal. Teachers of today have values and attitudes different from those of a generation ago. Therefore, principals cannot live in the past or wish for a past in which teachers were easier to deal with. The principals recognize that teachers are changing and will continue to change. Change is inevitable. The substance of this section deals with those principles necessary for principals to deal with current and future events with an emphasis on the role of the principal as a change agent who shares power with teachers, and serves as a social architect.

CHAPTER 1

Understanding the Requirements for Transformational Leadership

LEARNING OBJECTIVES

After studying and comprehending this chapter, you should be able to:

- Understand the need for transformational principals
- Identify the characteristics necessary to become a transformational principals

What Every Principal Should Know About Changing Schools Through Transformational Leadership.

Transformational leadership is about change, innovation and empowerment. This brand of leadership is a behavioral process that everyone is capable learning and managing. It is a leadership process that is methodical, consisting of purposeful and organized changes, systematic analysis, and the capacity to respect the personal needs of teachers and other school people by involving them in the change process. As such, the transformation will lead to principals who are:

- firm believers in the values of teachers and other school people;
- value-driven;
- committed to learning;
- courageous leaders;
- visionaries;
- change agents; and
- skillful in dealing with complexity, ambiguity and uncertainty.

All of these traits need to be learned in order to become a transformational leader. This chapter can help you to do so.

Why Are Transformational Principals Necessary To Change Schools?

A new generation of men and women will be needed to manage and operate America's schools as we move toward the twenty-first century. Schools with traditional structures, hierarchical levels and outmoded processes and concepts have for the most part failed to keep pace with the human outcry and demands made by teachers for more humanistic and participatory approaches. Schools may not make it into the next century with any degree of excellence unless future principals demonstrate a kind of innovative thinking similar to that echoed by the late W. Edwards Deming, Ph. D. when he said that "the destination of change is a transformation." You can either become a transformational principal or strengthen your transformational leadership skills, but either way, change is needed.

Schools in the United States are undergoing changes that are comparable to those that took place during the Renaissance Period. The Renaissance Period, which revitalized western civilization, was spurred by new ideas. These ideas were generated by champions who were tired of the status quo and who could visualize another course of action. The school management Renaissance Period, that is the process of implementing new ideas for treating the human beings in schools, will continue as long as schools exist to meet the changing needs of students as well as teachers. Transforming a school is a human drama that involves both joys and sorrows. Change can be exhilarating, but it also can be painful when teachers' personal goals are ignored. What worked in the past may have become the cause of failure in the present. This transformation also requires new vision; new frames for thinking about strategy, structure, and people. While a principal in a new school can start with a clean slate, the transformational principal must begin with what is already in place. They are social architects that must redesign an outmoded school for a new use. Transformed schools will create principals who are free in spirit, but self-disciplined in action; comfortable with uncertainty, but innovation-oriented; and empowering in their approach to improving the entire educational process.

A Transformational Principals Characteristics

Although most principals could cite numerous other characteristics of a transformational principal, the following appears to be the most important, based on the contemporary needs of teachers and other school people.

You must believe in the value of teachers and other school people.

The transformational principal is neither autocratic nor dictators. He or she is a powerful leader who is sensitive to the needs, interests, and aspirations of teachers and of other school people. They use power by empowering others to perform. Because of their people-sensitive orientation, they deal with the emotional side of teachers through the use of humor, symbolism, rewards, and punishment. They are also adroit at motivating human effort by performing as cheerleader, coach, mentor, counselor, and leader. The chief trait that seems to separate the transformational from traditional principal is that they really care for their teachers, which is demonstrated by how they treat them in and out of the school work environment. They trust their teachers by giving them power, autonomy, freedom, and entrepreneurship. And they tend to be intimate with their teachers by finding every occasion to meet with them, to eat with them, to socialize with them, and to get to know better their professional as well as their personal needs.

You must become value-driven.

All transformational principals are able to articulate a set of core values and to exhibit appropriate behavior that is congruent with their positions. Unlike the old guard of principals who let the school culture shape itself, the transformational principal pays close attention to the shared values of the school by creating exciting school environment. They do this through preaching and teaching, role modeling, empowering others, recognition and rewards; doing training and development; making appropriate structural changes; and sometimes through direct intervention. Some transformational principals may have as core values, "generating a team spirit," while others might have, "being mindful of all stakeholders of the school," and others might have "being the best in everything." Still others may have, "caring for everybody." The point here is that these super school leaders will be involved in the development of shared values, irrespective of their position in the school. This will be the backbone to their success, and it will be those values that will fuel their minds and propel their bodies in the performance of their jobs.

You must become committed to learning.

Transformational principals realize that there is no "right way" to manage all schools at all times. They understand that because management involves working with the variation in people, there is no set of rules that is appropriate when dealing with teachers. Therefore, in the absence of a single ideology of school management, their only alternative is to possess a flexible mind, an inquiring attitude, and a thirst for knowledge. To this end, they pursue several courses of action. They view their mistakes as learning opportunities and also be tolerant of others who might make mistakes when solving school-related problems. They seek to make the school a learning organization by enabling others to adopt a learning attitude in which inspiration is drawn from changes in the external environment. They allow others to apply what they have learned to improve the practices of the district. They continuously pursue learning by traveling around the nation visiting both innovative and successful schools and some of the best-run companies. They then bring back to their schools promising principles and practices. They establish training institutes or centers which foster a strong training and development program so as to prevent obsolescence from eroding the minds of the teachers. They will establish a recognition and reward program for those who take their training seriously.

You must become a courageous leader.

Transformational principals are prudent risk-takers and individuals who are not reluctant to take a stand, even if it is against the board of education or the superintendent. To be courageous means that, intellectually, transformational principals are able to gain a perspective over a situation and are able to confront reality, even if it is painful. In addition, it also means that, emotionally they are able to convey the truth to others, even though others may not want to hear it. Many of our transformational principals will risk being ridiculed because of their deviant behavior, much like our school champions who were and still are to a great extent misunderstood by our old guard of principals. Most transformational principals have healthy egos and will not need constant reinforcement to brave any future situation. Look for the transformational principal to change things even though all is going well, to share power and authority with others, to stick to their core values even during difficult times, to risk being pressured for short-range results, and to convince others above and below them to be innovative.

You must become a visionary.

Transformational principals are adroit at dreaming about the future and translating their dreams and images so that teachers can share in them. Although they are rational and analytical thinkers, they are also intuitive thinkers. They are able to conceive and help realize the vision by eventful imaging of possibilities drawn from information known about the various units and schools. They deal with symbols, create coalitions with shared understandings and build comfort levels. They keep the school on course to make the dream a reality. And, if necessary, they will also suggest areas where changes or improvements are needed.

They will even provide the date to substantiate their decision and will initiate a change effect.

You must become a change agent.

Transformational principals identify themselves as either change agents or school champions. They assume responsibility for making a difference in their school. They enable change to take place in the school in part by repetition; that is, by communicating the ideas and practices on every possible occasion, and in every conversation, presentation, and gathering of teachers. They may use catch phrases such as "fulfilling our promise of excellence, "everybody is a manager," and "we execute excellence." Transformational principals are strong prime movers of change. They often visit a particular school, ask questions about implementation, praise efforts, and help out with the change movement. They not only "talk up change," but also perform those acts that indicates a commitment to change.

You must become skillful in dealing with complexity, ambiguity and uncertainty.

All transformational principals are capable of coping with and solving problems during changing times and conditions. They are not only capable of dealing with the cultural and political side of school management, but also the technical side of school management. They have no use for "seat-of-the-pants" or "top-of-the-head" management or for principals who are reactive and let the situation or event control them. They do not let the culture of the school shape itself. The transformational principals embrace concepts, build and articulate principles and values and examine assumptions. These actions are congruent with the requirements of the complex school-related problems in an ever-changing, external school environment. The transformational principals balance their cognitive side with their emotional side when dealing with the problems they are likely to confront.

The transformational principals are beginning to emerge in America's schools. You can see it when a transformational principal challenges the intent of the board of education because it delays approving a plan for several months for no other reason than the fact that "we don't want to get into it now." You see it when a transformational principal delivers a powerful message to the school family entitled "We're On Our Way." You see it when a transformational principal develops and implements a plan for empowering teachers, and now, since it has been successful, everybody wants to be empowered. You see it when a cadre of principals postpone attending a national conference and instead visit several innovative schools in the west to gain firsthand experience on entrepreneurial skills. You see it when transformational principals brave the obstacles, deal with constraints, meet with the adversaries, and never, regardless of the consequences, give up.

Transformational principals are keenly aware that they have a long way to go. The race is by no means over. They don't know if they will win or loose, but they do know they have a good chance of making it. The transformational principals are passing several milestones. Some progress is being made, some failures are being confronted, and some surprises have been met.

All principals are asked to join the charge with the transformational principals. The old guard of principals continues to bury their heads in the sand because they are not willing to face the truth. The truth is that there is absolutely no place to hide. These principals cannot insulate themselves from the American school system's failure to offer kids the finest education possible. They first must initiate reform in terms of how to manage teachers in schools and then let them decide the best way to educate students. When teachers' higher-level needs are being fulfilled, the stage is set for them to do almost anything in terms of achieving excellence. Many principals have not yet come to grips with the plain reality_what has been can no longer be. They must deal with the past realities to move into the twenty-first century to create a vision consistent with what parents want for the future of their kids, and they must mobilize a commitment to it.

They must approach the issue of bringing reform to schools on at least two levels: 1) the school level, and 2) on an individual level.

At the school level, they need to prepare schools to engage in the struggle of reform. Each must accept the challenge regardless of position in the school. Pockets of excellence tend to be contagious if teachers who create them have the desire to continue the struggle. Their reward will not be for doing the right things, but for doing things right.

At the individual level, they need to develop the transformational leadership potential in themselves as well as in others because school and individual renewal are inextricably entwined. They must also be willing to learn to accommodate the need for change or the twenty-first century will be similar to the twentith century—but worse.

REVIEW

KEY POINTS TO REMEMBER:

- Transformational principals are tired of the status quo and can visualize another course of action far different than what schools look like today.
- Transformational principals believe in the value of teachers and other school people, are value driven, committed to learning, are courageous leaders, are visionaries, are change agents, and adept in dealing with complexity, ambiguity and uncertainty.

APPLICATION:

Based on the instrument appearing on the following pages, request that your teachers evaluate your traits and characteristics to determine the degree to which you are a transformational principal. Next, perform and score a self-assessment of your own traits and characteristics. A scale of 1 is the lowest and 5 is the highest. Use the composite score and denote your assessment in blue, beginning with item 1 extending down to item 7. Average out the teachers' assessment and extend their assessment in red from item 1 through item 7. Look at the composite instrument for large gaps between the principal's assessments and teachers assessments. Meet with your teachers, review the composite assessment, and discuss where large gaps appear. Request that they cite ideas as to what you can do to close the gaps in the composite instrument. Develop a plan to do so and schedule another meeting with them to discuss your progress.

Teachers' Assessment of Principal

Name:_____

Date:_____

School:_____

Principal:_____

Encircle the number that represents the traits and characteristics of the principal:

1. Belief in school people.   1 2 3 4 5

The principal is not an autocrat nor a dictator. He or she is a powerful leader who is sensitive to the needs, interests, and aspirations of teachers. He or she used his or her people-sensitive orientation. He or she deals with the emotional side of teachers through the use of humor, symbolism, rewards, and punishment. He or she is adroit at motivating human effort by performing as cheerleader, coach, mentor, counselor, and leader. The chief trait that seems to separate the principal from others is that he or she really cares for his or her teachers, which is demonstrated by how he or she treats them in and out of the school work environment. He or she trusts teachers by giving them autonomy, freedom, and entrepreneurship. And he or she tends to be intimate with teachers by finding every occasion to meet with them, to eat with them, to socialize with them and to get to know better their personal as well as their professional needs.

2. Value-driven.   1 2 3 4 5

The principal is able to articulate a set of core values and exhibit appropriate behavior that is congruent with his or her position. He or she pays close attention to the shared values of the school by creating exciting school environments through preaching and teaching, and by providing role modeling, empowerment of others, recognition and rewards, training and development, appropriate structural changes, and sometimes direct intervention.

3. Committed to learning.   1 2 3 4 5

The principal realizes that there is no "right way" to manage a school. He or she understands that because management involves dealing with variations in teachers, there is no set of rules that is appropriate at all times. Therefore, in the absence of a single ideology of school management, his or her only alternative is to possess a flexible mind, an inquiring attitude, and a thirst for knowledge. To this end, he or she pursues several courses of action. The principal views his or her own mistakes as learning opportunities and is tolerant of teachers who might make mistakes when solving school-related problems. He or she makes his or her school a learning entity by enabling teachers to adopt an attitude in which inspiration is drawn from changes. He or she allows teachers to apply what others have learned to improve the practices of the school. He or she continuously pursues learning by traveling around the nation visiting both innovative and successful schools and some of the best-run companies. He or she then brings back to their school promising principles and practices.

4. Courageous leader.   1   2   3   4   5

The principal is a prudent risk-taker who is not reluctant to take a stand, even if it is against the board of education or the superintendent. To be courageous means that, intellectually, the principal is able to gain a perspective over a situation and confront reality, even if it is painful. In addition, it also means that, emotionally, he or she is able to convey the truth to others, even though they may not want to hear it. The principal has a healthy ego and will not need constant reinforcement to brave any future situation. He or she changes things even though all is going well, shares power and authority with others, sticks to his or her core values even during difficult times, risks being pressured for short-range results, and encourages others to be innovative.

5. Visionary.   1   2   3   4   5

The principal is adroit at dreaming about the future and translating his or her dreams and images so that teachers can share in them. Although he or she is a rational and analytical thinker, he or she is also an intuitive thinker. He or she is able to conceive and help realize the vision by imaging eventful possibilities drawn from information known about the various units and schools that comprise the whole school organization. He or she deals with symbols, creates coalitions with shared understandings, and builds comfort levels. He or she keeps the school on course to make the dream a reality. And, if necessary, he or she also suggests areas where changes or improvements are needed. He or she even provides the data to substantiate his or her decision and will initiate a change effort.

6. Change agent. 1 2 3 4 5

The principal identifies himself or herself as either a change agent or a school champion. He or she assumes responsibility for making a difference in their school. He or she enables change to take place in his or her school, in part, by repetition; that is, by communicating the ideas and practices on every possible occasion: in every conversation, presentation, and every gathering of teachers. He or she may use catch phrases such as, "fulfilling our promise of excellence," "everybody is a manager," and, "we execute excellence." These principals are strong prime movers of change. They often visit a particular class, ask questions about implementation, praise efforts, and help out with the change movement. He or she not only "talks up" change, but also performs those acts that indicate commitment to change.

7. Skillful in dealing with complexity,
   ambiguity, and uncertainty. 1 2 3 4 5

The principal is capable of coping with and solving problems during changing times and conditions. He or she is not only capable of dealing with the cultural and political side of school management, but also the technical side. He or she has no use for "seat of the pants" or "top of the head" management or for school administrators who are reactive and let the situation or event control them. He or she does not let the culture of the school shape itself. The principal embraces concepts, builds and articulates principles and values, and examines assumptions. These actions are congruent with the requirements of the complex school-related problems in an ever-changing, external school environment. The principal balances his or her cognitive side with their emotional side when dealing with the problems.

Composite Teachers' and Principal's Self-Assessments

Name_____
Date:_____
School:_____
Principal:_____

Traits and Characteristics of an Ideal School-Based Management Principal

1. Belief in school people	1 2 3 4 5
2. Value drive	1 2 3 4 5
3. Committed to learning	1 2 3 4 5
4. Courageous Leaders	1 2 3 4 5
5. Visionary	1 2 3 4 5
6. Change Agent	1 2 3 4 5
7. Skillful in dealing with complexity, ambiguity and uncertainty	1 2 3 4 5

CHAPTER 2

Changing the Role of the Principal to Effect the Transformation

LEARNING OBJECTIVES

After studying and comprehending this chapter, you should be able to:

- Describe the various ways to change the principal's role from controlling to enabling teachers.
- Explain the essential difference between traditional and transformational principals.

What Every Principal Should Know About Changing the Role of the Principal to Effect the Transformation

It should be common knowledge that today's teachers have values and attitudes different from those of a generation ago. As a result, principals cannot live in the past or wish for a past wherein teachers were easier to deal with. Today's principals must recognize that teachers are changing and will continue to change. Change is inevitable. When teachers' values are significantly different from those of their principal, there is bound to be conflict, disagreement, and problems.

Michael Maccoby, author of *Leader*, indicates that new forms and styles of leadership are needed. He maintains that a model must be developed that will bring out the best in people, and he maintains that although a vast amount of money has been spent on management systems, those systems have not necessarily improved the production or the quality of service and cooperation. Quality and emotional climate are among the emerging values upon which systems should be built. The following traits and characteristics are necessary to meet the changing needs of teachers.

Responsibility Replaces Prerogatives

Gone are the days when principals could manage their schools by prerogatives. School-management prerogatives can be defined as rights based exclusively on authority. Whenever principals use prerogatives, they in turn evoke a requirement for teacher prerogatives. One force presents an equal but opposite force and as a result, teachers' prerogatives tend to be contrary to the mission and goals of the school. Therefore, today's principals will be self-defeating when leading by the authority of prerogatives. The divine rights of the almighty principal are being relinquished by forward-thinking principals. Experience has demonstrated that "prerogatives" kill initiative, alienate teachers, and lead to unachieved goals and objectives.

Today's prerogatives will give way to responsibility to kids, to school people, and to community people. To kids, the principal is responsible for delivering a superior education. To teachers, the principal is responsible for providing a meaningful life at work, one that will create and nurture excellence in education. And to community people, the transformational principal is responsible for maximizing return on tax dollars.

Proaction Replaces Reaction

In the past, a major portion of the principal's time was spent reacting to external stimuli, such as people, phone messages, etc., and responding to the needs of the school. Principals who are reaction-oriented forfeit their right to decide the nature of the problems in which they will be responding. Once this occurs, they being to lose control over the nature and direction of the school.

Changing the Role of the Principal to Effect the Transformation

As a result, the problems and events themselves will determine the objectives of the school, the activities to attain, them and the solutions to these problems. Because many principals in the twentieth century were reactive administrators, a number of negative consequences befell them as indicated below:

- Stability is worshipped and innovation and change is discouraged.
- Decisions are made in terms of the safety, security, and status quo.
- Decisions are made in terms of favoritism and protective trade- offs.
- Information sharing is sacred and prized.
- Power groups emerge as protective lobbies.
- Although short-range problems may be eliminated, the solutions used to alleviate them may have devastating effects on long-range results.
- School mission is displaced by the school's reaction to organizational needs, goals, and requirements.
- Principals and teachers acquire a behavior and attitude in terms of their own security, safety, and status. As a result, self-actualization of teachers, as well as students tends to become luxurious under these conditions.

If principals took time and used more effective short- and long-range planning to anticipate problems, they wouldn't need to spend an inordinate amount of time putting out fires. For example, the principal of an urban school got the board of education to approve an alternative school for problem students. Because he failed to anticipate problems in maintaining this program, he was severely admonished by the board when one of the students was molested on her way home from evening classes. As a result of this incident, he reacted by providing students with transportation to and from the program. To avoid reacting to problems, principals should not work in isolation from teachers, but with them in order to decide all of the variables that may impact the program. They can then create plans to deal with them.

The above dealt with anticipating problems on a short-range basis. In order to deal with issues and problems on a long-range basis, the principal should assist central administrators and scan the external environment of the district, paying close attention to the impact of the environment on his or her own particular school and engaging in the development of scenarios to address the various "what if..." situations. By being able to implement a contingency plan to deal with the event, he or she will not be caught by surprise or will minimize surprises. In this way, he or she is being proactive rather than reactive.

Today, the transformational principal who is proactive aligns goals, objectives, and activities of the school more directly with the purposes and mission of the district in an attempt to avoid or minimize reaction management.

Support Replaces Overseeing

Gone, too, are the days in which the principal oversees the operations of the school by evaluating, monitoring, and supervising the instructional program as well as the teachers. This overseeing behavior and attitude evokes certain assumed characteristics of teachers that were not valid in the twentieth century and certainly will not be valid during the twenty-first century. The principal assumes that it is natural for teachers to do as little as possible at work and believes that close supervision and a little fear are all that are needed for teachers to perform at an acceptable level. In his or her opinion, most teachers do not have much imagination and ingenuity and their perspectives are too limited to allow many substantive ideas and suggestions that would help move the school in a forward motion. In addition, this overseer interprets his or her role literally as "superior" and assumes that it entitles certain privileges, respect and prestige, denied to teachers. The principal also believes that if he or she asked teachers for their ideas and suggestions, it would weaken his or her position and status. The overseer also assumes that most teachers are irresponsible individuals who cannot be trusted with information and who are not able to cope with unfavorable information. The overseeing principal believes, that the more knowledge and freedom teachers are given, the more control is needed to keep them in line. Although a large number of principals are relinquishing their overseeing style of management, there still remains far too many principals who are following this mode. The needs of our teachers have changed tremendously throughout the last two centuries. Those principals who cannot alter their style to a more supportive one in the next century are doomed to fail.

Today, transformational principals demonstrate a balanced concern for the needs of their schools as well as their teachers. Their behavior reflects confidence in and respect for the ideas and suggestions of their teachers. They take time out of their busy schedule to visit each teacher daily to listen, talk, and facilitate information regarding all aspects of managing and operating the school. The transformational principals solve school-related problems by sharing information with teachers and involving them in problem-solving teams. Major decisions, in most instances, are achieved through consensus. They encourage teachers to reach out in new directions, assuming risks and learning from their mistakes. They manage by organizing their school around teams and provide the necessary time, encouragement, training, and information to enable teams to achieve success with a high degree of consensus. In addition, they become sponsors of teachers' innovations and run interference for their creative ideas. Whenever appropriate, they identify teaching and program champions and provide nurturing support, recognizing that school champions are important to the success of the school and that everything possible must be done to cherish and support them when they come out of hiding.

Change Agent Replaces Manipulator

Throughout the course of Americas history of education, whenever change had to be made in schools, principals either ignored the needs of teachers and made the change regardless of their feelings or superficially involved them in the act of change. Most of the changes that did take place in the past involved the principal obtaining the ideas and opinions of teachers and doing for the most part what he or she felt was good for the school, thereby equating what is good for the school as being good for teachers. In essence, the principal manipulated the teachers into believing that they had a voice in the change. As a result, teachers resisted being changed and did what they had to do. They either rebelled against the change or sabotaged the change.

The manipulation that the principal resorted to evoked manipulation by teachers when they played the "game" of going along with the system (change) even though they rejected, behaviorally and attitudinally, what was being done to them by the principal through the change process.

One of the roles transformational principals assume is that of a change agent. To this end, they are responsible for implementing participative management that involves teachers in identifying the need for specific school changes and planning and executing those changes. They establish teams in the school and use these teams as agents of change by acting as the "change masters." Change can be effectively carried out if it comes across as a problem-solving mode. This will require several things.

- Teaching teams must receive thorough training in such areas as problem-solving techniques, team building, group dynamics, etc.
- Teachers' teams must identify what appropriate information is needed and then collect it.
- Teaching teams must use the date to diagnose their own problems for the purpose of digesting the problem.
- Teaching teams must devise a plan of action for the implementation of change.
- Teaching teams, after a period of time, must evaluate the change and make modifications in the change if warranted.

The Differences Between the Traditional and the Transformational Principal

The following represents some essential differences in the principal's role, differences that have emerged as a result of changing times and conditions and changing needs of teachers and other school people.

Changing the Role of the Principal to Effect the Transformation

Traditional Principal	Transformational Principal
Oblivious of the role of school champions and often will punish them by bypassing them for a promotion or by admonishing them.	Supports and nurtures school champions by realizing that they personify the values of the school and are vital to its success.
Give teachers just enough information necessary to do the job.	Gives teachers access to any information desired by them.
Reach decisions either by autocratic leadership or majority rule.	Reaches decisions usually by consensus.
Infrequently meets daily with all teachers.	Meets with all teachers daily through practicing management by wandering around.
Tends to be oblivious to a school philosophy.	Very conscious of the school philosophy and performs as a culture-builder using the philosophy as a guide.
Rewards achievement and punishes failure.	Recognizes and records achievements and uses mistakes and failures as learning opportunities.
Solves school problems by isolation of teachers.	Participates with teachers in solving school problems and at times will allow them to solve school problems without direct intervention.

Traditional Principal	Transformational Principal
Seeks and uses a variety of power to make teachers perform properly.	Empowers teachers by sharing and equalizing power with them, thereby enabling them to be creative in the use of power.
Gets school work done through teachers.	Gets school work done *with* teachers.
Tends not to change even though all is not going well.	Has the courage to change things even when all is going well.
Seldom if ever trains a successor.	Installs a succession plan whereby the most promising teachers are enrolled in a formal career-path program to become a school administrator.
Tends to feel that he or she has all the answers and tells teachers what to do.	Creates a supportive school environment for teachers' personal growth.
Relies on a dysfunctional teacher-evaluation process whereby the principal observes the teacher and conducts a post-observation conference, which hardly improves teachers' performance.	Adopts peer and reverse feedback methods of teacher evaluation by which team members evaluate individual teacher's performance of the team, team leader's contributions to the team, principal's contributions to the team, team leader and the team as a whole.

Changing the Role of the Principal to Effect the Transformation

Traditional Principal	Transformational Principal
Tends to be primarily concerned with the goals of the school at the exclusion of teachers' personal goals.	Becomes a synthesizer of teacher's personal goals and school goals so that while teachers are fulfilling their personal goals, they will also fulfill school goals.
Fosters a notion that successful principals are cool, rational, and professional administrators.	Includes the notion that successful principals are obsessed with their kids, school, teachers, and other school people; that they have as much faith in their own gut feelings and intuition as they do in fact and analyses.

Visible Management (Management by Wandering Around) Replaces Secluded Management

Today's principals who think they can continue to seclude themselves from teachers are in for a rude awakening. No longer can principals spend from 50 to 70 percent of their time in the confines of their personal or main office. No longer can they limit most of their time and activities to paperwork. No longer can they eat lunch either in their private office or out in the community with other school administrators. No longer can they use their secretaries to act in their stead when dealing with either school-related or personal problems of their teachers. No longer can they resort to communicating with their teachers through memos, edicts, or the public address system. No longer can they make seat-of- the-pants or top-of-the-head decisions on matters directly affecting their teachers. And no longer can they treat their teachers as though paperwork is more important than people-work. Transformational principals practice visible management, a style of management in which they can engage in a number of varied activities that will enable them to be accessible to their teachers.

To implement visible management, transformational principals will need to institute the following activities:

- Manage by wandering around the school; connecting daily with every teacher; listening for one-minute more or less to their concerns; discussing issues and events; adjusting the process of sharing information and resolving problems.
- Have lunch-and or breakfast with individual groups and teachers on a frequent basis.
- Encourage teachers to use the district's open-door policy by discussing either school-related and/or personal matters with them or with the superintendent.
- Call teachers together periodically just to recognize and reward them when something good happens.
- Conduct informative sessions with teachers and share information regarding the performance program of the school; that is, the degree to which the school is meeting long-range goals, short-range objectives, and performance standards.
- Conduct various training services in an effort to update the skills of teachers.
- Manage by socializing. Don't just attend events, but also sponsor them on a periodic basis.

Philosophizing Replaces Administrating

Transformational principals are expected to perform less as administrators and more as philosophers. In the past, when there was an emphasis on the hard or concrete side of school management, the principal's primary role was to disperse power and authority to make things happen among school people. Today, when the emphasis will be on the soft or intangible side of school management, a principal's primary role will be to empower others to make things happen. As a result, it will be their chief responsibility to interpret the abstract principles, values, norms, and beliefs so that they become meaningful guidelines that govern human performance. You will then see a shift in management from the hard side to the soft side. Basically, this shift will require the transformational principal to perform as disciples of the superintendent, clarifying the vision of the school organization and monitoring school people as they help realize that vision, as well as helping to formulate and inculcate the philosophy to build a strong and healthy school culture.

As disciples of the superintendent, the transformational principal is committed to the future direction of the district as espoused by the vision of the superintendent. Because they have been thoroughly informed of the direction in which the district is headed, through a two-or three-day workshop conducted by the central administration team, these principals are known to thoroughly and frequently discuss and clarify with their school people where the district and school is heading and how they will get there. It will be their obligation to make certain that every grade, every team, and everybody is right on course so that the abstract vision can materialize into tangible results. Through these activities, they have subtle opportunities to articulate the vision, to evaluate the extent to which teachers are aware that the vision has been communicated throughout the school, and to do whatever it takes to guide teachers back on course if they happen to sway from the vision.

As disciples of the superintendent, transformational principals are expected to be active participants in the formulation and inculcation of the district's philosophy. First, they serve on the philosophy committee to help develop the purposes, mission, and shared values of the district. The intent of the philosophy is to arrive at a "constitution" that will guide all of the performance activities of everyone in the district. Second, they preach and teach the tenets of the philosophy in order to build a strong and healthy culture. To this end, they serve as role models, supporting the nurturing school chairpersons who personify the values of the district and school, assisting teachers whose personalities are consonant with the values of the district and school, establishing appropriate principles and practices according to the philosophy, and establishing training activities to serve as culture builders.

Cooperation Replaces Adversity

In the past, the relationship between principals and teachers' unions has traditionally been based on the assumption that the goals of the district, as represented by central school administration, are in conflict with the needs of its teachers. In fact, most union contracts between the administration and unions reflect an implied conflict of interest between the parties involved. For scores of years, school administrators assumed certain concepts or prerogatives that exploited and manipulated teachers. What ensued was a management style in which teachers were the oppressed and the school administrators the oppressors. In those states where laws were enacted, strong militant unions were organized and demanded and got what some people might call school teachers' prerogatives. As teachers' unions began to acquire more and more rights and protections, the tables turned and the teachers' union became the oppressors and the administration became the oppressed. What resulted is a school climate in which teachers' personal goals, which were subordinate to the district and school goals, became superordinate to the school organization's. Although this is a healthy sign, it did very little in terms of bringing excellence to the doors of the school.

Transformational principals and teachers' unions understand and appreciate the cycle that took place in the past and use that knowledge as a base to harmoniously co-exist and actively cooperate to attain both teachers' personal goals and school goals.

Good union-administration relations depend upon the principal's recognition of the meaning and value of the teachers' union. Today, transformational principals strive for co-existence with teachers' unions. Teachers' unions have made important improvements in the work life of teachers, and in many instances, they have made schools a better place in which to work and educate kids. If teachers were not represented by teachers' unions or someone else, many principals would "benignly neglect" their interest. Therefore, teachers' unions are important because their existence, reasonable actions, and sound policies improve the quality of work life for teachers.

Today, the teachers' unions and administration are beginning to share identical interests. Both are recognizing that without improvement in teachers' welfare, there can be no improvement or growth in the school. This is because without welfare improvements for teachers, their willingness to teach effectively will not be optimized; the quality of teaching will suffer and overall improvement in the school will be impossible to achieve. Therefore, it is beneficial to both principals and teachers' unions to cooperate and harmonize with each other. As a result, principals will begin

Changing the Role of the Principal to Effect the Transformation 27

to believe in the idea of harmony over opposition and harmony over conflict. Then the superintendent, by educating principals, unions, and teachers to appreciate the benefit of cooperation, can foster an administration-union relationship. One effective relationship that accomplishes this is when both parties have equal power and where improvement is the name of the game. When one party has power over another, it breeds a sense of arrogance and self-righteousness that will in time cause the other party to react with defiance and sometimes with destruction.

Cooperation can only replace adversity if the following takes place:

- Principals consider a strong teachers' union as an asset to the school district.
- Teachers' unions recognize that the welfare of their teachers depends upon the successful operation of the district and school.
- The teachers' union is strong, responsible, and democratic.
- Principals avoid interfering with the internal affairs of the teachers' union.
- Mutual trust and confidence exists between the teachers' union and principals.
- Negotiation tends to provide problem-solving opportunities.
- There is widespread sharing of information between principals and teachers' unions.
- There exists no serious ideological incompatibility between the parties involved.

Unions emerged as a protector of teachers or as a counter balance influence against arbitrary decisions made by principals. Therefore, the survival of teachers' unions would seem to require continued conflict between principals and teachers. However, when a school learns to negotiate peace and harmony with unions through cooperative pursuit of mutual goals, this achievement alone will not cause the demise of the unions.

People Orientation Replaces Authority Orientation

In the past, an authority-oriented management style reflected a high concern for the school or principals themselves, but little concern or respect for teachers. Principals established goals and objectives for teachers, and by not giving them the necessary information, made it impossible for them to set their own goals and objectives. The management style of principals tended to be manipulative. They proclaimed that they believed in Theory Y, which is democratic leadership or participative management, but their words were seldom supported with action. When confronted with conflict, they tended to suppress it or capitulated by trying to appease the troublemakers; thus, the problem appeared to be solved. Authority-oriented principals leave little room for mistakes, particularly those mistakes that may embarrass or take them by surprise. Whenever, something goes wrong in the school, these principals attempt to find the culprit and use an assortment of methods as punishment. Although many principals would not deliberately defend the traditional application of authority, in many ways, as a result of habit, tradition, policy, systems structures, insensitivity, and introspective myopics, many principals continue to use authority as their prime source of influencing and managing teachers.

The people-sensitive principals are characterized by being equally concerned about the goals of the school and the personal goals of teachers. They are very much conscious of the fact that the personal goals of teachers take precedence over all other goals, even those of the school. Therefore, the most important role of educational leaders is to make certain that while teachers attain their personal goals, they also fulfill the goals of the school.

Transformational principals have gained a better understanding of how they can foster the proper school environment that will enable teachers to attain their personal goals while realizing the goals of the school. One cannot be subordinate to the other; both must be mutually achieved for any semblance of excellence in education. Transformational principals usually assume the role of goal integrator, thereby embarking on people-sensitive management that enables them to propel the school in the pursuit of the transformation.

REVIEW

KEY POINTS TO REMEMBER:

Requirements needed to change the traditional principal to a transformational leader are:

- Responsibility replaces prerogatives
- Proaction replaces reaction
- Support replaces overseeing
- Change agent replaces manipulator
- Visible management replaces secluded management
- Philosophizing replaces administrating
- Cooperation replaces adversity
- People orientation replaces authority orientation

APPLICATION

- Hire a consultant or firm to conduct a survey among your teachers to determine the pros and cons of your management style. Prepare an action plan to update your management style. Discuss this plan with your consultant and make any necessary modifications. Implement the plan and have the same consultant conduct another survey in five months to assess the degree to which you have improved your management style.

- Obtain information on some of the best-run schools in the country and visit at least five of these sites. Interview various levels of teachers to gain insight into the management style of their best principals. Prepare a list of activities, principles, and practices that make them "good" administrators. Make an action plan to improve your management style by emulating, with or without changes, those activities, principles, and practices that are used by these principals.

CHAPTER 3

Identifying Change Management Skills to Transform Schools

LEARNING OBJECTIVES

After studying and comprehending this chapter, you should be able to:
- Define the term change.
- Identify the forms of resistance to change.
- Cite reasons why teachers resist change.
- Describe effective strategies for dealing with resistance.
- Explain some barriers to change.
- Describe the stages of change.
- Cite the steps for planning change.
- Discuss process skills necessary to implement change.
- Cite the characteristics of an effective principal.
- Discuss the "principal personal guarantee statement"

What Every Principal Should Know About Change Management Skills to Improve School Performance

Change has always been a disruptive force within schools. However, never before has school change been as widespread, deep, or continuous as it is today. The impact of change on teachers is often omitted. Frequently, teachers and other people within the school are neither considered nor given the opportunity to deal with the reality of change. Yet, it is these very people who will determine the ultimate success or failure of the new school. All effective schools must change in order to survive. Principals must lead the change. They must help teachers and others to survive and be productive through the change process. In order to do this, they must understand what teachers want and need in times of change. They must understand and practice the required change management skills necessary to create productive changes in school.

Defining Change

Change can be defined as a planned or unplanned response of a school to survive. This can occur as the result of individuals, team coalitions, interest groups, state departments of education, or the community as a whole. It may occur as the result of a new attitude, such as the current focus on total quality, or an idea, such as empowerment. It may be reflected in new procedures, policies, processes, or programs. It may also involve new functions and relationships. However, transformational change involves sweeping changes, not a piecemeal approach. Because change is an attitude, a state of mind, and a stance, transformational change requires transformational thinking. It's like a religion; it should embrace every fiber of your being. Because of your own commitment to transformation, you should be obsessed with the movement. You should sleep and dream about the vision: the transformational school. You should teach and preach the gospel to change by articulating the mission, vision, and shared values until they are inculcated throughout the school by your own management style. Some may call you a maniac with a vision, but you do not care. This statement attests to your strong desire to propel everyone in the school toward your quest for new and improving reality.

The Forms of Resistance to Change

Teachers react very differently to change. Some teachers easily adapt to change. Champion teachers usually become leaders driving the change process within their school. Many others resist change in one form or another. The resistance usually manifests itself in some type of negative behavior. Resistance can be placed in one of three categories: passive, aggressive, and covert.

With passive resistance:

- Either the school as a whole or a few teachers develop a school-improvement plan that no one follows.
- Teachers are trained in force-field analysis, but do not use the tools in school.
- Individuals within a team remain silent even though they disagree with other team members.

With aggressive resistance:

- Principals refuse to allow teachers to make decisions on their own.
- Principals cancel important staff development needs because he or she is too busy.
- Teachers say, "There is no reason to change; it has always been done this way."

With covert resistance:

- Some teachers try to prove that the new process or program will not work.
- Some teachers get other teachers to ignore the change.
- Teachers agree to complete action items in a team meeting, but do not follow up on them.

Why Teachers Resist Change

In order to effectively deal with resistance, it is important to understand the causes. Kotter and Schlesinger, in a 1979 *Harvard Business Review* article entitled, "Choosing Strategies for

Change," discuss the four most common reasons why teachers resist change, as follows.

1. *A desire not to lose something of value.* When change is implemented, teachers worry about potential loss. Some examples are: department chairperson may fear the loss of control or authority when a team becomes involved in the decision-making process; a new teacher may fear the loss of a job when total quality education is implemented.

2. *A misunderstanding of the change and a lack of trust.* Teachers resist change when they misunderstand the implications of the change. This most often occurs when there is a lack of trust between the principal and teachers involved in the change. When schools embark on change, they often run into resistance. The implication appears to be that the principal is trying to get "something for nothing" out of the teachers.

3. *A belief that the change does not make sense for the school* . Individual teachers may resist change because they assess the situation differently from the principal. A team that makes a recommendation to the principal may find resistance because the team is working with different or incomplete information. This would lead to a difference in the way the situation is analyzed, and, therefore, resistance to change would arise.

4. *A low tolerance for change.* Teachers also resist change because they fear they will be unable to adapt to the change. The autocratic principal who now has to act as the facilitator/coach of his or her team may feel threatened by the new skills and behaviors that will be required of him or her.

Some Effective Strategies for Dealing With Resistance

Change is not likely to occur without some resistance. The following are some strategies for dealing with resistance:

Active listening and Emotional Support

The first step in dealing with resistance is to recognize it. It is impossible to resolve resistance successfully without dealing with human emotions. Teachers need to feel understood. Active listening enables the principal to listen for feelings as well as for facts.

Once you recognize and understand the resistance, you need to get it out in the open. This is most effectively done through verbal communication. Let teachers vent their emotions (anger, frustration, trepidation) and talk about their feelings. Give emotional support by letting them know their feelings are valid. Then help them understand that it is their resistance (passive, aggressive, covert) that is slowing down the change process. Determine actions for new behaviors/outcomes with them, and help them to solve problems and set personal goals. This can be done in the form of one-on-one counseling sessions or meetings with groups or teams. The key is getting teachers to take accountability for change rather than to resist it.

Communication and Training

When teachers know beforehand that change is coming and fully understand why it must happen, their resistance will be decreased. It is also important that teachers know what their part in the change will be and are trained and prepared for it. Formal training in the use of quality tools as well as skills training (i.e., communication, facilitation/coaching, team building) can be beneficial. Individual coaching is an excellent approach that can help overcome the resistance to change.

Teacher Participation and Involvement

Teachers don't resist change, they resist being changed. For a decision or course of action to be effective, teachers must "buy-in." When individual teachers are a part of the decision-making process, they feel important and much more accepting of change. They will be resistant if they are not involved in areas in which they have control.

Steven Covey, in a 1994 *Journal for Quality and Participation* article entitled, "Involving People in the Problem" states that, "involvement is the key to implementing change and increasing commitment." He feels that teachers' involvement acts as a catalyst in the change process. He further states that principals often avoid using involvement as a proactive-strategy because they fear the risk of losing control.

Recognition and Rewards

The term WIIFM? (What's In It For Me?) is often used in the context of school improvement. In other words, what benefit will the teacher receive for changing his or her behavior and/or work processes? Rewards and incentives must support the change. Whether they be formal team awards or individual teachers' goals within the evaluation process, the new practices must create an incentive for teachers to change.

Some Barriers to Change

Havelock and Havelock, cite in their book, entitled, "Training for Change Agents," a number of barriers to change encountered by principals in very successful districts. They reported the following acceptance barriers to change in order of importance:

1. Confusion among teachers about the purpose of the change.
2. Unwillingness of schools and communities to change or listen to new ideas.
3. Shortage of funds allocated for the change.
4. Lack of precise information about the change by teachers and other school people.
5. Frustrations and difficulties encountered by teachers in trying to adopt change.
6. Lack of communication among teachers.
7. Inadequacy of school plant, facilities, equipment, or supplies.
8. Shortage of qualified personnel.
9. Feeling by teachers that the change would have little benefit for them.
10. Rigidity of school structure and bureaucracy.
11. Lack of communication between school, community, and students.
12. Lack of coordination and teamwork within the school.
13. Lack of adequate contacts with outside resources.

Identifying Change Management Skills to Transform Schools

14. Absence of promotion program to put the new ideas across.
15. Frustration and difficulty encountered by the students during the change.
16. Lack of contact with other schools that have considered the same innovations.
17. Unwillingness, or lack of effective resource groups, to help the school revise or adapt.

The Stages of Change

Whenever change is initiated, there is a series of stages or phases that will be experienced in implementing the change. Although the length of these steps vary with the situation, each will, no doubt, occur while coping with change. Each stage is described below.

Stage One: Denial

During this stage, teachers will feel that the change is not really new, or that it is more of the same thing, or if it is occurring, that it won't affect them. For some teachers, this stage is brief; in others it is prolonged. In this stage, teachers may fail to recognize or accept their part in the whole change process. You should build teachers' and administrators' awareness of the impact of the change during this stage.

Stage Two: Resistance

Resistance can take many forms, ranging from a negative attitude to opposition. In this stage, because teachers' and administrators' resistance can be so strong, they may resort to a number of ways to prevent the change from becoming a reality: by absenteeism, nonperformance work, slow-down, sabotage, "back stabbing," and irritability. Although resistance can occur at any stage, it is usually the most difficult to manage at this stage. To deal with it, your best method is conflict resolution.

Stage Three: Adaptation

In this stage, change is beginning to become accepted, and at times, welcomed. Teachers provide input in developing principles, practicing, and methods to implement the change not only for themselves, but also for others. To strengthen adaptation, you will need to engage in some goal setting and problem solving.

Stage Four: Participation

In this stage, teachers actively participate in the change by making suggestions and contributions, initiating work on their own, and seeing the change as it should be. Change begins to become stable at this stage. You should now engage in team building to enhance participation.

Development of a Master Plan to Implement Change

These are several steps used in developing a plan for change, including identifying the mission, components, and objectives.

Step One—identify the mission or purpose of your plan. The mission indicates exactly the intent of the plan. When preparing the mission, it should be done with brevity and clarity so that all those formulating the plan understand the reason for meeting, and for planning which change will occur. For example: The purpose of the design team is to plan and develop a plan to implement total quality in education on a pilot basis.

Step Two—create a schematic of all components necessary to meet your mission.

The following is an example of a schematic for installing a total quality education:

Step Three—establish a short-range objective and action plan/performance standards to fulfill each component to produce the desired change. For example: Explore Total Quality (TQ)

My goal is to become fortified with information on total quality from September 10 to November 30, 199X.

My performance standards are: (This objective is satisfactorily achieved when...):
1. A TQ resource center is established in the library, containing TQ tapes, books, professional journals, and training manuals by October 15, 199X.

2. Three model TQ schools have been visited by the design team by November 1, 1996.

3. A nationally renowned TQ consultant has been retained as a basis to assist the design team to develop and implement TQ at a stipend of $1000, plus traveling expenses. An orientation for the school family and a three-day workshop for members of the design team has been conducted by November 30, 199X.

For step four, obtain approval for the plan from the principal. Once all of the components of the plan have been completed as planned, it should be discussed with the principal. Any revisions should be made at this time.

Make duplicate copies for all teachers in step five.

Once the revisions have been made, a personal copy should be given to each teacher. Give teachers about a week to digest the plan, and arrange a date and time to discuss the plan with them.

In step six, Members of the design team conduct a presentation on plans to obtain teacher input Finally in step seven, in accordance with input from the teachers, revise the plan and initiate appropriate action to execute the plan.

Principles That Should Be Observed When Initiating Change

In *Dynamic Education Change*, Gerald Zaltman, David Florl, and Linda Sikorski have identified a number of principles pertaining to change that should be observed or considered by any principal who is initiating change. These principles are :

- Other things being equal, teachers will more readily accept change if they feel that it will increase student achievement.

- The principal should consider and collaborate with all major stakeholders and persons who are affected or can influence the change, as well as with those who will actually install the change.

- The principal should look for opportunities for support and assistance from those who can influence the change and should forecast conflicts and take action to prevent them.

- The principal's own perspective is not broad enough if he or she has not considered opportunities and potential problems as they may occur from : 1) the nature of the school climate; 2) the characteristics of school and community members; and 3) the attributes of the change.
- The principal should prevent the development of unrealistically high expectations for the changed school.
- The principal can use pressure from the external stakeholders to stimulate change in the school.
- The principal should determine whether a particular factor, such as values, attitudes, or characteristics of the environment in which the change will take place works to hinder or facilitate change, or both.
- Poor communication within the school and among schools may create important barriers to change.
- The principal should be mindful of attempts by central school administrators and union officials to alter change in a way that the change is more favorable to themselves but may have undesirable effects for the district as a whole.
- To prevent some of the resistance to change, the principal should clarify the nature of the change and the expected behavior for implementing the change.
- The principal should attempt to connect the desired change with the unmet needs of one or more interested stakeholders.
- The principal can publicize the change throughout the school through use of direct mail, articles, booklets, demonstrations, sponsors, telephones, meetings, action research, confrontation, use of computers, workshops, information systems, and training manuals.
- When possible, the principal should attempt to obtain endorsements or early commitment from key individuals in the district.
- Individual schools should be allowed to adopt and implement change to fit their own needs and circumstances.

- The principal should view teachers and other school people as creative people who are implementors of change and should convey this view to them.
- The principal should make every attempt to identify potential undesirable consequences of the change and develop contingency plants to deal with them if they should occur.

Process Skills Needed by the Principal to Install Change

There are several process skills that will help you to manage change. However, the most important ones are empathy, communication, and participation. The following is a brief description of each.

Empathy involves the ability to understand the impact of change on others; that is, to put yourself in the shoes of others. To perform this feat you will need to understand those who will be involved in the change. What motivates them? What is impacting them? What is happening to them internally? To enhance your abilities in this skill, you will need to ponder the following questions:

1. What would affect me if I were facing this change?
2. What would happen to my position in the school?
3. Would my job be in jeopardy?
4. How are my priorities impacted by this change?
5. Would my relationship with my peers be affected?

Communication, will enable you to understand who, what, when, and how things are occurring in the change process. The following are some questions that you should consider when initiating change.

1. What form of communication is better: oral communication or written communication, or both? Why?
2. Was the message clearly communicated? How did I determine this?

3. Were there opportunities to communicate about the change that I took advantage of ? Where? What time? What way?
4. Did I get effective feedback? How did I use the feedback?
5. How did I improve the communication process?

Participation entails adequately involving those who will be affected by the change.

Questions you should consider are:

1. What representatives can impact the change process the most?
2. Who are the major stakeholders and should they be involved within the change process?
3. Who can have the greatest impact on the change? How should they be involved? What should we be sensitive to?
4. Who should be involved in the change process in order to have broad representation?

Some of the activities that are ideal for involving teacher and community people in the process are as follows:

- Assessing teachers' and administrators' readiness.
- Developing plans, performance standards, and action plans.
- Assessing the decision-making process.
- Participating in developing the foundation, such as the mission, vision, and shared values statements.
- Assessing needs.

An Effective Model for Principals to Help Teachers Accept Change

Through transformational leadership that fosters empowerment, the following information can enable you to successfully lead teachers through the transition for change.

To communicate the change, you need to:

- Inform teachers as much as possible and as early as possible about the need for change.

Identifying Change Management Skills to Transform Schools 43

- Use a variety of ways to get teachers' input on change and act appropriately on it.
- Demonstrate concern for teachers' feelings and appreciation for their views.

To acknowledge the loss, you need to:

- Provide opportunities to vent their frustrations.
- Permit teachers to design their old ways of doing things in the school.
- Give opportunities for teachers to work through their grief over the change.

To provide the tools, you need to:

- Educate teachers about the change process.
- Provide stress workshops.
- Encourage behavior appropriate for change.
- Understand the differences between grieving and motivation and negative attitude problems.
- Create new rituals to help teachers to understand, accept, and believe in the new way of doing things in the school.

To deal with resistance, you need to:

- Create an appropriate school climate to enable teachers to capitalize on their strengths.
- Empower teachers to take charge.
- Encourage innovative behavior and creativity, and recognize and reward risk-taking.

To create a powerful vision, you need to:

- Involve teachers in creating the vision of the new school.
- Communicate the vision religiously and get teachers to support it.
- Provide opportunies for teachers to communicate the vision within and outside of the school.

Some Common Things Principals Miss When Introducing Change to Teachers

Several years ago, while I was researching the impact of change on teachers, I interviewed forty-two teachers from several districts. These teachers indicated that when their principal attempted to initiate change in the school, a number of key factors were neglected that they believed were important for producing change. In addition, some of these teachers stated they knew more about the impact of change on teachers than did their principals.

Principals must understand that teachers are aware of the need for change and are able to articulate conditions that have pushed the school to change. However, the principal must do a better job in communicating and discussing the need for change with teachers.

As stated previously, principals must also understand that teachers don't resist change; they resist being changed. As a result, teachers who participate in the decision-making process will realize a higher degree of comfort with change. Why? When teachers are not involved in the change process, the principal will have no way to determine if the change will help them to realize their personal goals. Obviously, when teachers participate in the change process, they are more apt to meet not only their personal goals, but also the goal of the school. The prudent principal must notably involve teachers early in the process of change and keep them involved throughout the transitional period.

In addition, principals must understand that teachers use metaphors to structure their school experiences and that they develop a concept or reality based on interlocking systems of metaphors. Therefore, as a school attempts to change its focus and priorities in pursuit of the change, new metaphors are introduced that often conflict with those with which the teachers felt comfortable. Further, new values and priorities emerge, creating resentment if the principal tries to implement a cultural change. Often during the new change, rituals were also reduced or eliminated, aggravating the condition.

Finally, principals must understand that the biggest block to effective change in schools is poor communication between the teachers and the principal. In fact, when I asked teachers why the change failed, many did not even know that the school was changing. In fact, fewer teachers had received any direct communication with the principal about the impending change. Those teachers who had received information up front usually indicated that they were more comfortable with the change. However, all teachers agreed that the communication process needed major improvement.

Characteristics of an Effective Transformational Principal

To be effective in overcoming resistance and influencing change within a school, the transformational principal exhibits a number of characteristics. One of these is the guts to take risks.

This is the opposite of one of the reasons for resistance : fear of losing something of value. What might happen if a teacher speaks out and gives an opinion on an issue in your school? Will he or she lose their job, respect of their co-workers, or career opportunity? Most of these fears are unfounded. Teachers are often nervous about consequences that are not real. In his book *Getting Things Done When You Are Not in Charge*, Geoffrey M. Bellman states that you must put your fears in perspective and build you own courage to take risks in order to influence change. Each principal should go through a mental process to determine if the risk and effort is work the potential reward.

Transformational principals must also have the ability to form good relationships with teachers. This will build a broad base of support with teachers in many areas and levels of the school organization. This relationship is built on trust and collaboration. In order to gain the support of teachers, the principal must provide support.

Resilience is another necessary characteristic. In his book *Managing at the Speed of Change*, Darly. R. Connor, defines resilience as the "ability to absorb high levels of change while displaying minimal dysfunctional behavior." He further describes resilient principals as positive, focused, flexible, organized and proactive; important attributes of an effective leader.

The transformational principal also serves as a role model for the shared values and beliefs of the school. Your treatment of teachers and other school people, the completeness of your work, your timeliness with promised deadlines, your seeking of input, and your offers of assistance are ways in which you must exhibit your belief in quality improvement. If you don't "walk the talk" and "talk the talk" (communicating the vision and values), you cannot expect another person to change their behavior.

A Principal's Personal Guarantee Statement

A principal's personal guarantee statement is a written and verbal proclamation by the principal to diminish any fears or trepidations teachers, other school people, and community people may have regarding the change by citing how their security and sensation needs will be accommodated through the program. Security needs refer to those guarantees that protect an individual from being personally harmed by the implementation of the change. Sensation needs refer to those benefits that will be forthcoming to those individuals who support the change.

Some security choices that are often used to arrive at security and benefits statements are job security, failure without penalty, training and development, teacher evaluation changes, personnel selection, role re-definition, pilot study, support system, decision versus consensus, development of a school-based management plan, accountability, and budgetary use.

Some benefit choices are: professional growth opportunities, budget preparation, budget for pilot schools, reverse evaluation, personal growth, sponsorship, waiver system, recognition, elimination of "dumb" rules, formalized feedback, planning time, and support services.

The following is a copy of a personal guarantee statement prepared by a principal with input from a teachers' committee to implement school-based management:

Principal's Personal Guarantee Statement

In accordance with the district's intention to establish a school-based management program for the school year, the principal and assistant principal are prepared to make the following guarantees to all teachers and other school people regarding participation in school-based management activities:

1. No individual will lose his or her position or have his or her employment status jeopardized in any way due to participation in school-based management activities. While the district retains the option to closely monitor the development of

school-based management plans chosen by each school (in order to protect the interests of all stakeholders in school communities), the results of this evaluation and the outcome of the school-based management activities will in no way threaten the job security of district personnel. Creativity and innovation on the part of council members will be strongly encouraged.

2. The school-based management model with be highly inclusive in that all constituencies within schools will be invited to participate. With the exception of administrators, all constituencies within schools (including teachers, paraprofessionals, school aids, secretarial staff, parents, food service staff, and students) will be invited to elect representatives to the school-based management council. The school will also elect one "process observer," whose primary responsibility will be to facilitate the resolutions of any conflicts/disagreements that develop among council members.

3. The decisions made by the school-based management council will be arrived at by consensus. That is, no individual on the council will have the authority to pass resolutions or make decisions without the agreement of every other member of the council. When disagreements among council members arise, the council must resolve these disagreements by arriving at a reasonable compromise or by convincing the dissenting members to accept the majority opinion.

4. The principal will retain control over decisions not related to issues being considered by the school-based management council. More specifically, the principal and assistant principals will continue to make those decisions which relate to the day-to-day functioning of the school. The decision-making capacity of the school-based management council will be limited (at least initially) to those issues that have been discussed by the council and on which consensus has been reached.

5. Intensive school-based management training will be provided for all participants. It is the position of the district that the successful implementation of school-based management procedures is greatly facilitated through the provision of appropriate training for council leaders, members, and process

observers. Pursuant to this point of view, the district will incur the costs of training and will also assist interested individuals in obtaining training.

6. Parents and students in the school will be strongly encouraged to elect representatives to the school-based management council and to be active participants on the council. The district's school-based management policy will assume that students and their parents should comprise an integral part of the decision-making process within the school. As such, their representation on the council is crucial. Moreover, as the recipients of instructional services, it is likely that students and parents will offer valuable insights to the functioning of their schools, which may not have been recognized by school staff. Consequently, the inclusion of parent and student representatives on the school-based management councils will be mandated.

7. School-based management council members may be rewarded through special recognition by the principal due to outstanding performance in the service of school-based management goals. While each school-based management council will be given the option to apply for payment for additional services via per session funds and/or stipends, budgetary and ethical considerations make it impossible for the district to provide additional monetary rewards to those council members whose efforts on behalf of school-based management have been judged to be exemplary. As the superintendent is still interested in rewarding the efforts of these individuals, however, efforts will be made by the district to find alternative means of recognizing the accomplishments of exemplary council members. The district will also explore the possibility of obtaining grants from private sources (i.e., foundations, corporation, civic organization, etc.) to establish a reward fund to which schools can apply to obtain additional funds for their school based management programs.

8. Through its school-based management council, the school will be given the responsibility to allocate their school-based management funds in the manner in which they desire. Further budgetary decisions should be made by the council.

REVIEW

KEY POINTS TO REMEMBER:

- Teachers resist change for a number of reasons, among them are: 1) a desire not to lose something of value; 2) a misunderstanding of the change and a lack of trust; 3) a belief that the change does not make sense for the school; and 4) a low tolerance for change.

- Some strategies for dealing with resistance are: active listening and support, communication and training, teacher participation and involvement, and recognition and rewards.

- The stages of change are: 1) denial; 2) resistance, 3) adaptation; and 4) participation.

- The steps for producing a plan for change consist of the following: 1) Identify the mission; 2) create a schematic of all components of the plan; 3) establish short-range objectives and performance standards for each component; 4) obtain approval of the plan from the principal; 5) duplicate copies for teachers; 6) make a formal presentation to teachers; and 7) revise the plan.

- Process skills that are needed to install change are empathy, communication, and participation.

- An effective model to help teachers to accept change consists of the following: 1) communicate the change; 2) acknowledge the loss; 3) provide the tools; 4) deal with resistance; and 5) create a powerful vision.

- Characteristics of an effective transformational principal are the guts to take risks, the ability to form good relationships with teachers, resilience, and being a role model.

- A principal personal guarantee statement consists of a list of security and sensation needs guaranteed by the principal to help teachers accept change.

APPLICATION:

Think of something you would like to change in the school. Initially, avoid a major project, such as installing competency-based education. Instead, select something small, such as decreasing incidents of student accidents in the school. Ask for volunteer teachers to serve on a design team to arrive at a plan to effect this change. Consider the content of this chapter and produce a plan.

CHAPTER 4

Understanding the New Role of Principal as Social Architect

LEARNING OBJECTIVES

After reading and comprehending this chapter, you should be able to:

- Identify the various roles of the principal when serving as a social architect.
- Understanding both the "hard" and the "soft" side of school administration.

What Every Principal Should Know About Becoming a Social Architect

Traditional principals tend to manage from the hard side of school administration. Today's principals must learn to manage from both the hard and soft side of school administration. They must make some radical changes in the future, changes that some of them will be reluctant or unwilling to make. Although traditional principals will have to function from the hard side of school administration to be successful, the principals must also lead from the soft side of school administration.

The Difference Between the Hard and Soft Side of School Administration

The hard side of school administration deals more with objects than with teachers. If focused on controls, that is, it is the principal's job to keep the school on some course by controlling the behavior of its teachers. The hard side makes use of the organizational chart to allocate resources. It favors formality and protocol in terms of who is reporting to whom. It does not make allowances for human mistakes. It means achievement or outright dismissal. It abhors those who upset the status quo and punishes them with reprimands or forced resignation. It requires strict adherence to the job description. It favors the "big is better" concept because of the economy scale. It believes in using power to suppress problems over conformity. It favors time management over people management. It advocates a rational role of school management even for those teachers who function in a nonrational school environment. Hard is hard and that's it!

On the other hand, the soft side of school administration deals more with teachers than with objects. It enables the principal to visualize and create a sound future direction for the school so that everybody is aware as to where the school is heading. It shapes core values and reinforces them through varied human activities to form a sustaining and healthy culture. It encourages teamwork to optimize performance by giving teachers freedom and opportunity to perform. It empowers others to become more innovative and creative in their performing efforts through sharing and equalizing power with principals. It enables the school to "grow its own" principals so that it can have at its disposal a cadre of people ready to help it achieve a high degree of success in the future.

The soft side of school administration is not devoid of controls. However, instead of relying strictly on external controls, it relies primarily on internal controls of principals who work in schools, because it assumes that they have the best interests of the school at heart and that its teachers can be motivated to perform well when they are cared for, respected, and trusted. Even though the soft side of school administration gives principals freedom to perform through flexibility, autonomy, and so on, soft is also hard. Soft is hard because it requires principals to keep their sights on the vision of the school; to strictly adhere to the core values of the school; to manage a tightly driven school culture; to plan always considering the external environment; to require high quality performance through teamwork; to hold teachers accountable for results; and to promote from within.

How Principals Should Perform as Social Architects

To perform as a social architect, the transformational principal must concentrate on the soft side of school administration. He or she must primarily be concerned with long-range achievement efforts of the school, knowing full well that it's the long-range results that are important and that short-range efforts are only important in terms of step-by-step style progression-in order to realize the vision, purposes, missions, and goals of the school. To perform as the social architect, the principal must shed certain common or traditional duties and assume those duties cited and explained below. The principal should: become the visionary leader; perform as cultural builder; assume the role of strategic actor; promote teamwork; and empower others.

Become the Visionary Leader

The transformational principal orchestrates the school in an effort to create and take advantage of future opportunities. As a result, school success depends, as never before, on the ability of the principal to visualize, participate, and realize change. Vision can be seen both as an offensive and a defensive maneuver; on one hand it will help you to map out a course that creates change, and yet on the other, it can help you to respond to changing times and conditions. Transformational principals are expected to invent excellent futures for their schools. Those who insist on remaining in the past will permit their schools to retrogress at a much greater rate that what may or may not be occurring presently.

What is a vision? A vision is a mental imaging from where a person comes from to where he or she desires to go, thereby creating the future from an assortment of facts, ambitions, aspirations, dreams, threats, and opportunities. If you can accept the fact that our schools are not meeting the needs of a large portion of our students, you must also accept that fact that what did not work in the past, certainly won't work in the future. What we need are visionary leaders who are fortified with new knowledge, new insights, and new skills, who can transcend a viable vision throughout the school organization that will bring an improved education for not only a small segment of our population, but also for all our students.

Transformational principals are expected to formulate a clear vision resulting from a profound understanding of kids and what they and their parents want for them, and from an understanding of the capabilities of the schools and the external environment. As a result, it will take a craftsperson, not a technician, to perform this feat. The transformational principal must visualize excellence in education and understand exactly what must be done to attain it. He or she is expected to use old and new knowledge and skills to visualize excellence for the school; to put tools and materials to work shaping the school; to adjust and adapt to changing times and conditions; and to keep in constant mental view the ultimate goal, the vision.

Vision distinguishes the transformational principals from the traditional ones. Transformational principals do not merely create a vision for the school, but rather the vision resides at their very core and governs all of their actions, words, and deeds. To this end, visionary principls perform the following:

- Create a compelling vision of the school's future.
- Translate the vision into reality by focusing on the key elements for success.
- Remain intimately involved at the heart of those matters essential to making the vision happen and to inducing actions from others necessary to realize the vision.
- Encourage teachers to embrace the vision.
- Constantly communicate the vision so that it permeates every level of the school, propelling it where it has never been before.

Transformational principals follow the three steps to become visionary leaders: Step 1, continually analyze the school by stepping back and taking a critical look at the programs and activities of the school and all factors that will affect it. This means that the principal will become involved in meditation and objectively weigh all factors that will perfect the school. Once the principal

Understanding the New Role of Principal as Social Architect

has critically analyzed the school and has meditated and objectively weighed all factors, Step 2 is to create the vision by building a scenario. This requires four activities. First, describe the vision with a simple statement including the shared values needed to support the vision. Second, identify all positive and negative potential outcomes of the new vision, including an analysis of the best and worst things that can happen. Third, identify the major key result factors that ultimately determine the realization of the vision. Fourth, develop an action plan for implementing the vision. Step 3, manage by wandering around, talking, listening, and facilitating matters pertaining to the school's philosophy, values, directions, and vision in an attempt to reach all teachers on all levels of the school. The following represents the distinction between the non-visionary (traditional) and visionary (transformational) principal. The nonvisionary principal:

- Solves problems on a daily basis and makes decisions
- Meets with teachers, but usually on a formal basis.
- Tends to be aloof, rational, and critical.
- Scrutinizes weaknesses.
- Concerns himself or herself mainly with current affairs of the school.

The visionary principal:

- Preaches and teaches the school's philosophy.
- Communicates with all teachers at all levels.
- Pays attention to the school's culture.
- Articulates the school's vision.
- Is receptive to new ideas and is supportive of teachers.
- Makes certain the school is making the most of its strengths, interests, and talents.
- Acts as a strategic agent for the purpose of ensuring that goals, strategies and activities will be realized in relation to the school's vision.
- Inspires teachers to attain their short-range objectives in order to realize the school's long-range goals.

Thus, the nonvisionary principal is today-oriented while the visionary principal is future-oriented, a necessary prerequisite to make the transformation.

Perform as a Cultural Builder

Today's principals are required to devote a great deal of their time to institutionalizing the mission, vision, and shared values that provide the philosophical foundation in order to meet the student needs. In the past, many principals prepared a philosophy. In most cases the philosophy was dead because it was never actualized through the efforts of the principal. This resulted primarily because many principals did not understand their role of giving the school a soul through the inculcation of the beliefs and values of the philosophy. It was not until such books as *Corporate Culture, the Art of Japanese Management, In Search of Excellence* and others that most managers of all organizations began to understand the importance of producing a sound philosophy and repeating it through a number of activities in a number of direct and indirect ways.

The transformational principal initiates a number of activities to institutionalize the philosophy. First, he or she convenes a philosophy committee of which he or she will serve as the secretary and orchestrator. After weeks of committee interaction, deliberation, and widespread contribution from teachers throughout the school, the committee should reach a consensus on the mission, vision. and shared values. The mission will address the students to be served and what services will be provided to them. The vision will identify the future direction of the school. The shared values statement identifies those hard-core values that spell out the management style of the school and how teachers should be treated. There is not single principal's duty that is more important than to build a strong and healthy school culture.

To reiterate, a culture is a set of informal policies and rules that identifies how schools are expected to behave in the execution of teacher's jobs. Teachers who know what is expected of them through a strong culture can then dance to the same beat as the principal. Therefore, time is not wasted and order and harmony can exist when the culture is strong. When the culture is weak, disorder and disharmony prevail and teachers waste a great deal of time trying to determine what is expected of them and what they should do.

Second, the transformational principal uses the shared values statement to preach and teach all teachers how thing are done in the school. He or she takes every opportunity to discuss, repeat, and clarify the shared values statement. His or her actions, words, and deeds are guided by these statements. Eventually, he or she is infused in the school, thereby producing the desired culture. However, a strong culture does not emerge overnight. This leads us to the next step.

Third, not only does the transformational principal serve as a strong role model, but he or she directs school administrators to implement a long-range training program whereby, either biweekly or monthly, as a series of fifteen to twenty minute seminars will be initiated to cover all the aspects of the philosophy and thoroughly indoctrinate all teachers as to how things are done in the school. Eventually, as the philosophy is being inculcated throughout the school, a strong culture will be produced, and teachers do not have to be told what to do because they will know what the values are that will govern their behavior.

Fourth, the transformational principal is not satisfied with either the philosophy or culture. He or she encourages all teachers to challenge the shared values and to assist in changing or modifying them if changing times and conditions warrant such a change.

Assume the Role of the Strategic Actor

The transformational principal should become a strategic actor; that is, not only does he or she articulate the philosophy, but much of his or her time is devoted to paying attention to the school's strengths, looking for opportunities and discussing the future at all levels of the school. Whereas the traditional principal of the past spent most of his or her time dealing with tangible and everyday problems and functions from one year to another, the transformational principal deals primarily with the intangibles and delegates day-to-day problems to his or her team and functions on a long-range basis. His or her primary role is to translate the abstract so that it is real to all teachers.

One of the essential roles of the transformational principal is to keep all teachers focused on the mission, vision, shared values, and strategic focus of the school. He or she does not become involved in the minute details of these activities, but reviews and monitors decisions, programs, and efforts to ensure that they are consistent with the vision. Thus, the principal is not only concerned with instilling the school's values, but with supporting them as well so that the vision can be realized through them.

To function as a strategic actor, the transformational principal articulates the shared values of the school on a frequent basis. To this end, the principal should be heard at meetings with the entire family of teachers present, explaining each shared value. He or she should also be observed doing this same thing at luncheon meetings, church affairs, PTA meetings, and board meetings. In fact, wherever there is an assembly of people, the transformational principal is expected to preach and teach the important values of the school.

They measure how well the values match reality. It is not enough for the principals to preach and teach the shared values. They are observers, monitoring whether or not the values are deeply seated beliefs of the school and doing whatever it takes to inculcate them. They remind other administrators of shared values when they do not comply with them, or send congratulatory letters to those who have complied with a core value.

They examine strategic focus to determine if it must be changed. The approaches the school uses to attain excellence are not embedded in rock. It's the transformational principal who finds time to encourage school teachers to challenge the strategic focus and to determine if changes should be made to stay in tune with realities.

They also act out the philosophy. As a strategic actor, the principal acts out the philosophy through actions, words, and deeds. If they are successful as actors, then the school has a minimum trouble inculcating a strong and healthy culture, which is an essential step toward attaining the transformation process.

The transformational principal reviews and monitors the school improvement plan. The strategic acting role of the transformational principal requires him or her to ask thought-provoking questions concerning the external environment so as to minimize surprises; to make certain that rules are developed that are flexible; to ensure that all the teachers who will be directly affected by the plan will be involved in the plan; and to ensure

Understanding the New Role of Principal as Social Architect

that long-range goals and short-range objectives are formulated. These will, in all probability, ensure that the vision is realized.

The strategic actor is characterized by such phrases as "creating a climate," "serving as a catalytic agent," "acting as the devil's advocate," "cultivating the proper attitude," and "stimulating collective thought." They work diligently so that teachers understand the real meaning of strategic planning. As the strategic actor titles suggest, the transformational principal carries out this role primarily by communicating face-to-face; meeting with teachers individually and collectively to focus their attention on the future; conveying his or her perception of the school; and persuading teachers to develop and refine their own perceptions of these critical matters.

Promote Teamwork

The transformational principal is expected to take an active role in promoting teamwork within the school. Promotion means promoting those processes that establish an improved synthesis of the effort among all teachers of the school. To this end, the principal is expected to do the following:

- Reorganize the entire school into teams. This includes all departments, all grades, and all subjects.
- Provide essential training to all teams in team building. Such training areas include group dynamics, teaching consensus, conflict resolution, communication, problem solving, etc.
- Be patient. Give teamwork some time to be realized. Implementing such a reorganization will take a great deal of time; therefore, everyone including the principal should be patient and give implementation problems time to be resolved.
- Provide teams with autonomy and freedom. Teams work best when principals are willing to share and equalize power with them. Therefore, by giving them autonomy and freedom, they begin to promote teamwork among themselves without it being imposed on them.
- Recognize outstanding feats of team building. Use recognition, rewards, or techniques to promote teamwork

through the school. For example, praise a team that has accomplished some outstanding feat through teamwork. The reward could be a citation in the local newspaper, or a dinner paid for by the principal.

- Saturate teams with information. It is far better to give teams too much information and let them decide for themselves what they need than to supply them with too little information. The most effective means to communicate with teams is to conduct informal and formal communication seminars as often as need be.

- Manage by wandering around. This concept is not only good for articulating the school philosophy and vision, but it can be useful in assessing the extent to which teamwork is being promoted throughout the school. One effective way in which the principal can use this concept to promote teamwork is by speaking only to teams of people, unless a team member has a personal problem.

- Evaluate team-building activities. The process of promoting teamwork is not only left up to the principal, but to all teachers and to other school people. If a team is not functioning properly, all team members are at fault. This thought should be emphasized over and over by the principal until it has permeated every fiber of the school. Team leaders and supervisors should be evaluated partially on how well they have organized and implemented activities to promote teamwork.

- Assess and correct. Hire an outside consulting firm to assess the degree that teamwork is promoted throughout the school and take whatever course of action is necessary to optimize team building.

Empower Others

The transformational principal relies more on empowering others than on using power to induce school people to perform. To do this, he or she practices the principle of delegation. This does *not* mean delegating those duties and tasks expected of the board of education, superintendent, and other school administrators. Although it could, delegating here does not necessarily mean empowering others to perform certain duties and tasks usually reserved for school administrators at the building level, such as curriculum development, school budget, instructional strategies, selecting teachers, etc.

To empower others to perform, the transformational principal believes in the concept and educates others to believe in it. Depending upon the school's readiness for empowerment, he or she decides desirable areas in which to establish the empowerment program. They then develop specific guidelines to ensure that teachers don't feel they are giving up power, but are making better use of it and that teachers are meaningfully involved in sharing and equalizing power with the principal. However, it will not be enough to establish guidelines for implementing empowerment. Empowerment will only reap maximum results if a strong training and development program is an essential component of the empowerment program. For example, what is the use of enabling teachers to prepare their own budget if they are not familiar with the budget codes or budget format, of if they are not aware of the various kinds of products available to them? Another appropriate title for the strategic actor is the "School Educator". He or she orchestrates all of the necessary activities to ensure that the transformation take place.

Empowerment is sometimes thought of and referred to as a process. Actually, it is a philosophy or a way of school work life consisting of giving others enrichment and added responsibilities to make decisions that directly affect them. In the true sense, it cannot be separated from school management and the culture of the school. The transformational principal does several things in an effort to implement empowerment, not only as a practice, but also as a philosophy in the school district.

- Grants teachers and other school people specific empowerment activities, duties, or tasks and hold those who have been empowered for results. These should be accepted by the principal first.

- Gives sufficient power to teachers to allow them to share power with their principal.

- Considers the role of the principal as an integral and important part of the empowerment program.

- Establishes controls or monitors by which the empowered can assess their own progress and make any necessary corrections.
- Creates the proper school climate.
- Communicates clearly the empowerment accountability to all teachers to minimize confusion and disagreement.

The prerequisites for empowerment, especially the management style and school culture, constitute the foundation on which the program is built. Empowerment is like any other type of structure; its ultimate soundness depends on the commitment of the principal and the soundness of the foundation on which it is built. A sure way to administer the coup de grace to empowerment is not to include all of the prerequisites in the proper balance when carving a foundation.

REVIEW

KEY POINTS TO REMEMBER:

To perform like a social architect, the transformational principal does the following:

- Becomes the visionary leader by helping to create and articulate the vision of the school.
- Performs as a culture builder by institutionalizing the mission and shared values of the school.
- Assumes the role of the strategic actor by paying attention to the school strengths, dealing with problems, and discussing the future at all levels of the school.
- Promotes teamwork by reorganizing the school into teams.
- Empowers others by sharing power with teachers.

APPLICATION

At the top of a sheet of paper list all of the hard responsibilities and tasks that you presently perform dealing with controlling the behavior of teachers. For example:

Hard Responsibility:

- Evaluate all teachers at least three times daily.
- Speak to returning absentees.

After you have exhausted this list, give it to your teachers and have them review the list and include any other controls. Make another list and jot down soft responsibilities. Review each control under hard responsibilities and develop it into a soft/hard responsibility. Make certain that each statement also includes a hard responsibility.

Soft Responsibilities :

- Restructure the school into teams and institute self-evaluation and reverse feedback (soft responsibility). Require teams to periodically report performance (hard responsibility).

Once you have replaced your hard responsibilities with soft/hard responsibilities, make a decision as to what other responsibilities should be coupled with soft responsibilities.

PART
2 Creating A Philosophy To Guide The Transformation

This section describes what some feel may be the "secret weapon" associated with great schools—the philosophy. The philosophy helps to determine the culture of the school, to focus the guiding light that governs the human efforts of the school activities, and to provide the glue that provides the proper fit for the soft S's of skills, staff, style and school goals. The elements of the statement of philosophy illustrated and discussed in this section are the mission, vision and shared values.

CHAPTER 5

Developing the School Mission

LEARNING OBJECTIVES

After studying and comprehending this chapter, you hould be able to:

- Determine the school philosophy.
- Define the mission.
- Identify the multiple purpose of the mission.
- Describe the common types of mission statements.
- Explain how to create a mission statement.

What Every Principal Should Know About Preparing the School Mission

The first and most important step the transformational principal must accomplish is to engage school people in a process to produce a philosophy to direct human efforts in the school. The philosophy is a network of aims that spells out the primary reason for the school's existance and ensures that everyone is working together. Developing a philosophy is an extremely difficult task because most principals take the aims of public education for granted. They have either oversimplified this task, failed to perform it satisfactorily, or completely ignored it during the change process.

The School Philosophy

Philosophy helps to determine the culture of the school; to focus the guiding light that governs the human efforts of the school activities; and to provide the glue that creates the proper fit for the skills, staff, style, and educational goals.

When producing the statement of philosophy:

1. It is developed involving a cross-section of school people;
2. It is thoroughly discussed with all school people;
3. It dictates all actions, words, and deeds for both school people and administrators;
4. It is inculcated continuously throughout the school; and,
5. It is periodically used as a basis for assessing and improving the school culture.

The first element of the philosophy is explained in the rest of this chapter.

The Mission

The first component of the philosophy identifies the mission of the school. The mission theorizes the operations of the school, is usually stated in abstract terms, and endows everyone in the school with a sense of direction. It is the formula for developing the other elements, preparing plans, and assessing the school.

Names used to describe the statement of the mission are: charter, purpose, and definition of the school. Mission is stated in order to mobilize every administrator, every teacher, and other people within the school into a concerted effort to fulfill its destiny. It also provides a focus whereby the principal nurtures the appropriate climate to attain cohesiveness and harmony among the human beings who comprise the school. A mission is:

- a statement of something desired, and a strong commitment to pursue the vision; it give guidance, direction, and life to a school.
- a statement that can withstand well-reasoned change.
- the basis for developing plans and allocating resources.

- the key for facilitating the identification of strength/opportunities and weakness/problems that must be addressed when planning.
- a statement that provides parameters for governing the actions of all people within the school.

A mission statement should incorporate features that are associated with how human beings function in a school. Basically these features would encompass the following:

1. Giving teachers broader discretionary powers.
2. Operating without close supervision.
3. Being free to be creative.
4. Trusting each other.
5. Being flexible.
6. Sharing of power and authority.
7. Union and management working together for the common good.

Review your mission statement in terms of these criteria to determine if they are implied directly or indirectly. If not, some discussion and rewriting may be necessary to produce an atmosphere of egalitarianism.

The Purposes Of A Mission Statement

One of the most essential decisions that any school can make is the determination of its mission. A failure to make this decision will leave the district, school, department, and team without the focal point needed to employ its goals and objectives. Schools do not determine their mission; the students, parents, and others should make this determination. Thus, effective mission statements always proceed from outside (the community environment) to inside (school administration, teachers, and other school people's response to the needs and desires of students).

The mission statement serves a multitude of purposes. The following appear to be most important:

- It describes the reason for the existence of a district, school, department, or team.
- It provides a basis for making the right kind of decisions.
- It serves as a vehicle for measuring success.
- It provides a belief that will foster a school's climate, which will produce the instructional program.
- It determines how resources will be allocated.
- It facilitates the task of identifying opportunities and threats that must be addressed.

The Key Elements of the Mission Statement

The mission statement should contain the following key elements, including the nature of the school. Ask yourself questions like: What is the primary purpose or function of the school? Why does the school exist? What needs in the community or greater society does it satisfy? How are these needs expected to change in the future?

The mission statement should also give a description of the students. Who are the students? How well does the school, department, grade, or team serve the students? What improvements should be made in meeting students' needs? What is the probability that the school can attract students?

Regardless of the approach used to develop a mission statement, it must include the services and/or product to be provided, and the students to be served.

Units That Should Create a Mission Statement

Most districts are neglectful in the area of creating units who will develope the mission statement. They usually develop a district mission statement, which is the statement used by all schools. True, a mission statement should be developed by the district, and should be the basis upon which each school, department, grade, and team develop their own mission statement.

The Four Common Types of Mission Statements

There are at least four common types of mission statements, including the standard format approach, the primary and secondary approach, the grand design approach, and the contemporary approach. All of these should be stated in terms of services and description of the students. If the student is not designated, the mission statement may encompass too wide a scope, thus depleting limited resources of the school or team.

Standard Format Approach

The most common form of a mission statement usually contains certain elements, like beginning with a description of the entity (district, school, department, or unit) such as the "Apex School", or you could specify the act the entity is responsible for carrying out by indicating: "The Unnatural School District will direct, support, and participate in the development an implementation of outcome-based education."

You should also indicate the students to be served by the unit, such as: the Apex High School will direct, support, and participate in the development and implementation of outcome-based education.

Primary and Secondary Approach

The second form of a mission statement involves the primary and secondary mission of the school as illustrated here:

"The primary mission of the Apex High School is to engage in success emulation in order to search for, and capitalize on the best practices so that we are better able to meet our primary mission."

Grand Design Approach

The grand design approach to preparing the mission statement involves a general statement about the thrust of the school and specific statements regarding the stakeholder, school people, students, providers, community, and governments.

The following is an example of the mission statement using the grand design:

"The mission of the Apex High School is to provide our students with the best education possible as compared to our contiguous schools. More specifically, the school shall endeavor to:

1. provide students with top-quality services and resources at reasonable cost to the community.
2. consider stakeholders' varied interests when effectuating change in the school.
3. provide teachers with a top-quality working life, including the opportunity for solving school and unit problems.
4. be perceived by providers as a school that is appreciative of their products and services.
5. actively support the community in order to improve its people's quality of life, and to assist in the improvement of the community.
6. convince the governments in which the school operates to give constructive support to our progress.

Contemporary Approach

The contemporary approach is an out-growth of the other three approaches. It contains three sections: section one, which includes an opening statement of no more than two sentences identifying your school and describing what it will do or provide for students; section two which declares in simple two to four statements the services and activities the school will provide for students; and section three which indicates what the school is dedicated to doing for the students.

Compare the following standard format approach with the contemporary approach and it will be easy to see the latter is an improvement over the former:

Standard Format Approach

The Zenith High School is dedicated to serving the educational needs of all students within the community. The bond of district, school people, the state education department, and community all share in the responsibility for the education of your students. Our commitment is to provide a free public education

Developing the School Mission

to maintain a literate community, which is the keystone for a democratic society.

Contemporary Approach

In the Zenith High School, we are dedicated to providing the necessary teachers, resources, and inspiration for each student to develop:

- a command of learning
- society reponsibility
- emotional stability
- critical thinking

We are committed to motivating students to achieve more than they ever hoped to achieve and to value life-long learning.

Some Important Guidelines When Preparing the Mission Statement

Important guidelines for preparing the mission statement are as follows.

1. The mission statement should be developed by a cross-section of school people and other stakeholders of the school district.
2. It should be prepared after a lengthy discussion has taken place.
3. A consensus should be reached concerning the content of the mission statement.
4. Enough time should be allotted to disseminate a copy of the mission statement, and to clarify it throughout the school, by discussing each of its key elements.
5. Be prepared to make minor revisions, if warranted.
6. Whenever possible, use a consultant to facilitate the school in the preparation of the mission statement.

These guidelines are essential for creating an "active" school mission that will motivate teachers before and during the transformation process.

Gain Commitment to the Mission

All teachers—in fact all people in the school as well as parents should be involved in the development of the mission statement. Your school will probably go through several drafts to arrive at one that is satisfactory in meeting school and community requirements. When a draft is completed, prior to arriving at another draft, it should be reviewed by as many people in the school and community as possible. One way a school accomplished this task was by organizing a design team consisting of representatives of each group and department to prepare and refine the initial draft of the mission statement. Then the entire school tested and critiqued the mission. It was then presented to the design team who refined the mission statement, making certain the essence of what the entire school felt was important remained in the mission. It took the school four months before arriving at an acceptable mission statement. If your mission statement takes less than three months, it is probable that you have not involved enough people in its creation.

REVIEW

KEY POINTS TO REMEMBER:

- The mission statement theorizes the operations of the school or team, is usually stated in abstract terms, and endows everyone in the school with a sense of direction.
- Some of the purposes of a mission statement are:
  1. It describes a reason for the existence of the school
  2. It provides a basis for making the right decisions
  3. It is a vehicle for measuring success
  4. It provides a belief system for preparing the instructional program
  5. It determines how resources are to be allocated
  6. It facilitates the identification of opportunities and strengths.

Developing the School Mission

- There are four types of mission statements: 1) standard format approach; 2) primary and secondary approach; 3) grand design approach; and 4) contemporary approach.
- The guidelines for developing a mission statement involves six steps: 1) it should be developed by a cross-section of school and community people; 2) it should be prepared after a lengthy discussion; 3) it should be reached by a consensus; 4) it should be disseminated and posted throughout the school for discussion purposes; 5) minor revisions should be made where warranted; and 6) consultant should be retained to facilitate the preparation of the mission.

APPLICATION

Obtain a copy of the school mission statement and rework it to conform to the contemporary approach, to give it more energy using the following:

Open statement:

_____
_____
_____
_____
_____

Description of education activities:

_____
_____
_____
_____
_____

Dedication of the school:

_____
_____
_____
_____
_____

CHAPTER 6

Creating a School Vision

LEARNING OBJECTIVES:

After reading and comprehending this chapter, you should be able to:

- Define a vision.
- Identify the principles that foster the school vision.
- Describe why a district vision is created.
- Explain how the school vision is created.
- Explain why creating a school vision is not enough.
- Identify tools for creating the school vision.
- Cite the criteria for producing a powerful school vision.
- Identify the benefits associated with creating the school vision.
- Identify the traits of a visionary principal.

What Every Principal Should Know About Creating the School Vision

I've already discussed the first element of the school philosophy, the mission. The second element of the school philosophy is creation of a vision. A vision is the deepest expression of what a school desires. This declaration of a desired future creates the conditions for producing an aligned school. It is the interaction about the vision that helps to connect the school with school and community people in a way that matters. Only then can the school and community support the school's effort. Although a vision can be a source of conflict, in most cases, it is a source of connecting and pulling forth in a united effort.

A vision is a person's mental image of the future, based on a collection of information, knowledge, ideas, aspirations, dreams, dangers, and opportunities. A school vision is a picture of what the school would like to be in the future. It is a dynamic picture of a future and it is more than a dream or a hope. It is truly a commitment in which both the principal and everyone in the school will aspire to make the vision a reality. Thus, the vision provides the context for designing and initiating the essential changes that are necessary to enable everyone in the school to help the transformation happen. It is extremely important for the principal to be able to engage all teachers in the creation of the school vision so that everyone within and without the school will know where it is heading. In addition, you must be able to communicate the school vision not only to teachers and students, but also to everyone within the school community. This chapter will not only demonstrate how the principal can enable teachers to create the vision, but also how to pursue it with a great deal of vigor and enthusiasm.

Creating a vision is a two-stage operation. The first part is the intuitive imagining of a possible desired achievement. The second part is the most difficult, yet crucial aspect of planning: converting the intuitive vision into an action plan. These two aspects of creating a vision must be carried out alternately, with the right, or creative side of the brain thinking of an ideal to help realize the desired achievement, and the left, or analytical, side of the brain determining the concrete implications of the intuitive vision.

The vision of a principal is not simply a vague idea of a desired end, nor is it a clear picture of a single aspect of the school that is being created, and the actual steps taken that are necessary to make that model a reality. To pursue greatness requires much time building and testing the mental mode of existence. The ability to visualize the steps from an idea to realization is one of the most important jobs of a school.

The Traits Of a Visionary Principal

The traits of visionary leaders are identified in the book *Creating Excellence* (New American Library, 1984) by Craig R. Hickman and Michael A. Silva. They use the work of Abraham Zalenik of the Harvard Business School to identify traits of visionary principals. The ten traits are as follows:

- Be able to search for knowledge, ideas, concepts, and ways of thinking until a clear vision crystallizes.

- Be keen at articulating the vision into an easy-to-grasp philosophy that integrates strategic direction with the values of the school.

- Be adept at motivating all teachers to embrace the vision by providing constant encouragement, and by performing as a role model.

- Be able to relate to all teachers and students in a warm, supportive, and expressive way, always communicating to others that, "We are a family; what affects one affects all of us."

- Be adroit at keeping in contact with both students and teachers in an attempt to understand their concerns and the impact of the vision on them.

- Be able to translate the vision so that everyone is able to relate to his or her own individual interests, concerns, and position.

- Be astute at remaining at the core of the action so as to be the primary source for shaping the vision.

- Be able to evaluate the progress of the school in terms of the degree to which the vision has been actualized.

- Be adept at focusing on the major strengths of the school in an effort to centralize the vision.

- Be cunning in seeking ways to improve, augment, or further develop the vision of the school by carefully monitoring changes within and outside of the school environments. Study these tracts carefully. Take one at a time and practice until you feel that you have mastered that tract, then go to the next one and do the same.

Principles That Foster the School Vision

The elements for the creation of a vision of a school are as follows:

- The principal's personal image of the kind of school he or she wants to create
- The principal's agreement is committment to the vision
- The prevalence of openness and creativity and freedom throughout the visionary statement
- The teachers and all school people see, hear, and experience the vision
- The principal and other school administrators are of the same mind regarding the school vision
- The principal and other school administrators speak of the vision with a sense of purpose
- School meetings and workshops are conducted on implementing the school vision and communication meetings on the school vision
- Vision is integrated into the regular school meetings
- The school's imperatives and descriptive statements define the school vision

The District Vision

To inform all interested parties where the district is headed, a vision, called a district vision, is developed and articulated for the entire district by the superintendent. Every school serves as a miniature district. Each school must create and communicate its own vision. Therefore, a transformational district requires two types of visionary statements: the superintendent's vision and the school's vision.

The district vision is usually stated in a simple statement, such as, "To enable our students to realize their unconscious potential." It is used as a base or starting point for each school to create and realize its own vision.

Creating a School Vision

When the district vision has been completed, approved by the board, disseminated and articulated throughout the district and community, the next process involves having all schools create their own vision. A school vision is the mental image of the future direction of a school, based on the district vision and other information relevant to each school and community area. This requires the following steps:

1. **Review Pertinent Information.** The school as a whole reviews the district vision, plus other information that reflects on conditions within and without the school.

2. **Ponder Appropriate Questions.** When sufficient information has been collected and digested, the school ponders the following questions for introspection and projection:

   - What can we do to maximize the number of our students going to college?

   - Why do any of our students fail and what can we do to minimize failures?

   - What do our students want? Do they value what we do for them? Can we enhance our values? How should we change our curriculum to fortify them for the future?

   - What do we do well? What do we do poorly? How can we improve? What constrictions keep us from improving?

   - What is our potential? Where could we be in five or ten years?

   - Why have we succeeded or failed in the past? Do we really understand the reasons for our success or failure? Are we being honest with ourselves?

   - If we could rewrite our school history, what would we change?

   - What are other schools doing to improve the instructional program?

   - How can we use the frustration and disappointment of our students as learning experiences to improve our school?

- What can we do to enable our students to be more than they ever hoped to be?
- How do we handle situations in which our students let us down?
- What do our students want from us?
- What can we do to help our students to be prepared for the future?
- How do we treat the majority of our students and how should we treat them?

However, before generating the vision, it may be appropriate to review with the teachers how visionary statements should be written, by sharing with them the following tips, which are expressed by Peter Block in his book: *The Empowered Manager:*

Tip 1: Don't try to be better than any other school. Your school vision should express the contribution it wants to make to the school.

Tip 2: Begin with your students' long-term survival. The growth of the school is dependent upon how well the school becomes close to students and how well it serves them.

Tip 3: Treat students and teachers alike. If you treat your students well, you are most likely treating your school people well, too.

3. Identifying Key Visionary Areas. Key visionary areas are highly selective visionary statements that depict the future direction of the school that must be realized in order for it to become what it aspires to be. These key visionary statements are usually arrived at by using brainstorming or the nominal group process.

The total number of key visionary areas is equal to the vision. This means that the results of the introspection of the past and projection into the future must lead to those crucial and essential issues and activities that describe a reference point in the future to which all efforts of the school and community must be directed. This does not mean that other areas may be neglected, but it focuses on what key issues and activites on which the school should be concentrating its efforts. Design teams should be established to deal with any other areas. Each statement is an expression of hope, desire, and aspiration. However, it is not

Creating a School Vision

enough just to create a vision, not even a vision of excellence. What we should be striving for is a vision of greatness. A vision of greatness demands that you hold nothing back, that you set no limitations, that you push faith with everything you have, that you eliminate caution and reservation, and that you have faith in the future.

Key visionary statements are created by merely writing a single statement describing what is desired for the future for students. The following are some examples: "Function as a synergistic team in which everyone feels responsible for the success of the team." "Develop, implement, and continuously improve on a strategic curriculum."

When using either brainstorming or the nominal group process to generate key visionary statements, the problem should be stated similar to the following: "Describe in single sentences those key visionary statements you think and feel should define the future direction of our school."

The school must be careful not to include values statements as key visionary areas. An effective way to do this is to understand the differences between the two statements: 1) key visionary areas indicate where the school is going as related to the future (or "the name of the game"), and 2) values statements indicate how the school will get there (or "the rules of the game."). The main reasons for separating these statements are that all key visionary statements must be realized through a program strategy or action plan. Values statements are usually expressed with indicators for evaluation purposes. In addition, values statements are challenged periodically in terms of the culture, whereas the vision is not necessarily challenged, but is reviewed and modified based upon internal and/or external environments. To separate key visionary areas from values statements will require the school as a whole to review each statement, to consider the above definitions, and to select those statements that indicate where the school is going or the future direction of the school. The values statements should not be discarded but saved and considered when either challenging existing values or preparing a shared values statement

4. **Link Each Key Visionary Statement to a Program Strategy**.
   In order to realize the vision, a plan must be developed and executed. This is accomplished by developing a program

strategy. A program strategy is a series of long-term action plans designed to guide human efforts in realizing a key visionary area. The following is an example of a program strategy for the following key visionary area:

KEY VISION AREA

Function as a synergistic team in which everyone feels responsible for the success of the team.

PROGRAM STRATEGY:

Teacher and principal recruitment

The teacher will interview all new teachers and administrators so that each member shares responsibility in the selection process. The key basis upon which teachers and administrators will be selected is that their personality and character are consonant with the shared values of the school.

Training and development

All teachers will undergo a minimum of six, thirty-hour training sessions per year in process skills and sixty hours of training per year in technical skills. The school council will attend most training events as a group.

Evaluation Performance

Teachers will be evaluated based on how well each one has contributed to the success of the school. Teachers will also evaluate all support staff, including the superintendent, in terms of how well they supported the efforts of the council.

School Improvement

A school development plan will be jointly developed quarterly by the principal and the teachers to improve the school's effectiveness in carrying out its charge.

Preparing the Vision Realization Plan

Once the program strategy is in place, a vision realization plan is developed for each key visionary area. The purpose of the plan

Creating a School Vision

is to have some visible evidence that appropriate steps are being taken to realize the vision. The plan contains four elements as described below:

1. The specific key vision area in which a program strategy will be developed.
2. Name of the council member/s assigned and responsible for carrying out the program strategy.
3. A description of the program strategy that was created by the collective action of the school council.
4. A progress report used to determine if the program strategy will realize the key visionary area.

Why Creating a Vision Is Not Enough

A number of schools have created a vision to direct the performance efforts of their school and community people. However, unfortunately, it stops there. The vision must also be preached and taught to everyone in the school and community. It is the responsibility of the principal and other school administrators to communicate the school vision throughout the school and community. It is also the responsibility of the school team leader and school members to create and communicate the school vision throughout the school and community.

All principals should take a lead from Peter Drucker, one of the country's most noted scientific management consultants, who said that when he wants something done, "give me a maniac with a mission." This statement is applicable to preaching the vision. Transformational principals are visionaries who have become maniacs with a mission. They teach and preach the vision anywhere and everywhere, in the streets, in the home, in the banks, in the supermarkets, in the churches, and in the office buildings! No place is off limits when it comes to preaching the vision. The following are some activities that transformational principals use to communicate the vision:

- They institute a vision awareness that focuses on the school vision and they use the visions to capture local media coverage.

- They organize parades in the center of the community consisting of local groups, students, parents, and teachers, all carrying signs depicting the vision. They make use of cheerleaders and the school band. Tots are at the forefront who will be directly affected by the realization of the vision.
- They require all school administrators and school team leaders and members to preach the vision at least twice weekly and submit a brief report.
- They manage by wandering around and periodically stop school and community people and ask them to give a direction in which the school is heading in the future. If the person is unable to do so, they spend several minutes with him or her to preach the vision.
- They prepare a video on the vision and insist that each department head, grade leader, or team teacher spend forty-five to sixty minutes with his or her staff explaining the vision.
- They establish a vision suggestion award program in which the persons submitting the best ideas for improving the future direction of the school will receive an award.
- They create a newsletter entitled "The Vision" and include articles relevant to realizing the vision.

Transformational leaders institute these activities and others so that all school and community people eventually become maniacs with a vision to preach the essence of the vision to everybody in and out of the school and community. They encourage others to be a maniac with a vision. It is not enough to create a vision; it must come alive by the presentation of the vision through a number of five- to ten-minute "stump" speeches. This means that visionary statements must be "preached" to both school and community members by the principal, by teachers, by anyone within and outside the school and community. The goal of every council member should be to preach the vision on a daily basis, at least twice a day, through a variety of settings. Some settings in which the vision should be preached include: churches, homes, public meetings, stores and supermarkets, schools, athletic events, musical events, banks, anywhere and everywhere in the school and community.

The following is an example of a "stump" speech delivered by a principal of a school in Longmont, Colorado:

"I want to thank you for giving me five minutes of your valuable time to hear my vision for our school.

Our strategic vision is to enable our students to become more than they ever hoped to be. When I say that I mean, WE WILL NOT BE:

- a school that cares only for the success of some students, the bright ones.

- a school that closes its doors to the community or invites them in only for token PTA appearances or to bake cookies for the school carnival.

- a school where students merely memorize material, not developing the essential thinking skills they need for life.

- a school where students sit as passive receptacles at their desks, bored and uninvolved with the learning process.

- a school where teachers and staff are burned out, lethargic, and counting their paychecks until retirement.

- a school where an elite few make decisions that impact many.

- a school where students have no sense of their potential because they have never been stretched and nurtured to think about the possibilities for their lives.

- a school that permits students to fall through the cracks, leaving them for society to handle.

TO REACH GREATNESS, we will not be any of these things.

Instead, I offer you a vision for our future epitomized by the expression, "every child a promise." For every child is a promise in:

- a school that cares passionately about the success of all students be they learning disabled, possess an offbeat learning style, in the minority, or gifted.

- a school that opens every door to the community to sit on councils and task forces and committees to engage in meaningful dialogue and to make significant decisions.

- a school where creative students master critical thinking skills for lifelong learning.
- a school where all students can comprehend, evaluate, and act on what they learn in their everyday life, communicating their zest for new ideas.
- a school where every student succeeds beyond his or her expectations.
- a school that reaches for success by fostering the academic and social and emotional development of each child.
- a school where there are no cracks to fall through.

Every child is a promise in this school. I offer you that vision. Join me in offering your support."

Instilling the School Vision in Students

It is not enough for the principal and teachers to create the school vision, to defend the district vision before a task force, and to deliver several "stump" speeches throughout the district and community. It is not enough for the school to use the district vision as a base to create a school vision. It is also not enough for the principal, teachers, and others to deliver "stump" speeches to communicate the vision to school and community people and to develop program strategies to realize the school vision. The school vision must be used to encourage each student to develop his or her own personal plan to realize this vision. To perform this feat, the following activities must be initiated by the school:

1. Require teachers to discuss the school vision and the need for students to develop their own personal plans to realize the school vision.
2. Require the librarian to accumulate a wealth of resources on various alternatives for students to realize the school vision.
3. Request all teachers to frequently refer to the school vision in the teaching process.
4. Consider making the school vision a pledge that students will recite periodically.

Creating a School Vision

5. Stop students in the halls and test them for reciting the vision and their plan for realizing that vision.
6. Conduct contests in which those students reciting the most realistic and creative plans for realizing the school vision, and who demonstrate concrete steps to do so are rewarded. Make certain a large number of students receive this reward.

Everybody Plays a Part in Actualizing the Vision

It takes a visionary superintendent and visionary councils to achieve greatness in education. The superintendent and councils must conceive of separate visions. The board of education must act on the superintendent's vision. And council members and teachers must perform harmoniously to actualize the school vision. If any one of these stages is poorly executed, the quest for greatness is lost. Therefore, the superintendent, as well as the councils are the key. They must have the knowledge and skills necessary to create a vision that when actualized will produce greatness.

The best way to teach the vision is simply and directly. Tell everybody in and out of the school about its quest for greatness. What steps are presently being taken? How long will the quest take? What evidence will indicate that the vision is becoming a reality? The principals and teachers must embody the dreams, values, and aspirations of the school. They must be true believers and must characterize that vision through words, actions, deeds, and thoughts.

The most essential step for planning for the future consists of depicting the future direction of the school based upon a collection of information, knowledge, ideas, facts, aspirations, opportunities, and dangers. In their book, *In Search of Excellence*, Tom Peters and Robert Waterman say about the importance of having a vision that, "A vision must always . . . start with a single individual . . . the raw material of the vision is invariably the result of one man or woman's searching." Howard J. Leavitt, author of *Corporate Pathfinders*, maintains the vision "usually starts in a fumbling, groping way, reaching toward one shadowy dream that cannot easily be verbalized or defined." He goes on to say, "For a vision of the future to be more than a dream, for a creative idea to translate into a useful innovation, hard work has to be done."

The principal is not only responsible for producing a visionary statement, but for getting other school people, as well as the community, to buy into the visions.

Some Guidelines for Creating A School Visionary Statement

These guidelines have been practiced by hundreds of companies and schools throughout the United States. They seem to produce necessary statements that inspire and motivate teachers and teams to perform at a high level. They consist of the following:

- Allow design team members to be in a relaxed state of mind, preferably away from the school where there is no pressure. Play soft relaxing music during the envisioning process.
- Focus on what really matters to the school as a whole.
- Try to focus on the right side of the brain, the creative side first and switch to the left side, the practical side, to establish a plan to implement the dream.
- Focus on imagining what is happening.
- Avoid focusing on present-day problems..
- Give some sample abstract visionary statement, such as "To enable students to become more that they hoped to be."
- Design a result-orientated plan to implement the school vision.

Some Visioning Tools for Creating the School Vision

The following are several tools useful in thinking about the school vision. It may be necessary for you to use all of them. However, try at least two or three of these tools. These tools can be very effective in helping your design team to envision what the school can become:

Symbols

Symbols are images or visual pictures that represent the vision. They mirror an image of the future. Each person on the design team draws an image of what the vision should be like. When each person has completed this task, the design team leader takes all of the images and puts them together into a composite symbol. Crayons, flipchart paper, colored pens, tape, scissors and other supplies are used to create a team image from the individual images that have been created.

Storytelling

An interesting tool to help create the school vision is to create an enactment of the school vision of the future by involving the design team members in a direct experience of dialogue, actions, and behaviors that will be needed to make the school vision real. This can be accomplished by asking members to create a play that demonstrates what the school would look like when the vision is achieved.

Students' Wants

Complete a paragraph that begins with a stem statement such as, "If I were a student in this school, I would want..."

Values

The design team is asked to think about what it individually and the team as a whole values most. Then, list five ways of completing the stem statement, "In our school (or class) we really care about..."

Physical Challenge

Quite frequently, active experience can release design team members from their usual patterns of thought. Several games and outdoor activities have been effective in getting individuals and teams in the mood for new ways of thinking. Sometimes an exercise is used to allow individuals and/or teams to think differently about how they solved the exercise.

Imagery

Imagery is effective in getting individuals and teams to think differently. It invites the use of the mind by team members to project themselves into the future when the school vision has been achieved. Imagery, basically is the mental process of creating sights, sounds, smells, tastes and sensations in the absence of external stimuli. It is a means of improving communication between conscious and unconscious levels of the mind.

An effective way to do this is to select one of the key shared values of the school and allow someone to imagine how he or she personally embodies this value from the beginning of school to the close of school. Another way is to asks members of the design team to imagine that they are journalists writing an article for a school publication and to create a story that vividly describes the successes the design team will achieve ten years from now.

The Criterion of Powerful School Vision

A powerful vision statement has the following criteria that can be used to evaluate your school vision. These are:

- Indicates where the school wants to go.
- Comes from the heart.
- It is easy to read and comprehend.
- It is radical and compelling.
- Captures the desired spirit of the school.
- Begins with students.
- Gets teachers and other's attention.
- Is apt to be impractical.
- Describes a preferred and meaningful future state.
- Provides a motivating force.
- Is used as a guide to direct human efforts.
- Gives the school a soul.
- Is pie in the sky.

The Benefits Associated With Creating A School Vision

To the teachers, teams, and the school as a whole that have created a vision, the following benefits have accrued:

1. *Alignment.* Teachers and teams that have participated in creating the school vision have acquired a sense of purpose and an overall congruence with the school's goals. There was also an increased sense of energy and excitement. In addition, school has a deeper meaning in teams that have created a vision.

2. *Empowerment.* Creating a vision increases a sense of personal worth, team empowerment, and school vigor. Because the experience of teachers assuming direct responsibility for results that they have planned and implemented increased their ability to act.

3. *Commitment.* Teachers who have participated in the creation of the vision usually notice that the school vision often replaces standard operating procedures. Thus, the vision is used to make decisions and give direction. Teachers work out of commitment rather than compliance.

4. *Innovation.* Teachers who have participated in creating the school vision usually increase their ability to generate different ideas about the future. They usually are able to think beyond short-range objectives and imagine the future.

5. *Respect.* Creating the vision provides an opportunity for shared participation. All contributions of team members are treated equally. The school vision is an image in which each team member can make a contribution.

6. *Interdependence.* Creating and orchestrating the school vision is a format for school teams to experience how they are connected with other teams. It provides the larger picture in which individual team members can place individual efforts.

Differences Among a Vision, Mission, and Shared Values

Sometimes people get confused about what differentiates vision, mission, and shared values from each other. A vision is similar to a dream created to describe the future direction of a school. For example, "To enable our students to be more than they ever hoped to be," means that you desire to reach a point in the future in which all students achieve beyond their expectations. It differs from the mission in that the mission statement indicates what businesses you are in and the population you serve. For example, the statement, "Our mission is to provide quality education and experiences to all students who knock on the portals of our schools," means that *all* students who desire to go to your schools will be admitted, regardless of whether they live within or without the school district. Shared values which will be discussed in the next chapter, are norms and belief statements describing how school people should be treated as they achieve the mission and realize the vision. For example: "Trust in the goodness of people" is a value statement, meaning that most people can be trusted to do what is right.

REVIEW

KEY POINTS TO REMEMBER:

- A school vision is a picture of a future state of what the school would like to be some years from the present.
- The superintendent should first create and communicate the district vision and the principal *should* engage teachers and parents in the creation of the school vision.
- Some guidelines for providing the school vision are: 1) allow teacher team members to be in a relaxed state of mind; 2) focus on what really counts; 3) try focusing on the right side of the brain first and then the left side; 4) focus on inquiring; 5) give some samples; 6) develop result-oriented implementation plan.
- The principle steps for creating a school vision are as follows: 1) give the task to a design team; 2) use visioning tools; 3) create a draft; 4) discuss the draft; 5) redraft the

Creating a School Vision

school vision; 6) repeat steps 4 and 5; and 7) promote the school vision.

- Some tools for visioning consist of symbols, storytelling, students' wants, values, physical challenge, imagery, and five-ways worksheet.

- The benefits associated with the creation of a school vision are: alignment, empowerment, commitment, innovation, respect, and interdependence.

APPLICATION

Once your school vision has been created and communicated throughout the school for six to nine months, get some feedback on what the school vision represents. Look for gaps and rework the vision.

A force-field analysis is an excellent tool to perform this feat. Identify and list all of the forces that are working to make the vision happen and all the forces that are keeping the vision from happening. (Read Chapter 29 to understand how to construct a force-field analysis.)

There are three types of forces that are likely to impact the visionary process:

1. Things that have to involve students
2. Things that have to involve teacher teams and other school people
3. Things of a nonpersonal nature, cultural assumptions, environment, etc.

Negative forces impacting the vision

_____
_____
_____
_____

Positive forces impacting the vision

_____
_____
_____
_____
_____

After the force-field analysis has been completed, determine the top three negative forces impacting the vision. Now, develop an action plan to eliminate these negative forces.

CHAPTER 7

Identifying the Shared Values of the School

LEARNING OBJECTIVES:

After reading and comprehending this chapter, you should be able to:

- Define shared values.
- Identify the chief reasons for creating shared values.
- Describe why shared values are important.
- Identify guidelines for creating shared values.
- Understand the various approaches for writing shared values.
- Explain how shared values should be formulated.
- Inculcate shared values in the school.

What Every Principal Should Know About Creating Shared Values

If all teachers have the same values with the same priorities, it will be relatively easy to work in school without any conflict or problems. However, if not, all teachers will have a diversity of values and beliefs. To help teachers to work better and to arrive at decisions that lead to commitment and action, it is necessary for the school as a family to arrive at a set of key values that will influence decision-making progress and thus improve the school's performance.

The transformational principal is keenly aware of the importance of assisting the teachers to reach agreement on these values to ensure that everyone is marching to the beat of the same drummer.

The Definition of Shared Values

Webster defines values as "a principle, standard or quality considered inherently worthwhile or desirable." The root for value is valor, meaning strength. As a result, values are sources of strength to the school because they give teachers the basis and power to take action. However, values may be deeply rooted and emotional and can be difficult to change. Shared values are belief statements that most, if not all, teachers agree are important to give direction and guidance to all efforts in the school. Sometimes shared values are created to include both how adults should treat other adults and how adults should treat students.

A district or school must clarify its mission, create a vision, and identify shared values. When values are not stated or shared, the district and school find it difficult to unify individual components. As a result, each operates as a separate entity, creating conflicts and disunity among its segments.

Shared values are the fundamental and common beliefs that unite a district, a school or a team, integrating its work efforts, guiding its actions, and channeling its energies so as to bring fulfillment to all members and to the system as a whole. To accomplish this, it is necessary to develop a value statement on the district and school levels. More specifically, values:

- Provide guidelines for governing the behavior of administrators, teachers, and others within the school system.
- Provide a sense of direction for those associated with the district and schools.

Identifying the Shared Values of the School

- Are the basis for guiding teachers and other school people's decisions and actions.
- Help teachers perform better (because they are influenced by the substance of each statement).
- Communicate to others what is expected from the district and school.

The Underlying Theory About Shared Values

Shared values define the fundamental character of the district and school—the attitude that distinguishes it from others. In this way, they create a special sense of identity for those in the district and school, giving meaning to work as something more than simply earning a living. Values should guide human behavior.

Shared values affect school performance in three ways:

1. The principal gives extraordinary attention to whatever matters are stressed in the value system. This in turn tends to produce extraordinary results.

2. The principal regularly makes better decisions, on average, because he or she is guided by their perception of the shared values.

3. Teachers simply work a little harder because they are dedicated to the cause.

In a district and school, a shared value of "excellence in education" becomes a reality in the minds of all teachers and other school people. Shared value acts as an informal control system that tells everybody what is expected of them and gives a sense of everyone pulling together towards a common goal.

Once the superintendent's value statement has been developed, it is presented to each central school administrator to study prior to a meeting that will take place during a designated weekend off school grounds. During this meeting, each values statement is discussed, clarified, defended, and/or modified until a consensus is reached between the superintendent and central school administrators.

The district's shared values statement is global in nature, and is used as an umbrella for each school to create its own value statements. Its purpose is to:

- Describe how the district should be managed.
- Identify the values, beliefs, expectations, and attitudes of the superintendent.
- Be used as a basis for synchronizing the values of the central school administrators with the superintendent.

The Chief Reasons for Creating Shared Values

The mainspring for achieving shared values in a school is the creation and clarity about it shared values, but there are also other reasons for achieving shared values. Today, with emphasis given to empowerment and more autonomy given to individual teachers, they need to be guided not by rules or the principal, but by understanding the shared values of the school. If an action or decision fits the shared values, then it is correct. If not, the action is incorrect and should cease.

Shared values are a set of beliefs or understandings in a school about how teachers should work together and how the principal should treat teachers and others in the school. Shared values are also motivators. When teachers or the principal feel that something is right and important to the success of the school because they agreed to them, they will spend a great deal of time and energy to achieve it.

To be effective, the teachers need to reach a common understanding about what they value. Their values must be put into practices, policies, and standards for acceptable behavior. Shared values are the essence of a school's philosophy for reaching success. They are the foundation for providing the school culture. They provide teachers and other school people with a sense of common direction and guidelines for day to day acceptable behavior.

When the principal's values are congruent with the shared values of the school (this is a strong reason why the principal plays an important part in participating in the creation process arriving at shared values of the school) teachers' sense of what

Identifying the Shared Values of the School

is important strongly influences their commitment and motivation.

The Importance of Shared Values

The school philosophy is incomplete if it only includes the mission and vision. These elements only define the major external focus. Shared values describe the underlying foundations for action. In addition to the previous two elements discussed in this part, the philosophy must indicate how the people within the school will work together to carry out the philosophy, how they will treat teachers and other school people, and what will bond them together. Teachers and others within the school work for a variety of reasons and discuss different things with each other and the school itself. It is possible for teachers to agree on a mission and vision, but to have a conflict when it comes to shared values, because different teachers have different values about students and about the school. Some teachers might want to work independently, while others might enjoy working in teams. Because of conflicts and needs, a consensus must be ready among all teachers as to what values they can share and have in common. Creating shared values helps the principal to do so.

Some Guidelines for Preparing a Shared Values Statement

Some general guidelines for preparing the school shared values statement are:
- Include only brief statements.
- Review the statements for clarity, impact, and accuracy.
- Limit each statement to effective (attitudes, values, beliefs) matters. Avoid behavioral and cognitive matters.
- Use a directive to construct values statements, regardless of the approach selected.

The following technique can be used to develop values statements for the school.
- The team requests its members, facilitators, community people, and a consultant to serve on its shared values task force.

- The task force arranges the nominal group process and other techniques to arrive at a semifinal shared value statement.
- The task force discusses the semi-final shared values statement with designated school and community people to get their input.
- Based on this input, the statement is modified and/or revised. The entire school family is requested to appear at a meeting to receive, review, and discuss the final document. Minor adjustments are then made.
- Once the generated list of indicators for each values statement has been completed, each indicator is used as a topic for training in a series of ten- to fifteen- minute workshops conducted over a period of several months.
- Districts and schools should include value statements for both teachers and students. If value statements indicate how people are to be treated in school, this applies to how school administrators should treat teachers, and how teachers should treat students.

When all of the activities have been completed, the district and school are in a state of readiness to determine if school administrators and teachers walk like they talk. This is determined through challenging each value statement on a yearly basis, and taking appropriate action when warranted.

The Various Approaches for Writing the Shared Values Statement

There are perhaps several dozen methods for depicting values statements, including the simple statement approach, the action-oriented approach, the quality standard approach, the whereas approach, and the key value card approach.

Simple Statement Approach

The simple statement approach is probably the most common method through which schools prepare shared value statements, and it is the least prepared by practitioners. It consists of two steps. The first is to identify a list of shared value statements.

Identifying the Shared Values of the School

"Teamwork" is an example of a value. Next, define each core value, such as "Teamwork and cooperation are essential."

Action-Oriented Approach

Perhaps the best method to declare a shared value statement is the action-oriented approach. There are two basic steps to this approach. First, meet and mutually agree on a set of shared values, such as "Research, facts, and data are better than hunches and guesses."

Next, reach mutual agreement on all appropriate actions necessary to support the shared value, as demonstrated below:

SHARED VALUE

Research, facts, and data are better than hunches and guesses.

ACTION STATEMENTS

- Base all decisions on research
- Train team members to follow fact-based, problem-solving techniques.
- Provide diagnostic support, and help teams locate needed data.

The action-oriented method identifies activities mutually agreed on by teachers to engage in to support the values. It therefore minimizes guesswork. In addition, each shared value can be assessed periodically to determine the extent to which they are being inculcated throughout either the district or the school.

Quality Standard Approach

An effective method of creating shared values is to attach standards of quality to each value. There are four steps for creating shared values using the quality standard methods. First, identify single core value terms to perform this task, and reach a consensus on key value terms that represent the district or school quality focus, like caring, respect, integrity, empowerment, and intimacy.

The next step involves describing each term with no more than two to four words, such as:

Caring:
1. Reach Out
2. Be friendly
3. Care for each other.

For the third step, now that the core value has been briefly described, use short, descriptive statements to indicate how each will be carried out. For example:

Caring:
1. Reach out. Welcome all irate parents appearing in school for an audience. Acknowledge their presence. Make eye contact and smile. Introduce yourself in a pleasant tone of voice. State your name and your position. Whenever possible, use the parent's name to address him and/or her. Above all, engage in active listening by paraphrasing what the parent(s) said. Try to reach a solution to the problem. Be attentive, genuine, and positive.

Whereas Approach

Another effective approach to creating shared value statements is to describe the values, then further change the values with "therefore" statements.

There are three steps to this process. First, use consensus to arrive at a list of shared values to depict the district or school focus, such as, "quality is our number-one concern."

Second, precede the sample value statement with a "We believe" or another appropriate phrase, such as, "We believe quality is our number-one concern."

Finally, complete the "We believe..." values statement with "therefore," followed by a statement further clarifying the value statement, such as "We believe quality is our number-one concern; therefore, quality is everyone's responsibility."

Some districts and schools may desire to proceed further with this correctly written statement and amplify the words "quality is everyone's responsibility." To do this, brainstorm or use the nominal group process to generate evaluation indicators for the word "expectations." Such a list may resemble the following, us-

ing the stem statement, "All school people demonstrate a responsibility for quality when they ...
1. ... either as individuals or teams engage in activities to improve performance on a continuous basis."
2. ... attend a minimum of sixty hours of education and training on statistics, problem solving, and meeting management."

Key Value Card Approach

Another effective approach for realizing shared values is the key values card approach, which consists of four steps.

Step 1: Cite Key Value.

Request teachers to cite and sort key values that should be used as guidelines for the principal to treat teachers and other school people and/or how the teacher should treat students in the school. After everyone has written their key values, ask the group to select the five most important values that should govern how teachers and other school people should be treated, and/or how students should be treated by teachers and other school people. Use the following stem statement to identify these values:

Teachers and other school people should be treated in school ... and/or students should be treated in school . . .

Step 2: Sharing Key Values.

Circulate around the room and request individual teachers and other school people to read their most important value statement. Record each value on a flip chart. Combine value statements that are similar. Get agreement on the similarities. Complete three to four rounds of voting on the values statements. Ask the group to decide on a specific number of key values that represent the school shared values statement. Prioritize this list.

Step 3: Discuss Gaps.

The group should at this time discuss each ranked shared value statement and agree to restate, re-prioritize, or modify them if necessary. The following should help:
Which shared values are not expressed as often as they should?_____

Which shared values are often neglected in crisis or during times of pressure?_____
_____

Which shared values are considered dispensable?._____
_____

Step 4: Neglected or Unexpressed Shared Values.
Sometimes you might find that certain shared values are espoused, but are not really enacted. Cite ways each shared value should be practiced in the school (or team).
Action plan to shared this shared value:

Shared Values No.	Description	How Should It Be Practiced
_____	_____	_____
_____	_____	_____
_____	_____	_____

Finally, it is not sufficient to list core values. Each year, a process must be put in place to determine the degree to which the core values are being inculcated in the district or school. Some techniques for assessing core values are as follows:

1. Conduct a general session with the district or school and use the values and quality standards for discussion purposes.
2. Request that those monitoring the values assess the extent to which the values are being carried out.
3. Request a team to perform an assessment.

Writing Meaningful Student-Oriented Value Statements

Thousands of schools have written student-oriented value statements so that they are virtually meaningless. Value statements should be written so that they are meaningful and can be evaluated periodically. The following is a typical value statement: "All children can learn."
This is a value statement, which has been written by hundreds around the country, but how can it be measured? The following is a procedure to do so. First, use "We believe" at the beginning

Identifying the Shared Values of the School

of "All". Second, add the word "therefore" after the word "learn" and include a statement as to what should be performed in order to accomplish this value statement, e.g. "...all teachers will demonstrate high expectations for all students." Thus, a meaningless values statement is now meaningful since it can be measured, such as the following: "We believe all children can learn; therefore, all teachers will demonstrate high expectations for all students."

Some schools may desire to proceed further with this correctly written statement and amplify the words *"high expectations."* To do this, brainstorm or use the nominal group process to generate evaluation indicators for the word "expectations." Such a list may resemble the following, using the stem statement "Teachers demonstrate high expectations for students when..."

- No students is ridiculed for making an error."
- All students are encouraged to succeed and are recognized and rewarded for doing so."
- All teachers display a caring attitude for all students."
  The generated list of indicators becomes the basis for evaluating each of the value statements.

Once the generated list of indicators for each values statement has been completed, each indicator is used as a topic for training in a series of ten-to fifteen-minute workshops conducted over a period of several months.

Schools should include values statements for both teachers and students. If values statements indicate how people are to be treated in school, this applies to how the principal should treat teachers and how teachers should treat students.

When all of the activities have been completed, the school is in a state of readiness to determine if the principal and teachers walk the talk. This is determined through challenging each value statement on a yearly basis and taking appropriate action when warranted.

The task force discusses the semifinal shared value statement with designated school and community people to get their input. Based on the input, the statement is modified and/or revised. The entire school family is requested to appear at a meeting to receive, review, and discuss the final document. Minor adjustments are then made.

An example of a final shared values statement is as follows:

School People

We believe that people are our most important resource; therefore, we must continually train and cultivate our entire school family.

We believe that it is all right to fail; therefore, we must praise students and appreciate all of our teachers who do things for students and fail for the first time.

We believe in a win-win relationship; therefore, we shall seek consensus in all of our major decision.

We believe that all school administrators exist to serve and support teachers; therefore, all school administrators are expected to support all efforts and activities of teachers.

Students

We value each student as an individual; therefore, each student is expected to be taught at his or her own individual level rather than at a group level.

We believe that every student is precious; therefore, not only is the school interested in the education of students, but also in their health and welfare.

We believe that there are no failures, but degrees of success; therefore. all students shall be praised and rewarded for what they have achieved rather than what they have not achieved.

We believe in making "educational miracles" the routine, rather than the exception; therefore, all students shall be required to pursue their own individual vision and the school is expected to actively support his or her vision.

Shared Values Are Inculcated in the School

The following are useful techniques for inculcating shared values to build a strong school culture:

1. **Principal Performing As Role Model.** If the words and deeds of the principal are consistent with the values of the school, a strong culture will result, if not, a weak culture will be evident. Role modeling can be demonstrated in written docu-

ments, as well as through the use of audio-visual aids. It is also useful to have the principal present skits in which he or she assumes roles to demonstrate various aspects and stages of certain value statements. For example, the principal may "act out" the behaviors associated with the value: "Criticism is viewed as a training opportunity." Teachers will then identify the element of the value that was represented.

2. **Recognizing Compliance.** Recognize a teacher who exemplifies an element of shared values. Send a note of praise to this person. In some schools, teachers who exemplify the desired elements of the shared values are given a gift certificate that can be exchanged for merchandise at a store, membership in a health spa, etc.

3. **Communicating the Shared Values.** Prepare a manual containing statements of the school's shared values and use it as a tool during orientation. This manual is invaluable when implementing the varied training activities associated with orientation and career growth. Some schools have produced newsletters to help spread the gospel, others have produced "white papers" and essays, and distributed and discussed these with their teachers.

4. **Implementing Long-Range Training Activities.** This refers to training programs conducted over two to three years, which involve regular monthly training sessions lasting for twenty to thirty minutes.

5. **Other Subtle Techniques Designed to Help Inculcate Shared Values of the School.** Some schools use tests and interviews to screen prospective teachers. If the individual's personality and character are compatible with the school's values, the candidate is hired. Another subtle form for inculcating involves adapting practices that are consistent with the shared values. These may involve an open-door policy, career development path, etc. Perhaps the most subtle technique for inculcating shared values is physically designing school facilities that embrace the values of the school.

REVIEW

KEY POINTS TO REMEMBER:

- Shared values are defined as belief statements in which most, if not all teachers agree are important to give direction and guidance to all human beings in the school.
- The chief reasons for creating shared values statements are: they cite beliefs that are important; they indicate how people should work together; they are motivators; they are values that are put into practices, policies and standards for acceptable behavior; they are essential for reaching success in school; and they give teachers a sense of what is important.
- Guidelines for preparing shared values statement include the following: include brief statements; review statements for clarity, impact, and accuracy; liimit each statement to attitudes, values, and beliefs; and use a directive to construct values statements.
- The various approaches for writing shared values statements are the simple statement approach, action-oriented approach, quality standard approach, the whereas approach, and key value cards.

Application

1. Organize a team of three teachers and two parents, and discuss the need to revise the existing shared values statement so that the school can evaluate the extent to which the shared values are being inculcated within the school. Use the action-oriented approach to format your school shared value statement. Assess each shared value within six months by engaging teachers in a discussion regarding the effort to which each action is being realized to inculcate each value.
2. There is a high probability that your shared values statement was created using the simple statement approach. Redesign your shared values statement and use either the action-oriented, quality standard, or the whereas approach. Use the redesign as a means to evaluate the extent to which each

shared values statement has been inculcated in your school. To do this, take the outcome or objective indicator for each shared value and use a scale from 1 to 5, with 5 being the highest to assess the shared values statement. For example, using the shared values statement cited earlier in the quality standard method, "Reach out", develop a five-point scale based on the following:

1. Welcome all irate parents appearing in the school for an audience.
   1 2 3 4 5

2. Acknowledge their presence.
   1 2 3 4 5

3. Make eye contact and smile.
   1 2 3 4 5

Once your instrument is completed, think of a way you would use it to determine the degree to which the shared values are being inculcated in the school.

CHAPTER 8

Building a Strong and Healthy School Culture

LEARNING OBJECTIVES

After reading and comprehending this chapter, you will be able to:

- Define a school culture.
- Identify the teachers for building a strong school culture.
- Cite subtle techniques for assessing the school culture.
- Identify the attributes of a good school culture.
- Explain the technique for building and shaping a healthy culture.
- Describe the procedure for inculcating the school culture.
- Prepare a philosophy awareness questionnaire.

What Every Principal Should Know About Building a Strong and Healthy School Culture

Merely preparing a comprehensive statement of philosophy will not produce an excellent school; the philosophy must come alive. All teachers and school people must be given a copy of the philosophy, each aspect must be thoroughly discussed and digested, and all elements must be practiced by the principal, other school administrators, and teachers. A living philosophy is one that has been inculcated throughout the school, thus giving it a soul.

A prevailing problem in far too many schools in this country is the stagnation that takes place when a philosophy has been formulated. Usually, the principles and guidelines that have been evolved, sometimes with adequate teacher involvement and deliberation, and sometimes without, are not shared with teachers. As a result, it is as if no philosophy exists. The principals and other school administrators alike go about performing their jobs with no set of macro-principles and guidelines. To increase the philosophy of a school, its principal must plan and execute a formal program to make this essential step to excellence a reality.

Defining School Culture

The *Random House College Dictionary* defines culture as "the sum total of a way of the living built up by a group of human beings and transmitted from one generation to another." Culture as it applies to schools can be defined as ideologies, values, assumptions, beliefs, expectations, attributes, and norms that unite teachers and other school people together. All of these interrelated psychological qualities reveal a school's agreement, implicit and explicit, as to how to approach behavior, decisions, and problems. In other words, culture is the way things are done in the school.

The Elements of a School Culture

What is it about the Johnson City Schools in Johnson City, New York, that exerts a grip on its teachers and other school people? In order to determine this, you will have to visit the district and examine each element of its culture. A brief description of the elements are as follows:

School environment.
Each school faces a different reality in the education area depending on its students and procedures. The environment in which the school operates determines what it must do to be a success. This school environment is the single greatest influence in shaping a school culture.

Building a Strong and Healthy School Culture

Shared values.

These are the basic concepts and beliefs of a school that form the heart and soul of the school culture. Shared values define "success" in concrete terms for teachers and other school people. They state, "If you treat teachers and students like this, you will be successful." Shared values become the established standards of the school.

Heroes.

These teachers, sometimes known as champions, personify the shared values of the school, and as such they serve as role models for other teachers to follow. Some heroes are born, such as the visionary builders of public education in the United States. Others are made by memorable moments that occur in day-to-day school life. Thomas Dewey was a born hero, while Marcus Foster (former superintendent of schools in Oakland, California) was made a hero.

The Rites and Rituals.

These are the systematic and programmed routines of day-to-day life in school. They show both the principal and teachers the kind of behavior that is expected of them. They also provide visible examples of what the school stands for.

The Cultural Network.

The cultural network is the informal means of communicating the shared values and champion-like behavior throughout the school. This network consists of storytellers, spies, priests, cabals, and whispers from a hidden hierarchy of power within the school.

The Person Responsible for Building a Strong and Healthy School Culture

In a school, the principal is the person ultimately responsible for building a strong and healthy school culture, and he or she should be held accountable when a strong and healthy culture does not exist. Creating such a culture should be one of the top priorities of the principal, but because of neglect, lack of knowledge, or incompetence, principals in many schools, both public and private, have not done their duty in this area. Consequently, the culture in these schools has been determined by a variety of disparate influences and the result is cultural uncertainty. This in turn has produced a multitude of negative consequences, some of which are cited below:

- Day-to-day life in the school is disorganized, with everybody more or less doing his or her own thing.
- Teachers function not to further a shared system of beliefs and values but to placate the principal or to look good.
- Morale is low many teachers are unhappy and have become readily and loudly critical of the school.
- Strong unions and other associations of subcultures have emerged, with their own purposes and agendas.
- The principal and other school administrators are inconsistent in the manner in which they treat their teachers, and as a result teachers don't trust them.

It is imperative that the principal recognize that one of his or her most important duties is to build a strong and healthy culture.

When doing so, there are several facts about school culture that will be helpful to keep in mind.

Any existing school already has a culture, even though it may be, and probably is, a weak and unhealthy one, and this culture must be recognized and taken into account in building a new culture. But building or rebuilding a school's culture is a long and continuous process.

Problems will occur if the culture of a school is vastly different from that of the district's. Because members of the school are first and foremost members of the district's culture, anger, dissatisfaction, suspicion, and rejection will likely occur if there are large gaps between the two cultures.

External stakeholders-those people outside of a school who nevertheless have a stake in its welfare—can be powerful shapers of the school's culture. These people should be identified and used in developing the school's culture.

A school culture is built and shaped by beliefs and values communicated again and again, day in and day out, through the words and actions of the principal and administrators in the school. To build a school culture, all school administrators must organize more or less in the same manner; must be consistent in

Building a Strong and Healthy School Culture

their behavior and in their treatment of teachers; and must communicate and perform in a way that makes teachers feel that they are all members of the same larger family.

The school culture is something in which every person in the school contributes to and has a role in, either by perpetuating or changing it over a period of time. This can be done by:

- The collective action of all teachers and other school people.
- Years of actions taken, decisions made, policies implemented and discarded with each successive generation; the new generation adds something new and discards some of the old.
- Both formal policies and procedures that identify "how things are done here."

The Attributes of an Effective School Culture

The best school philosophy is one that has the following attributes:

- Decision-making authority and responsibility are at the lowest level of the school.
- Problem-solving policies are not developed, but are anticipated and addressed before becoming problems.
- There is a relentless persistence to improving the quality of education while at the same time enhancing the school climate.
- There is a focused attention on the vision of the school that is held by most, if not all teachers.
- In terms of teachers, there is a widespread attitude of wanting to excel and a willingness to do whatever it takes to improve. Teachers going beyond their duty to do things right; there is a school-wide spirit of discovery; teachers are excited about their work and happy with the principal; and there is a certain amount of impatience to succeed.
- Although teachers are actively involved in the improvement process, efforts are directed by the principal.
- Most of the improvement process is made in teams.

- Teamwork is the operating morale by which things get done.
- The principal constantly informs teachers of school progress, successes, and failures
- While the principal is dedicated to helping teachers, a great deal of concern is also given to parents.
- School champions or heroes emphasize student satisfaction, outstanding service, and taking risks to improve the school's performance.

The principal has a major role to play in the improvement process by:

a) Believing that the teachers have the right and responsibility to improve the school environment and to change whatever affects their ability to do the right job.

b) Giving teachers a sense of ownership in serving students and parents.

c) Giving teachers the opportunities to innovate and create something new to add value to what is being done.

d) Nurturing a family relationship among teachers and other school people; the attitude that we are all in this together.

e) Encouraging teachers to change and to improve what currently exists even if it doesn't need changing.

f) Creating in teachers the commitment to commonly help school vision. Not only does the prical play an important role in the important process, he or she must lead the charge and inspire others to join in the change process.

Not only does the principal play an important role in the important process, he or she must lead the charge and also inspire others to join in the change process.

The Techniques for Building a Strong School Culture

The inculcation of the philosophy is intended to build a strong school culture. Here are useful techniques for building a strong school culture.

Principals should perform as role models. If the words, actions, and deeds of principals are consistent with the norms and values of the school, a strong culture will result; if not, a weak culture will be evident. Role modeling can also be demonstrated through written documents, as well as through the use of audiovisual aids. Some schools have found it useful to have principals present skits in which they assume roles to demonstrate various aspects and stages of the philosophy.

Recognize philosophy compliance of principals who are observed exemplifying an element of the philosophy. Send a note of praise to a teacher who is seen practicing a desired value or norm; if the deed has a significant impact on the reaction of other teachers. In some schools, teachers or teams that exemplify the desired elements of the philosophy are given a gift certificate which can be exchanged for merchandise at a store, membership in a health spa, or free lunches, served by principals.

Communicate the philosophy by preparing a philosophy manual and use it as a tool during teacher orientation. Such a manual contains all of the essential elements of the school's philosophy. Each element is segmented; sometimes questions follow each element to test the teachers' understanding of that aspect of the philosophy. This manual is invaluable when implementing the varied training activities associated with orientation and career-path growth. Some schools have produced newsletters to help spread the gospel of the philosophy; others have produced "white papers" and essays, and distributed and discussed these with the employees.

Implement long-range training activities. A number of schools have a long-range training program, designed to cover all of the elements of the philosophy. This training program usually is conducted over two to three years, and involves regular monthly training sessions lasting for twenty to thirty minutes. (Some of the substance of this chapter is devoted to the kinds of training activities that can be implemented for this purpose, one of which is becoming increasingly popular.) The principal reads a book that is consistent with the desired values and norms of the school, and holds meetings to discuss its contents.

Use subtle techniques designed to help inculcate the philosophy. Some schools use tests and layers of interviews to screen prospective teachers. If personality and character are compatible with school values and norms, the candidate is hired. Another subtle form for inculcating the philosophy involves adapting certain practices and school designs that are consistent with the philosophy. Some common practices of excellent schools may involve an open-door policy, no lay-off plan, promotion from within, career development path, etc. Perhaps the most subtle technique for inculcating the philosophy is physically designing the facilities to embrace the values and norms of the school. In an egalitarian school, there would be no reserved parking spaces, and, in an open school, offices would be replaced by open work stations.

Ways in Which the School Philosophy is Inculcated

Inculcating the philosophy of a school is the process of impressing upon teachers the importance of certain macro-principles and guidelines or expected behavior, attitudes, and parameters for the successful operation of the school. As a result, these macro-principles and guidelines are frequently repeated throughout the school by numerous and varied activities. When the philosophy has been fully inculcated throughout the school, a strong organizational culture has been produced and, as a result, teachers are aware of its principles and are working within the guidelines. Thus, the school is achieving an essential step in the pursuit of excellence.

The purposes of an inculcation are:

1. To build and nurture a strong culture to be passed down from one generation of teachers to another.
2. To transmit values of the school.
3. To define the philosophical weak spots in order to initiate corrective actions.
4. To enable individual parts of the school to come together to fulfill their intended purposes.
5. To enable all teachers to have similar beliefs.
6. To foster shared understanding of what is really important to the school and its activities.
7. To promote continuity throughout the school.

The Principal's Role in Inculcating the School Philosophy

Every principal has two basic training functions: to inculcate the philosophy of the school, and to train teachers in the basic skills to perform their jobs. In excellent schools, both functions take place continuously throughout the tenure of teachers. In other schools, the inculcation of the philosophy through training and other means is virtually nil, while some training in the basic skills is provided to some teachers on a short-term basis.

The inculcation of the philosophy usually takes place before skill training and is expanded through formal and informal means. Teachers hired directly after graduation from college are less likely to have to be "decontaminated" and then indoctrinated in terms of the principles, practices, and guidelines of the school. The principal is responsible for the formulation of the statements of philosophy in collaboration with a cross-section of teachers. Another mission of principals is to develop appropriate policies and procedures that inculcate the philosophy, then to make certain periodic analyses are conducted to determine the extent to which the philosophy has been implemented, and to take any appropriate corrective action. The principal is also responsible for bringing attention to various elements of the philosophy through his or her actions, words, and deeds.

The principal is also responsible for the execution of the policies and procedures regarding the inculcation of the philosophy. To this end, everyone in the school will spearhead the formal and informal activities to inculcate the philosophy. This means that they will conduct numerous appropriate training activities involving teachers in assessing the extent to which they are adhering to the philosophy, and to recommend changes and corrective actions to the principal.

The Procedure for Inculcating the Philosophy in School

The inculcation of the philosophy of a school must proceed through six steps:

Step 1: Preparation of the Statement of Philosophy.

The principal determines what elements of the statement of the philosophy should be incorporated into the school philosophy. Some common elements contained in the philosophy are mission, vision, shared values, and organizational objectives.

Step 2: Develop a policy and procedure statement for inculcating the philosophy.

The principal makes basic decisions relating to how the statement of philosophy should be inculcated. Below is an example of a policy and procudure:
1. How should teachers be introduced to the philosophy? What is the best way to get maximum interaction from teachers?

   How much time should be devoted to the introduction; when and where it will take place?

   Should audio-visual aids be used to introduce the philosophy?

   1) Who should prepare the aids?

   2) How much should be budgeted?

   3) How much planning and development time should be allocated to the preparation of aids?

   What activities should be used to inculcate the philosophy?
   1) Should a school song be written and by whom?

   2) Should a school creed be prepared and by whom? How often should it be recited and on what occasions?

   3) How and when should the principal focus on the philosophy?

   4) What training activities should be initiated to inculcate the philosophy?

   5) How much time should be devoted to training activities and how should the activities take place?

   6) How should teachers' feedback be used to strengthen the inculcation of the philosophy?

What process should be used to evaluate the extent to which the philosophy has been inculcated?

1) Should an outsider or an insider be used to evaluate the inculcation of the philosophy?
2) How much should be budgeted for the evaluation?
3) How much time should be devoted to the evaluation?
4) How should corrective actions be taken?

When all pertinent questions have been considered, organize a team of teachers to prepare a comprehensive policy and procedure statement on the inculcation of the philosophy. From time to time, it may be necessary to revise this statement.

Step 3: Disseminating and discussing the philosophy.

Once guidelines have been developed to inculcate the philosophy, copies of the philosophy must be distributed to all teachers and discussed. The principal is responsible for introducing the philosophy and initiating the various activities to inculcate the philosophy.

Step 4: Initiating varied activities to inculcate the philosophy.

Use a variety of activities to inculcate the school philosophy. These should be well-designed and planned prior to their execution. They include teacher orientation and training activities. Some excellent schools have begun the inculcation of the philosophy during the orientation process when new teachers are first hired. Although the substance is brief, all elements of the philosophy are covered.

Each training activity should be designed to be completed within fifteen to twenty minutes. Depending on the amount of interaction generated, you may need two or three more sessions. Some activities will require the principal to prepare questionnaires or other instruments for discussing specifics of the philosophy. Below are some training activities for inculcating the philosophy:

Self Indoctrination

Request each member to become familiar with an essential point of one of the elements of the philosophy, then give a ten-to-fifteen minute persuasive presentation. The presenter must persuade the team membership that a particular detail of the philosophy has been realized. Team members must be convinced not only by words from the presenter, but also by the deeds and actions of the principal. The principal is responsible for conducting an interesting and thought-provoking meeting.

Using Sentence Stems

After the principal explains an element of the statements of philosophy, he or she requests a teacher to think about what has been presented. The teacher is then asked to use any one of the following sentence stems to share with team members his or her personal feelings about the element:

"I believe the mission is..."

"I don't believe that our mission is . . . because . . ."

"Our principal doesn't practice what they preach because..."

"I believe that... is a desirable school value because..."

Responding to Vignettes

The principal introduces this activity by initiating a discussion about an element of the philosophy. Teachers are then presented with a specific situation or vignette, which calls for some appropriate action. Each teacher is requested to write a brief description of what he or she would do in that situation. Teachers then divide into mini-teams of three to discuss their proposal and to determine which of the three decisions is considered the best. After ten to fifteen minutes, all teachers reconvene as a team to discuss the decisions and to reach a consensus on the most desirable course of action. The situation used by the principal should be based on an actual condition existing in the school.

Sharing the Philosophy

An effective way for a principal to get team members to focus on the philosophy is to have them identify or cite situations in which someone was abiding by any one or more elements of the philosophy. The principal convenes the team and asks members to share with the team an incident in which he or she has observed either a teacher or an administrator abiding by an element of the philosophy. Some team members may have some difficulty remembering such incidents.

Guess-What Elements

The principal identifies and explains each element of the statement of the philosophy. An excerpt from one of the elements is recited to the team. Individual team members are requested to identify the element in a guess-what procedure. Sometimes the list of the elements is posted so that the individual can refer to them before responding. When a correct response is given, positive recognition is exchanged and the respondent is asked to elaborate on it. When an incorrect answer is given, the principal will ask the team if the response was correct and seek another individual to give an answer.

Response Questions The principal provides teachers with a worksheet containing a series of belief statements about an element of the philosophy. Team members complete the worksheet on an individual basis, after which they are divided into three-member teams to share and discuss their individual responses as in terms of SA = Strongly Agree, AS = Agree Somewhat, DS = Disagree Somewhat, and SD = Strongly disagree.

Some examples of appropriate response questions are:

1.	People are our greatest asset	SA AS DS SD
2.	The school fosters initiative and creativity by allowing freedom in the performance of their jobs.	SA AS DS SD
3.	Teachers are genuinely involved in the decision-making process.	SA AS DS SD
4.	The principal trusts teachers.	SA AS DS SD
5.	Criticism is viewed as a training opportunity	SA AS DS SD
6.	Most team decisions are reached by consensus.	SA AS DS SD

Management Assessment

The principal sits on a chair in the center of a circle composed of team members. Each individual team member gets a chance to cite five ways in which that principal bides by the philosophy of the school. Team members are asked to identify how the principal abided by the philosophy and, after the entire team has recited, individuals are asked to cite five ways in which the principal has not abided by the philosophy. One team member is selected to act as a recorder, indicating the substance of the recitations, which is given to the principal at the conclusion of the activity.

This activity is not for the weak of heart, and should not be used by principals who are timid or do not wish to improve their performance.

Schedule training for inculcating the philosophy in short durations, spread over two or three years. Each training session, with the exception of the orientation, should last from fifteen to twenty minutes and can be conducted once a week, bi-weekly, or monthly.

Step 5: Evaluating and taking corrective actions.

Because of the short duration of each training activity, it will take from two to three years to complete the inculcation of the philosophy. At the close of the training activities, a formal method must be employed to evaluate the extent to which the philosophy is a reality within the school. Regardless of whether an insider or outsider professional consultant is retained to complete the evaluation, each element of the statement of the philosophy must be used as the basis for the evaluation. This document should be used to prepare instruments and interviewing questionnaires. The evaluation should encompass the following positions: the principal, assistant principals, any supervisors, and teachers.

Once the individual assessments have been completed, all of the above positions should be combined to arrive at a school composite report. The consultant should meet and discuss the substance of the first draft of the report with the various teams to make any necessary adjustments before the final report is completed.

When the evaluation has been competed, the next stage of the inculcation of the philosophy consists of taking corrective actions, which should take place on the school and individual levels. Long range plans should be developed to improve the school over a three-year period. The principal should be required to develop improvement plans to accommodate the recommendations stated in the evaluation report.

Every school, excellent as well as not-so-excellent ones, should initiate a formal and comprehensive program to periodically assess the degree to which cultural gaps exist in the school, and then take appropriate steps to close these gaps. One effective method is the development of a school value improvement plan. To do this, first identify desired school culture values and norms. If a statement of philosophy exists, extract the specific norms and values that will be used to assess the extent to which the desired culture exists. If a philosophy is not available in written form, the principal may decide to perform the next step first, and, after learning what presently exists, to prepare the statement of philosophy or specific norms and shared values.

Next describe present school culture norms and values. Conduct an audit using an outside consultant who can critically review the following areas in order to determine the present norms and shared values of the school: performance standards and practices; communication flow; goals and objectives; empowerment; teampersonship; leadership styles and practices; student services; training and development; performance evaluation practices; peer relationship; innovation practices; school pride; productivity and quality of service; and relationships with stakeholders and community.

Once these areas have been reviewed, specific statements of present school norms and values can be produced to identify the unwritten philosophy of the school. If step one has not been completed, the principal must now determine what he or she considers to be acceptable or desired cultural norms and values and write them in the first column of the plan. An effective technique to prepare the desired norms and shared values should involve an assessment of what presently exists, related to what should exist. To collect information pertaining to existing cultural norms and shared values, audit the school culture by sending teachers a questionnaire and/or interviewing them to determine their impressions of the school.

Next, describe school cultural gaps. When desired cultural norms and values have been matched with existing cultural norms and values, cultural gaps, if any exist, may be identified and described with rigorous analysis and intuitive judgment. Once the gaps have been determined, rank them in order of importance to focus on those that need priority consideration.

Then, identify improvement strategies. Based on the ranked cultural gaps, consider the previous techniques discussed in this chapter when examining improvement strategies. Because these strategies are methods for improving the culture and inculcating the philosophy, both long- and short-range strategies should be identified and cited. To improve the culture, place major long-range emphasis on role modeling and training.

You will then need to develop an action plan. Designate someone or some department to head development of a school action plan for implementing the improvement strategies. The human resource department or staff development departments are good prospects for this charge.

Periodically assess the school culture. Audit the school every three to five years. Some practitioners feel the audit should be done every ten years; but external environments change so rapidly that a school waiting ten years to assess its culture may find itself in need of major surgery to eradicate obsolescence.

Assessing the school culture can be an enjoyable and fruitful process, especially if all teachers become involved in the process. The more people who become meaningfully involved, the more valid the results, and the more likely cultural gaps will be closed and the school will be persuing excellence.

Preparing a Philosophy Awareness Questionnaire

The following questionnaire can be used to assess a school's efforts to inculcate its philosophy. Questions one through eight can be used as a checklist by the principal and other administrators to make sure the appropriate steps have been taken to inculcate the philosophy. Questions nine through fourteen can be distributed and used as the basis for discussion at meetings of teachers to determine whether or not they believe that the philosophy is being or has been successfully inculcated. (The greater the number of positive responses, the more successful inculcation has been.) 4 = yes; 3 and 2 = to some extent; and 1 = no.

1. Was a cross-section of school and community people involved in developing the school's philosophy?

4   3   2   1

2. Does the philosophy contain at least a statement of mission, vision and shared values?

4   3   2   1

3. Is the philosophy discussed during the orientation of new teachers so that they are aware of how things are done in the school?.

4   3   2   1

4. Has a long-range training program been developed and executed to educate and train teachers in the beliefs and values of the school?

4   3   2   1

5. Has a formal program been established to recognize and reward teachers whose manner and actions best embody the essential beliefs and values of the school?

4   3   2   1

6. Are any written documents periodically disseminated to teachers in an effort to perpetuate the school philosophy?

4   3   2   1

7. Is there a formal process by which the school's philosophy is discussed on an annual basis, and, if necessary, modified by teachers?

4   3   2   1

8. Is some action taken to bring uncommitted teachers in line with the philosophy of the school?

4   3   2   1

9. Do you have a copy of the philosophy and has it been fully discussed with you and other teachers?

4   3   2   1

10. Can you state in writing your school's purposes, mission, and values?

4   3   2   1

11. Does the principal and assistant principals refer to the essence of the philosophy when conferring with teachers?

4   3   2   1

12. Is the school's' philosophy consistently applied in the decisions and actions of the principal and assistant principals?

4   3   2   1

13. Are you personally committed to the school's mission, vision, and shared values?

4   3   2   1

14. Do you think that 90 percent or more of the teachers in your school fully grasp its mission, vision, and shared values?

4   3   2   1

An Informal Technique for Evaluating the School Culture

Use the following to determine where you stand as a school. Some of the evaluation to follow will be subjective in nature. Keep in mind that in those circumstances, there is not a right or wrong answer; it's simply what is right for you!

1. Walk down your hallways. What do the teachers' bulletin boards look like? Has there has been thought and effort put into them?
2. What is the overall feeling you get while you are walking those halls? Trust your instincts and leave your brain in your office. Is there positive or negative energy?
3. Do you receive a lot of parent complaints about the teaching in your school? (Don't single out one or two teachers. Look for the big picture.)
4. Does your school receive a lot of bad press? Although the media tends to sensationalize, their stories may be grounded in some fact. This could easily divide your school.
5. How is the attendance at social functions? Do teachers appear comfortable with one another? With administration?
6. Are teachers' meetings characterized by candor (a sign of comfort in one's surroundings), or are they tense?
7. Do you get many volunteers for non-paying projects that may require some out-of-school time?

REVIEW

KEY POINTS TO REMEMBER:

- The school culture is defined as ideologies, values, assumptions, beliefs, expectations, attitudes, and norms that unite teachers and other school people together.
- The elements of a school culture are: school environment, shared values, heroes, rites and rituals, and the cultural network.
- The principal is the person fully responsible for producing a strong and healthy school culture.
- Some effective techniques for building a strong and healthy school culture are: using the principal as a role model;

recognizing philosophy confidence; communicating the philosophy; and implementing long-range activities and subtle techniques to inculcate the philosophy.

- The procedural steps for inculcating the school philosophy are to 1) prepare the philosophy; 2) develop policy and procedures for inculcating the philosophy; 3) disseminate and discuss the philosophy; 4) initiate training activities to inculcate the philosophy; and 5) evaluate and take corrective action.

- Training activities to inculcate the culture consist of the following: 1) self-indoctrination: 2) using sentence stems 3) responding to vignettes; 4) sharing the philosophy; 5) guess-what elements: 6) response questions; 7) teacher-principal assessment.

APPLICATION

To surface and assess cultural norms do the following:

1. Divide the school into school teams of 12 or more members each.
2. Instruct each team to generate the following:

    a. A list of existing unwritten cultural norms.

    b. A list of desirable cultural norms.

    c. Describe any culture gaps.

    d. Formulate strategies to close the gaps.
3. Reconvene as a full school; each team leader will discuss the outcome of his or her culture assessment.

Part

3
Identifying Practices That are Designed to Assist in Transforming Schools

This section identifies a number of practices that can help to achieve the purposes of the school and positively affect its mission. These practices are intended to empower teachers and other school people to do what is necessary to transform the school, to communicate more with the principal, to be considered as an equal members of the school family, to arrive at a consensus on decision which everyone agrees to abide by, to capitalize on the great things being performed by other schools, and to be involved in the decision making process in a meaningful way.

CHAPTER 9

Empowering Teachers in School

LEARNING OBJECTIVES

After studying and comprehending this chapter, you should be able to:

- Define empowerment.
- Describe the difference between power and empowerment.
- Identify the different forms of empowerment.
- Cite how the powerful can foster the empowerment process.
- Explain the procedural steps for implementing empowerment.
- Identify various empowerment interventions.
- Learn how to empower teachers.
- Describe problems that emerge when implementing empowerment.
- Explain the best vehicle for implementing the empowerment process.

What Every Principal Should Know About Empowering Teachers

Schools in the United States are constantly under attack from the outside and from the inside. Externally, in subjects such as math and science, our schools rank very low when compared to other countries. Internally, teachers are feeling let down and burned out, as they feel frustrated by districts that are making more demands on them and on changing administrative problems and guidance. At the same time, teachers are also demanding more decision-making opportunities, participative management, and more fulfillment from their work. As a result, the school must adapt, grow, and implement new ways to improve the instructional process. In addition, teachers are uncertain of their new role and responsibilities. Caught in the middle between the superintendent and teachers is the principal, who feels pressured by new demands and must involve teams of teachers to make the school operate more effectively.

In transformational schools, the principal and teachers become partners. Everyone not only feels responsible for their own jobs, but feels a sense of ownership of the school as a whole. Thus, school teams are not just a reaction to school needs, but are also initiators of action. Teachers become decision makers not followers. The principal is an enabler not a controller. Everyone feels that a school environment is created whereby they are continually learning and developing new skills to meet new school demands.

Defining Empowerment

In simple definition, the term is a verb to empower, which means to enable, to allow, or to permit, and is enacted either by the person himself or herself or can be enacted by another person. In school, as a social agent, empowerment is the act of building, developing, and increasing power through teams, cooperation, sharing, and working together with others. It is an interactive process based on synergy. It is not zero-sum assumption of power. It is the process of enlarging power in schools rather than redistributing it.

Whereby traditional principals really define power as their ability to control or change the behavior of teachers, the concept of empowerment is that traditional principals can influence or affect teachers' behaviors so that the interaction process produces more power for the school. In fact, everybody in the school has the potential power to empower each other, so that the net result is an increased power for the entire school.

An effective use of power was illustrated when an inexperienced principal prepared the duty schedule for his teachers. Because, the schedule did not meet the personal goals of many teachers, they became dismayed and voiced disapproval over the principal's schedule. The principal gave some thought to the situation and called a teacher representative into his office. He submitted some guidelines to the representative and requested that the teachers use these guidelines to develop their own schedule bearing them in mind. He also related to the representative that any problems in their schedule would have to be resolved by them. The next day, the representative appeared at the principal's office with the teachers' schedule. A review of the schedule revealed that it was an improvement over his schedule. He accepted the teachers' schedule. The teachers were delighted and so was the principal. You see, the teachers' personal goals were met as well as those of the school. All parties were satisfied.

Empowerment is a fundamentally different way of operating a school in which each teacher begins to control how things are done as indicated below:

1. Teachers feel responsible not just for teaching, but also for making the school work better. Teachers are *problem solvers* who help plan and control how to get things done and do them.

2. Teams are organized to improve performance on a continual basis, thereby containing a higher level of productivity.

3. Schools are structured in such a manner that teachers feel that they are able to achieve desired results, and that they can do what needs to be done without approval.

The empowered school is characterized by:
- Enhancing the content of the teachers' job;
- Expanding their skills and tasks that comprise their job;
- Liberating teachers' creativity and innovation;

- Giving teachers more control over decisions concerning their jobs;
- Enabling teachers to complete a whole task rather (managing and controlling) than a portion (teaching only) of it; and
- Generating more teacher satisfaction.

The empowered school creates a new relationship between teachers and the principal. A partnership is developed. Every teacher not only feels responsible for their jobs, but feels some sense of ownership for the total performance of the school. Teams do not just react to the principal's demands; they must initiate what has to be accomplished. The principal's role shifts from a controller to an enabler. Teachers are decision makers, not followers. Everyone feels that they are continuing to learn and develop new skills to meet changing times and conditions.

The Principal Shifts From Power to Empowerment

Most principals' styles are based on the person "in charge" being in a position of "power" or authority. That person, in the case of the school, is the traditional "boss." He or she is the one that makes or enforces "the rules," and is generally seen as having more of "a say" about the workings of the school than perhaps a teacher might. As such, they are thought of as ultimately responsible for the bottom line. Traditionally, teachers were thought of as "employees" or "subordinates." They had a role to play, a task to perform within the structure of the school, but, in the final analysis, were seen as replaceable cogs in the system's machine —not as important as management.

Synonyms for power include force, potency, and control. Seen from this light, power is domination, the triumph of one side over the other. When viewed in this traditional, hierarchical manner, power carries with it underlying assumptions of "abuse of power," including dominance, manipulation, victimization, and violence, which may or may not be true in any given situation, but which tend to cause defensive reactions in individuals. Given this, how do we shift from this perception of power to a more effective, positive form of power that best serves the school organization?

Other synonyms for power include ability, prerogative, and potential. Here, the terms refer to issues of competence and achievement, a concern for results. In the process of "empowerment," a principal is interested in tapping into this definition as he or she attempts to elicit the maximum potential from the available human resources. Below is a chart that draws the distinction between power and empowerment as it applies to the relationship between the principal and teachers.

Power	Empowerment
Principal gives teachers only the information necessary for them to teach.	Teachers get access to whatever information they need and desire.
Principal provides training or arranges for teachers to receive training on how to teach effectively.	Principal and teachers create situations that maximize learning opportunities for teachers.
Principal clarifies rules and regulations and administers discipline to ensure conformity and to suppress conflict.	Teachers dictate rules, regulations, and consequences of violations; teachers and principal mediate conflict.
Principal motivates teachers via persuasive leadership.	Teachers encourage and stimulate teachers through self-management, goal setting, autonomy, and entrepreneurship.
Principal effects change sometimes with and without teacher participation.	Teachers effect change with support from the principal.
Principal rewards success and punishes failure.	Teachers recognize individual and collective achievement and use failure as a learning opportunity.

Until principals begin to think about school results first, they are not very interested in the empowerment column. If they cannot yet place the good of the school first, it is likely that they are more involved with resolving dependency issues in their own growth and development. That is, they are concerned with their being dependent on others, being counterdependent against others (most notably, authority figures), and being independent from others. When you, as principal, are comfortable with these dependency issues, you are ready to make a quantum leap to the stage of interdependence with others.

Interdependent behavior requires a high level of sharing, which follows naturally as you are more and more comfortable with your own strengths and identity as a leader. As you reconcile these issues for yourself, you will enter into empowering relationships with your teams. In their article, "The Power Failure in Organization," (*Training and Development Journal*, 1984, 38 (1), pp. 35-38) authors Rubin and Berlew identify behavioral traits of individuals who are empowered, who feel powerful and believe that they can make a difference. (The characteristics below are what would be the end result of effectively empowering your teachers.) Empowered people:

- Are more concerned with achieving results than avoiding mistakes.
- Do what needs doing rather than waiting for someone else to take action.
- Accept the risks required to achieve innovative results.
- Look for opportunities to contribute, even outside their defined area of responsibility.
- Use a wide range of contacts and resources to get the job done.
- Expect to influence peers and superiors as well as subordinates.
- Communicate directly and forcefully.

As mentioned above, in order for you to elicit this type of behavior from you teachers, you must first come to grips with your own relationship to power.

Here are some tips:

Be aware and allow yourself to recognize how you normally perceive power.

Direct your power. Power in and of itself is neither "good" nor "bad." You have the choice to focus it in one way or the other. Make it a point to use your power in a positive manner, with a true concern for having others become more powerful in the process.

Share your thoughts. Strong, silent principals do not empower others. The more you share of yourself, in a non-threatening manner, the more comfortable others will be to do the same.

Be confronting and supportive. If you are truly interested in the results of the school, and not about preserving or strengthening your own personal power, others will recognize this. You can then confront them and make suggestions to them without being arrogant or degrading them. You will always be mindful of producing positive results for the school, and will confront your teachers in such a way that you reinforce their self-esteem and have them recognize their value to the school. One suggestion, always remember that your personal power is meaningless unless you use it to empower others.

The Different Forms of Empowerment

Empowerment relates to some general forms and specific activities such as, educating, leading, mentoring/supporting, providing, structuring, and actualization. Each is discussed below.

Educating

The process of education is an empowerment act that asserts that information is power. Therefore, providing information to teachers through either sharing information or training is an empowerment act. Education is beneficial not only to the transformational *principal* but also for teachers. As a result, both are able to capitalize on the education by creating a more accurate picture of the school situation, and therefore are able to make better decisions.

Leading

Another form of empowerment is effective leadership. The transformational principal is able to execute, energize, motivate, and liberate teachers and has in effect demonstrated the essence of empowerment. Transformational principals allow themselves to empower teachers to exceed their own accomplishment and help the entire school to benefit from those who are empowered.

Mentoring/Supporting

Mentoring and supporting is a form of empowerment that is personal in nature, and is based on a closer emotional attachment than leading. The transformational principal serves as a mentor and also gains increased power from observing teachers excel and from providing a role model for the school. When the principal and teachers perform the mentor role for other teachers, the net result is increased power for the school as a whole.

Providing

Providing is locating and supplying resources to teachers that are necessary for school success. Although it may not be possible to provide teachers with everything, they need a school that doesn't provide its teachers with the minimum tools to educate students is not serious about empowering its teachers. An effective teacher, that is, one with an excellent education and leadership skills, is limited by the resources available to perform the job.

Structuring

A teacher is only as powerful as the structure will allow. The best program in the world will not produce an empowered school unless the structure provides for it. An excellent example is the U.S. Constitution, which provides a structure of empowerment for the political system. Structuring pertains to school arrangements and procedures. It also pertains to a teacher's job or work life in school. For example, job description *is* an empowering *structure*, if it represents a good fit between the teacher and position and it if allows for growth and development in terms of new and creative ways of empowering.

Actualized Spirit

Actualized spirit is a form of empowerment that builds in all of the previous forms. It creates an actualized spirit in which the teacher performs at a high level in school. Such a self-actualizing process is a joint responsibility of the teacher and the school and is therefore geared toward good psychological health. A teacher who feels good about his or her job performs with a higher quality.

What The Principal Can Do to Foster Teacher Empowerment

The implementation of empowerment will necessitate a new kind of principal, called a transformational principal who has the traits and characteristics cited in Chapter One. Tannenbaum, et al (1954) has described school traits and characteristics that are applicable to the empowering principal:

1. Create a school environment conducive to learning. Empowerment is a developmental process. The principal's role of establishing the required learning environment is an essential aspect of empowerment.

2. Become a role model. The principal must be willing to take risks, change work habits, recognize his or her own strengths and weaknesses, actively integrate self and school, and provide teachers with a model to emulate empowerment.

3. Introduce new values. During the empowerment process, the principal implicitly and explicitly introduces new values that undergird empowerment. Part of the empowerment process allows for value clarification and the inculcation of appropriate values.

4. Inculcate the communication process—an essential ingredient of empowerment—by sharing information. It also requires information relevant to getting the job done in the best possible manner. Research seems to dictate that the principal's role in the empowerment process is to facilitate the flow of information. If he or she fails to carry out this role, it will hinder the process.

5. Participate as an expert. The key function of the principal is to empower teachers by sharing his or her knowledge and expertise derived from experience, research, etc. However, knowing how to become an expert is a critical factor in the empowerment process. On the other hand, too much expertise increases dependency and reduces empowerment behavior. One role of the principal is to eliminate blockage, which prevents empowered teachers from moving in a forward direction.

6. As early as 1967, when empowerment was not in fashion, Gordon, Lippitt, and Lee published an important article indicating the variables affecting the trainer's roles in a laboratory education setting. These factors can be an effective guide for the principal striving to empower teachers. They prepare and structure the school; strategies for implementing empowerment, including the self empowerment plus healthy school teams; group composition; practice the philosophy of the principal; expectations of team members; school's expectations, system, and culture; school goals and teachers' personal needs; influence of the team leader's peers and role expectations in general; current style of research and experience with empowerment; needs of the principal.

The Procedural Steps for Implementing Empowerment

There are numerous ways to implement empowerment in a school. The following is a recommended course of action that includes the most important steps.

1. Gain an initial commitment. The best way is to educate the superintendent and principal as to the benefits that will accrue from an empowerment program.

2. A two-day orientation program should be conducted for principals desiring to initiate the process. The session should include appropriate reading materials, a discussion of the empowerment program, and a question-and-answer period led by a consultant who has had experience in empowerment.

Empowering Teachers in School

3. Conduct a workshop for teachers. Give teachers a chance to learn about and understand empowerment and how such a program will work in a school.

4. Identify empowering interventions in the case of systemic, structural, and programmatic changes becoming empowered, the principal for enabling empowerment and evaluation criteria. Empowerment interventions are intended to be the skeleton to plan for empowering teachers. For example, a systemic intervention could be a belief and trust in people; one in structural could be operated in school teams; one in programmatic could be a reward and recognition program, etc. Once either you as the principal or a design team decide empowerment interventions under each of the categories, the interventions become the "bones" for constructing your empowerment process plan. The next step involves putting some "meat" on these interventions which represents your action plan for activating the empowerment process. Obviously the bones and meat of your plan should be representative of the needs and strengths of your school.

5. Seek volunteers to initiate the empowerment program. Select the best teachers, particularly your champion teachers, to inaugurate the program.

6. Implement the program. The best way is to restructure the school into teams. Select team leaders and provide opportunities for each team to self-manage. Start with one area of empowerment to be used to implement the program.

7. Evaluate the empowerment program. Assess it in both quantitative and qualitative teams.

The Uses of Empowerment Interventions

Empowerment interventions are useful because they give a principal an opportunity to select those components he or she feels are important to customize an empowerment process for their particular school. There is no such thing as a standardized empowerment process. As a result, the principal (or a design) team will need to combine those intervention strategies that he or she feels are appropriate to use in an empowerment act, and plan to implement the process. What may be appropriate in one school may not necessarily be appropriate for another school. The interventions cited below are not complete, but are only used as starters to enable you the principal to use your creativity to cite others that are appropriate for your school setting.

Intervention acts of empowerment are identified to enter a "frozen school". That is, a school that is not amenable to change and to help the principal assisted by teachers to "thaw" out the school. Although there are no specific number of interventions required to be implemented in a school, the plan for empowerment should contain those acts the school has the necessary resources to implement. There are acts that need to be enforced to be fulfilled, and there are acts that meet several preconditions in helping the school to implement empowerment.

Systemic empowerment interventions are: belief and trust in people; training in leadership skills; creation of a school vision; creation of shared values; belief in egalitarianism; plan for changes in school culture; belief in total quality; freedom from fear; mistakes used as learning opportunities; wide availability of information; cllimate of mutual respect, trust, and support; publication of individual and school team successes; and atmosphere of openness, authenticity, and acceptance.

Structural empowering interventions are: flattening of the school hierarchy; open communication channels; decentralization; open-access to information; and built in assessment systems.

Structural empowerment interventions are: participation-management structure; increased availability of resources; commitment to respond to the external social environment; staffing patterns reflective of empowerment values; interdependence/network norms; pyramid mode of communicating; and consensus decision making.

Programmatic empowering interventions are: training and development motivation; benchmarking; policies and procedure supportive of empowerment values; tries management as well as new programs; creative use of sponsorships, role models, peer coaches, and mentoring; reward and recognition program; planned change program; periodic school structure review; teacher assessment programs; teacher preparation of job descriptions and performance standards; and modeling of empower behaviors in all activities.

Interventions for teachers to become empowered include: willingness to become empowered; improvement in listening and communication skills; willingness to risk new behaviors; personal openness/reduction of facades; openness to feedback; increased tolerance for ambiguity; self-aware; look thyself; ongoing self appraisal through review of the past; clarity about self; seeking increased responsibility; appreciation of new ideas and experiences; valuing others and demonstrating; being interested in interactions; describing self actualization; and high stress tolerance.

Empowering Interventions for the principal include: regarding empowerment as a way of life; passion for empowerment; committed to and support of empowerment motivation; modeling empowerment behavior attitudes; listening actively to others; coaches and mentoring; openness and willingness to connect; provide timely assistance to teachers; clear statement of own values; being and encouraging teachers to be direct; delegation of responsibility, power, and work; recognizes and values individual differences; willingness to share self with teachers; ability to praise self and others; appreciation of good work; clarifying expectations of all teachers; ensuring teachers' rights to disagree and be different; appreciate school champions; gaining new interpersonal skills through practice; willingness to confront and explore issues and conflicts; influence over school performance; and reinforcement of teachers' creativity.

Criteria for Evaluating Empowerment Interventions

- Value uniqueness
- Curiosity
- Concentration
- Values
- Trust
- Willingness to listen
- Flexibility
- Challenge
- Risk taking

- Patience
- Tolerance for ambiguity
- Enthusiasm
- Interpersonal skills

School Criteria

- Elimination of dumb rules
- Egalitarian atmosphere
- Professional security
- Freedom
- Common code of conduct
- Availability of resources
- Improvement of school culture
- Valuing of dreamers and visionaries
- Recognition of interdependence

Learn How to Empower Your Teachers

There are two types of principals. The first is one who gets teachers to do things through the use of scare tactics. The second has an uncanny ability to get his or her teachers to comply and be happy about it. It goes without saying that the second type is the most effective. How does he or she do it? By instilling the desire to do well within their staff. Follow the five guidelines below to learn how to empower your teachers.

Organize School Teams

You must understand that each and every teacher is an essential part of your team., and you must treat them that way. To illustrate, let's look at an ice football team. The coach appears to be the most important person in a game, however, he is not, THE TEAM is.. Rather, he is the most knowledgeable about how football is played. He then uses this knowledge in such a way as to direct his team members towards reaching the same goal: winning! He does this by helping each player develop his own strengths and minimize his weaknesses. The coach is in fact entirely dependent upon every member of that team. Think of yourself as that football coach.

Care About Your Teachers

Trust your teachers and don't smother them with overbearing supervision. Also, spend more time developing personal relationships with your teachers. At least 50 percent of your time should be spent interacting with them. Finally, take time to publicly praise your champion teachers. It will do wonders for their self-esteem.

Build Upon the Strengths of Your Teachers

Focus upon the positive with your teachers, and don't harp on weaknesses. Remember, we all have them.

Make an Investment in Teacher Happiness

Create a formal orientation into your school district for new hires. Also make sure good training is provided along with curriculum and material changes. The benefits will include lower turnover and absenteeism, as well as increased competence.

Share Information Readily With Teachers

By making information available to teachers, you will foster an attitude of caring on their part for the fate of the district. It is the responsibility of the administrators to let everyone know exactly what is going on.

Use Peer Pressure to Your Advantage

Publicly display information about things like attendance records to motivate them to do better. Again focus on the positive. Identify those with good performance, instead of singling out those with poor performance.

Some Likely Problems When Implementing the Empowerment Process

Empowerment is a new process for both the principal and teachers. As a result, some problems will occur during the implementation of the process. Inertia, self-doubt, anger and chaos are the four most likely problems.

Some school teams will experience some difficulty in getting started. As a result, the principal should work closely with the school team leaders and members to help them get over their inertia..

Another likely problem is self-doubt among teachers or teams who believe that they cannot create an empowered school . To deal with this problem, the principal should select an easy problem for the school team to work on, such as creating a teachers' duty schedule.

Whenever there are multiple school teams operating in a school, some will make more progress than others. As a result, some team members are apt to get angry at others for not "pulling their weight." Sometimes, school team members will blame others for having to go through the empowerment process. To help with this problem, a principal should bring the teams together and mediate the problem.

Because the process is new, innovative, and can be implemented in numerous ways, some school teams may get lost or confused while installing the process. This can create chaos. School principals should be patient with teachers and give them time to adjust to new ways of doing things.

The Most Effective Vehicle for Empowering Teachers

The best way to transform a school using empowerment lies in the form of effective school teams. The empowerment process, combined with a transformation principal, will help school teams to establish a three-logic competency: trust, proactive skills, and clarity of school purpose. The school team's development process allows, encourages, and supports both individual and school actualization.

First, through school teams, the trust foundation is established and made possible in the face-to-face group encounters. Because trust is the prerequisite for sharing information, the encounter acts as the platform for structure empowerment development. Proactive skills operates at all levels of the school which allows issues, concerns and problems about school-related matters be dealt with accordingly. However, these problems cannot be resolved unless the third empowerment principle, clarity of school purpose is well inculcated within the school. Therefore, where trust is built, proactive skills can be developed and clarity of purpose and structure can be established from the information and knowledge that is shared among the empowered school teams.

School teams serve as major links with other teachers and groups within the school setting whether they are above, below, or lateral. As a result, how well school teams network among themselves, recognize their interdependence and strive to improve it is a major factor for producing and effective school.

REVIEW

KEY POINTS TO REMEMBER:

- Empowerment is the act of building, developing, and increasing power through school teams, cooperation, sharing, and working together with others.

- There are six forms of empowerment: 1) educating; 2) leading; 3) mentoring/supporting; 4) providing; 5) structuring; and 6) actualization.

- The principal can foster the empowerment process by creating a school environment conducive to learning, becoming a role model, introducing new values, and participating as an expert.

- The procedural steps for implementing improvement consists of: 1) gaining a commitment; 2) providing an orientation seminar; 3) conducting a workshop for teachers; 4) identifying empowerment interventions; 5) seeking volunteers; 6) implementing the process; and 7) evaluating the process.

- Empowerment interventions fall into several categories: 1) systemic empowerment interventions; 2) structural empowerment interventions; 3) programmatic empowering interventions; 4) the teacher interventions for becoming empowered 5) the principal empowering interventions; 6) criteria for evaluating empowerment interventions.

- Some effective ways to learn how to empower teachers are to organize school teams; care about teachers; build upon the strengths of teachers; make an investment in teachers' happiness, share information with teachers; and use peer pressure.
- Problems that are likely to emerge when implementing the empowerment process consists of inertia, self doubt, anger, and chaos.
- The most effective vehicle to implement the empowerment process is to organize and actuate school teams. To perform this feat, the principal will have to build trust within the school, provide for proactive skills, and clarify the school purpose.

APPLICATION

The empowerment process works on three levels: 1) the mindset; 2) relationship; and 3) school structure. Review and mark those pathways you have made to empower the teachers in your school:

1. Mindsets

Principal

- Assists teacher to get the job done
- Fosters a learning environment
- Encourages risk
- Concerns about training and developing teachers
- Accepts ambiguity as a step toward helping teachers
- Listens actively to teachers
- Accepts mistakes as learning opportunities
- Willing to give, receive, and request feedback
- Models empowerment behaviors and attitudes

- "Walk the walk" and "Talk the talk"
- Appreciate diversity
- Delegates authority and responsibility
- Willing to be open and to connect to teachers and others
- Regards empowering as a way of life
- Believes in nonzero-sum view of power

Teachers

- Assume responsibility for actions
- Solves problems rather than puts the blame on others
- Seeks increased responsibility
- Appreciates new ideas and experiences
- Willing to be empowered
- Open to feedback, to be heard, and to be confronted
- Value other teachers and demonstrate it
- Patience with self and others
- Values change

2. Relationships

- Commitment to participatory management and collaboration
- Shared responsibility
- Mutual trust and respect
- Focus on process and learning
- Helpful and supportive to each other
- Engagement of principal and teachers in decision making
- Mutual respect for school and timely information
- Communication at all levels of the school
- Shared accountability
- Shared recognition and rewards

- School-wide learning

3 School Structure

- Recognition and reward systems: recognition and rewards are consistent with the shared values of the school.
- Clarity of purpose: commonly accepted school mission, vision, and shared values.
- Facilitative problem solving: school is organized around cooperative working teams.
- Freedom and flexibility: school is responsive to teachers' school-related demands and committed to training and development opportunities of teachers.
- Commitment to total quality: the school continually strives to improve products and servises to students and teachers.
- Commitment to communication: principal shares timely information with teachers and teachers' input is elicited and responded to .
- Use those unmarked pathways (start with others) and develop a plan to do so with teacher involvement.

CHAPTER 10

Managing by Wandering Around

LEARNING OBJECTIVES

After studying and comprehending this chapter, you should be able to :

- Define managment by wandering around.
- Describe the steps for managing by wandering around.

What Every Principal Should Know About Managing by Wandering Around

The only way a principal can know the "pulse" of his or her school is by staying close to teachers. The transformational principal is an ardent fan of wandering around his or her school talking to teachers, listening to what they have to say, and resolving problems. In fact, some transformatinal principals have been known to spend 75 percent of their time managing by wandering around the school. This process is not as easy as the term implies. It takes time, patience, understanding of human behavior, and good communication skills to perform this role in an effective manner.

Most superintendents give their principals complete freedom to meet as frequently as possible with teachers. One of the roles of the transformational principal is to stay informed of new principles and practices in managing people, and the principal who does not wander around the school cannot be performing this role effectively.

Far too may principals do not make efforts to meet with their teachers on a daily basis. This happens for one (or more) reasons. First, they have become accustomed to managing the school the traditional way, using their offices as command posts. Second, some principals are lazy and don't want to put forth the extra effort to get out of their seats and meet with teachers. Third, some principals either don't plan or are poor planners; thus they engage in reactive management or crisis management, which leaves them exhausted and with little time to become people-sensitive leaders.

Defining Management by Wandering Around

Management by wandering around is a practice by which the principal makes frequent, informal contact with teachers in all parts of the school in order to stay in touch with their needs and concerns. This practice was first used at Hewlett-Packard and has been used in a variety of forms in many of the best-run companies. Management by wandering around is not easy; it is an art that requires the execution of four critical steps: connecting, listening, facilitating, and follow-through.

Connecting

The first step in managing by wandering around is to connect with teachers. Get out into the school and meet them. The best way to do this on a consistent basis is to set aside certain days and times to wander around. In this way, this practice will become a routine part of your schedule and not something that is incidental to it.

Once you have made contact with a teacher or a small group of teachers, explain why you are there. For example, "To keep in touch with our most important assets." The point of the meeting is to hear their concerns in order to learn what they think about their jobs and the school district. It might help to start off the meeting with a leading question, such as, "What are some of the most pressing problems in the school?" "What do you like least about this school?" "What should I do that I am not doing?" "Are you satisfied with how I treat you?"

Listening

After you have connected with teachers in the school and have begun the meeting with some questions, the second and most crucial step in the process is listening. Listening means taking an interest in what is being said without judging or evaluationing. It calls for openness and objectivity. Listening is a form of caring. No principal can be caring and concerned about people unless he or she knows them as human beings. No principal can know his or her people unless they disclose, reveal, and unveil themselves. And no principal can initiate meaningful dialogue with people unless he or she seriously listens. Genuine listening is a very difficult task. It takes a conscious effort and hard work to become an effective listener. Whenever a principal is preoccupied or concerned solely with himself or herself, receptivity is at a low level. Unless a conscious effort is made to get attuned to an individual, real listening cannot occur.

There are several keys to successful listening. First of all, stop talking. A principal cannot listen if he or she is busy talking or thinking about what to say next.

Next, be attentive.

Some principals seem to be listening, but they are thinking about something else and thus are not connected to the other person who is talking. A true listener is one who is quiet and sensitive to what is being said in an active, open, receptive, and genuine manner. A true listener is one who is inwardly silent. A true listener does not immediately evaluate or judge what is being said, but acts as a receptacle for verbal and nonverbal messages.

Be patient.

Teachers need to reveal themselves at their own pace and in their own manner. If a principal tries to force the listening process, the connection with the speaker will collapse.

Obtain clarity.

At times, the creative listener will respond, reflect, express understanding, or request clarity. During this process, which Carl Rogers calls reflective listening, the principal may request more information or may paraphrase what is being said in order to determine what the speaker is really thinking and thus facilitate communication.

Show empathy.

Teachers will open up to a principal more freely if they feel that he or she shares or is sensitive to their thoughts and feelings.

Be attentive on two levels.

Teachers or people in general tend to converse on two levels. The first level is the superficial one. On this level, people will often voice concerns, interests, desires, and aspirations that are petty or that have nothing to do with their true thoughts or feelings. It is as if they needed a springboard to propel them into the next level. This is the level at which the real intent of the conversation and the teacher's real goals are expressed. The only way to detect which level a teacher is communicating on is to let him or her continue talking. Sooner or later, you will learn of the real intent of the conversation. A listener needs a great deal of skill to decipher when a teacher has moved to the second level in the conversation. If a principal does not allow a teacher to move from the superficial level to the second level because of impatience, lack of time, or preoccupation, the real intent of the conversation may never be revealed.

Observe nonverbal communication.

Teachers tend to express almost twice as much nonverbally as they do with words. Therefore, one effective listening technique is for the principal to read the nonverbal actions of a teacher. A greater understanding of how we all communicate nonverbally will also help the principal to improve his or her own body language, and eliminate body language that transmits negative cues.

Avoid arguing or interruptive behavior.

Some principals have a tendency to get overly involved or to react emotionally to what is being said. This will do nothing but stifle the communication process. The effective listener will avoid falling into this trap by not jumping to conclusions.

Facilitating

There are several reasons principals should manage by wandering around. One of these is to become aware of the concerns of teachers. During conversations with teachers throughout the school, the principal will occasionally learn of concerns or situations that if left unaddressed could develop into full-scale problems. When this kind of concern is expressed, the principal must move into the third phase in the process of management by wandering, around facilitating. Facilitating involves two skills: 1) asking probing questions that will help a teacher convey his or her thoughts, attitudes, and feelings accurately and completely, and 2) paraphrasing the teacher's words so as to ensure that the principal has interpreted those words correctly.

Follow-through

The fourth step in management by wandering around is a very deliberate one that must be executed with a great deal of sensitivity. Upon arriving back at the office, the principal asks to review the notes of his or her meetings and conversations and looks for similarities in the concerns teachers have expressed. Once a problem has been identified, the next step is to take action either directly or by delegating authority. If the identified problem lies in the domain of one particular supervisor, the appropriate course is to inform him or her of the concern and its intensity (without ever divulging sources), discuss possible courses of action, and request that he or she address the concern within five days and submit a written report on the solution. Meanwhile, the principal should report to the teachers involved, indicating steps that are being taken to resolve the concern. A word of caution: When discussing the concern with the supervisor involved, be very cordial, avoid arguing, and use the discussion as an opportunity to explore alternative solutions to the problem and what can be done to prevent the situation from reappearing. After a common understanding has been arrived at, thank the supervisor for his or her time. Later, send the supervisor a note of thanks for his or her cooperative efforts.

The Procedures for Managing by Wandering Around

There is no set procedure for implementing management by wandering around. However, the following steps should enable any school to implement the practice with a high degree of success.

- Endorse the practice of management by wandering around in the school's statement of philosophy.
- Bring in a consultant to train the principal and supervisors in listening and facilitating skills. Make certain that the training involves everyone in role-playing.
- Help teachers to identify who the major stakeholders of the school are, and emphasize the need to stay in touch with them in order to achieve excellence. Indicate what activities should be engaged in to stay in touch with the stakeholders.
- Prepare guidelines that suggest the minimum time that should be devoted to managing by wandering around.
- Take into consideration the degree to which the supervisors manage by wandering around when evaluating their performance.
- Make certain all teachers are informed of the principal's schedule for wandering around.

Rambling is not the same as wandering. When a principal rambles, he or she walks around without having a specific goal in mind. In contrast, there are goals to management by wandering around, the most important of which is to keep in touch with teachers and to address their concerns. Sometimes a principal may intend to manage by wandering around, but actually ends up simply rambling. The principal who does this ends up in aimless chit-chat. Management by wandering around is a systematic process that involves seeking out teachers to connect with, actively listening to them, facilitating their conversation, and following through on their concerns. The principal who is merely rambling usually fails to carry out the last step of following through, whereas true management by wandering around is not a complete process until action is promised and carried through within a reasonable time span. The principal who merely rambles ends up talking mainly to teachers and other administrators. True, management by wandering around involves meeting with all types of people during the course of a school year. Mere rambling will not necessarily contribute to a thorough grasp of details about the school. Management by wandering around, because it is systematic, will help the principal stay well informed. Finally, mere rambling around the school will not necessarily contribute to an atmosphere of caring and trust. On the contrary, it may make teachers feel as though they are being "spied on." But true management by wandering around will help nurture a caring and intimate relationship among all the teachers in the district, because it is systematic, because its purpose is to allow teachers to express themselves openly, and because it is not mere conversation, but action as well.

REVIEW

KEY POINTS TO REMEMBER:

- One of the most important roles of the principal is to manage the school by wandering around.
- There are four steps for wandering around: 1) connecting (get out into the school and meet teachers); 2) listening (taking an interest in what the teacher is saying without judging or evaluating his or her comments); 3) facilitating (ask probing questions that will help the teacher to convey his or her thoughts, attitudes, and feelings accurately and completely, and paraphrasing the teacher's words so as to ensure that the principal has interpreted the comments correctly); and 4) follow-through (report back to the teacher and indicate how the situation was resolved).
- Rambling is not wandering around. When a principal manages by rambling around, he or she does so without having a special goal in mind. Managing by wandering around is a systematic process that involves seeking out teachers and other school people to connect with, actively listening to them, facilitating their conversation, and following through on their needs and concerns.

APPLICATION:

Obtain a pedometer and establish a base mileage by going to every class in your building, spending about 5 to 10 minutes with each teacher. Visit the school support staff as well. Calculate the total mileage for managing by wandering around your school. Use that base as a minimum mileage to manage by wandering around your school on a daily basis.

CHAPTER 11

Practicing Egalitarianism in Schools

LEARNING OBJECTIVES

After reading and comprehending this chapter, you should be able to:

- Define egalitarianism.
- Identify school egalitarianism principles.
- Describe the benefits associated with egalitarianism.

What Every Principal Should Know About Practicing Egalitarianism in Schools

Transformational principals are aware of the fact that when they treat teachers as equals, teachers will be amiable to change and transform the school. They are also aware that the terms empowerment, consensus, and participative management have one thing in common. And that term is respect, respect for their ability to make decisions, respect for them to do whatever is necessary to get a job done, respect for them to meaningfully participate in the decision-making process and respect for them to reach a common decision in all parties can agree with the best interest of the students and the school. If a principal truly desires to make the transformation, he or she should be fortified with the appropriate knowledge and be able to relate this knowledge to teachers in their daily lives in school.

To become highly effective, principals must decrease hierarchy, external controls, specialization, and status indicators, and allow teachers to control their own lives on the job. The more the principal respects teachers, the more self-respect teachers develop. The more teachers are trusted, the more trustworthy they become. Principals can demonstrate that they respect and trust teachers by increased caring and intimacy. The thrust towards improved school performance requires two primary considerations: 1) a high level of concern for school people by creating conditions for maximizing self-actualization while on the job, and 2) the achievement of school goals through the conditions created for self-actualization. These conditions are created through a management style called egalitarianism.

The egalitarian school, through its humanistic principles and practice of equality for all, makes it possible for teachers to graduate to a point where the school environmental conditions allow them to be motivated to self-actualization rather than to a lower-level need. When the conditions of the school allow this, forces are created that generate more self-actualized teachers, which in turn produce the synergistic work environment that is necessary to pursue excellence in education.

A vision of the great school reveals that teachers' main goals are not self-seeking, but rather mindful of the school and its purposes. Cooperation replaces competition; teamwork replaces individual effort; love replaces hate; harmony replaces discord; and higher goals replace lower-level goals. To some extent, the school life and family emerge into a social-economic life that benefits the teacher, the school, and the community. The main thrust of the egalitarian school is directed toward creating a spirit of humanship and mutual help for the teacher and the school. As a result, teachers become complete and respected individuals, who enjoy full participation in the success of the school.

Defining Egalitarianism

Egalitarianism in terms of education means that all teachers have equal economic, social, and political rights and privileges as conditions to fulfill their basic human needs in the school environment. By economic rights I mean the equality of opportunity that all teachers have so as to maintain a job in consonance with their personal characteristics and intelligence in order to obtain food, clothing, shelter, and other amenities. Social rights refer to equality of opportunity for teachers to participate in groups and to engage in social welfare and recreational activities. In the context of the school, political rights refer to equality of opportunity for teachers to assist in the operation of the school through decision making and problem solving - in effect, opportunities to influence decisions that affect them.

When these rights are given to teachers, three conditions will be prevalent: 1) they have equal dignity, rank, and privileges; 2) they are treated as equals in power, ability, and achievement; and 3) they are treated fairly, impartially, and equally.

The School Egalitarianism Principles

There are six egalitarian principles that seem appropriate in the treatment of teachers. They are: equality of treatment, equality of opportunity, equality to satisfy basic needs, equality for meaningful work, equality for equal distribution, and equality of power.

Equality of Treatment

Despite differences in characteristics, traits, and intelligence, all teachers are entitled to be treated equally in terms of respect, concern, and value. Some ways in which principals can perform this practice are:

- Type their own letters.
- Answer their own telephone.
- Insist that everybody be on a first name basis.
- Encourage principals and teachers to eat together in the same cafeteria.
- Remove all time clocks.
- Abandon all reserved parking spaces.
- Replace all enclosed office with action stations.

Equality of Opportunity.

All teachers have opportunities to occupy any position, regardless of differences in social status, economic resources, personal characteristics, and intelligence. This principle, although it is supported by federal and state legislation, guarantees each teacher opportunities to compete and be considered for any position in the district. This principle is founded on the basis that if everyone has an equal start, the position he or she attains depends on his or her abilities and aspirations.

The transformational principal performs this practice by committing themselves to the following:

- Hire more minority and women teachers and school administrators.
- Provide sufficient opportunities for all teachers to receive training and development in a variety of areas to enhance their chances of getting promoted.
- Increase teachers' job satisfaction through an assortment of practices, such as solving problems, participating in decision making, involving them in instituting change, etc:
- Recruit minority teachers on the high-school level.

Equality to Satisfy Basic Needs

All teachers should be entitled to use their physical and intellectual endowment to satisfy their basic needs. This principle is extremely important because it promotes the satisfaction not only of economic needs, but of safety, social self-esteem, and self-actualization needs. Therefore, these needs set parameters for principals in establishing a school environment whereby all of these needs could be fulfilled. As a result, the philosophy, the principals, and the total school environment reflect the accommodation of these basic needs. To this end, principals can perform the following:

- Provide adequate wages and supplemental benefits.
- Be impartial, consistent, reassuring, friendly, and fair.
- Provide adequate orientation for teachers.

- Provide adequate facilities, such as, lighting, bathrooms, cafeteria, etc., for all teachers.

Equality for Meaningful Work

All teachers are provided with opportunities to find meaning in their work. This principle supports the need to satisfy the basic need of self-actualization; that is, opportunities are afforded to everyone on the job, regardless of status, to find the job he or she is best suited for, which will enable him or her to be all that he or she can be according to his or her abilities, talents and limitations.

Some positions that enable teachers to obtain this right are as follows:

- Encourage all teachers to find their own career path.
- Pay teachers for becoming proficient in more than one area.
- Provide for a cooperative training and development program for all teachers.
- Institute a succession plan for all teachers.
- Enable teachers to solve problems.
- Reward teachers for making an outstanding contribution to the school performance.
- Recognize and reward teachers religiously.
- Enable teachers to set and achieve their own goals.

Equality for Equal Distribution

All teachers receive equal shares of the benefits or burdens. With this principle, everybody counts for one and nobody counts for more than one. This important operating principle provides the foundation for the distribution of income, fringe benefits, and other benefits. To do this:

- Recognize and reward a high percentage of teachers for their exemplary performance, thereby enabling everybody to become a winner.
- Don't reward teachers at the exclusion of other teachers and school people.

- Make beginning teachers' salaries competitive with other professions.

Equality of Power

All teachers are provided with opportunities to share power with those in the power position. This principle is founded on the basis that all teachers have something to offer to the school, and, whereas power can be either good or bad, those in power positions should look for and make opportunities to share power with their teachers whenever possible. This principle is also defined as empowerment in and means that attempts should be made to equalize power between principals and teachers. A principal provides this right for their teachers by doing the following:

- Eliminate titles, levels, and symbols.
- Provide opportunities for teachers to engage in consensus decision making.
- Encourage all teachers to become involved and to participate in daily conduct of the school.

The Benefits Associated With Egalitarianism

There are two major benefits associated with the concept of egalitarianism. One, egalitarianism is intrinsically desirable and morally right. "All teachers are treated as equals" is a normative conclusion and is a sound base for formulating rules and principles for governing human activities. Any deviation from this proposition must be, and should be, based on solid ground. Two, egalitarianism is an "ideal" to be realized by human effort. Teachers are more apt to perform better when they feel better about themselves. If power is used to subordinate teachers through privileges reserved for a few, it diminishes their self-concept and self-esteem and delays their growth toward self-actualization. As a result of such subtle constraints, teachers do not optimize their performance on the job.

It is good and humane to institute egalitarianism in the school, but other than that, why should the principal implement this concept by giving up power or equalizing it with teachers and other school people? This is a frequently asked question. However, egalitarianism does not advocate that the principal give up his or her power. It is recommended that the principals make better use of their power by spreading it throughout the school.

The best way to get maximum results is through an egalitarian approach. In fact, in one of the most comprehensive studies ever conducted, it was revealed that egalitarian organizations tend to produce better performance results than inegalitarian ones. The study was conducted by Hay Associates and was entitled *Hay Report: The State of Human Resources in American Industry.* This study involved 1,200 organizations, totaling two and one-half million people, covering the years 1975 to 1983, and examined trends relating to employees and management. This report concluded that there were two different cultures across United States' industry: an egalitarian culture, perpetuated by "faster-growth" organizations, and an inegalitarian culture perpetuated by "lower-growth" organizations. Hay identified faster-growth organizations as having sales/revenues and profit of an average of over 25 percent across industries and lower-growth organizations as having sales/revenues and profit of an average below 5 percent across industries. To meet the egalitarian criterion of "being concerned for people," Hay used employee rating of the company's desirability as a place to work. Their study revealed that more than 80 percent of the employees over an eight-year period rated higher-growth organizations as a desirable place to work. Based on this data, faster-growth organizations are cited as being egalitarian and slower-growth organizations are cited as being inegalitarian.

There is no reason why similar results cannot be achieved by schools. Therefore, transformational principals who implement egalitarianism in their school look forward to the following:

- Principals tend to be more in touch with their teachers than those in an inegalitarian school.

- Teachers of egalitarian schools have better attitudes and self-confidence.

- Higher-achieving schools foster an egalitarian culture and low-achieving schools do not.

- Teachers' attitudes in egalitarian schools become more positive toward the school.

- Egalitarian schools place greater value on human resource development than inegalitarian ones.
- Teachers in egalitarian schools are more concerned with challenge and learning, while those in inegalitarian schools are more concerned with security and authority.
- Egalitarian schools share information with their teachers more freely and fully.
- Credibility of information in egalitarian schools is higher than in inegalitarian ones.
- Teachers in egalitarian schools believe that they are the school's most important asset.
- Principals in egalitarian schools reinforce a culture that emphasizes a high level of performance.
- Egalitarian schools seek teachers who value challenge and growth.
- High-achieving schools foster egalitarian attitudes and low-achieving schools respond to hierarchical situations.
- Egalitarian schools make teachers feel that they can be much more than what they were and will go out of their way to remove barriers that restrict performance results.

REVIEW

KEY POINTS TO REMEMBER:

- Egalitarianism in schools means that the teachers have equal economics, social, and political rights, and privileges and conditions to fulfill their basic needs in school.
- School egalitarian principles consist of equality of treatment, equality of opportunity, equality to satisfy basic needs, equality for meaningful work, equality for equal distribution, and equality of power.
- The main benefits of egalitarianism in schools are its intrinsically desirable and morally right and it is an idea to be realized by human effort.

APPLICATION

Discuss the egalitarianism principles cited in this chapter. Now ask teachers individually to identify egalitarianism practices they would like to use. Request teachers to describe some egalitarian practices utilized in your school. Then have the teachers identify inegalitarian practices. Discuss each of these incidents thoroughly. After the discussion, request teachers to individually identify more egalitarianism practices and give you some time to think about this list and indicate when you will get back to them. After reviewing the list, identify those you can live with and those you cannot live with. Prepare to explain to teachers which you cannot live with. Reconvene a meeting with the teachers and discuss your acceptable egalitarian practices and those you cannot accept at this time. Practice the acceptable ones and inculcate them throughout the school.

CHAPTER 12

Arriving at a Consensus

LEARNING OBJECTIVES

After reading and comprehending this chapter, you should be able to:

- Define consensus.
- Compare majority rule with consensus.
- Identify the procedural steps for reaching a consensus.
- Discuss three consensus models.
- Describe the attitudes that support consensus.
- Describe the alternate forms of consensus.

What Every Principal Should Know About How to Engage Teachers Consensus Decision-Making

The consensus movement began in this country about thirty to forty years ago. However, because the process takes a long time before decisions are reached, it was soon abandoned for either the autocratic rule or majority vote. School organizations never did use this decision-making mode to arrive at decisions until the advent of school-based management and total quality management. Today, it tends to be the only acceptable way to make decisions in many schools.

Defining Consensus

Consensus is a decision-making process in which members of a school cooperatively arrive at a mutually acceptable decision, which all members will agree to support.

More specifically, consensus means:

1. Every member of the school may not be completely satisfied with the decision, but it is the best that can be reached at the time and under the existing circumstances.
2. Each teacher has consented to the decision.
3. A single teacher with a strong objection to a decision has the right to block the decision.
4. The school must continue searching for an acceptable team decision.
5. The focus is on being attentive to each teacher's ideas, and taking all the members' reservations and concerns into consideration in an attempt to reach an acceptable team decision.
6. A teacher who relinquishes the right to block a school's decision has, in effect, agreed to abide by the decision of school.

Inherent in the use of consensus decision-making are basic assumptions about the confidence in human beings and groups. For every problem, there is a best decision for a particular time and circumstance upon which all teachers can unite, if enough time is spent in discussion. The aim of the school is to develop a sense of cooperation and belonging. And every teacher participates and shares in the decision.

Some conditions or prerequisites must be understood to make the process work. These are:

1. The superintendent or steering committee must clearly indicate when it is appropriate or inappropriate to use consensus as a decision-making process.
2. Teachers must be trained to implement the consensus decision-making process.

Arriving at a Consensus

3. The principal should be trained as a facilitator of the process and in other areas, such as conflict resolution, school building, motivation, and school dynamics.
4. A manual on consensus decision-making should be developed and made available to all teachers for future referral.
5. Everyone who will be affected by the decision should be involved in the process.
6. There must be a common bond uniting the school, such as similar areas of responsibility, linked goals, etc.
7. Each teacher must accept the belief that everyone has something to offer the school, that conflict can be healthy, and that any problem can be solved if enough time is spent in discussing it.

Common Terms Related to Consensus

There are some terms associated with the consensus decision-making process. These are blocking, incubation period, unanimity and compromise. A consensus is considered blocked when one or more teachers who have gone through the synthesizing process oppose the decision. Their action is termed "blocking." Since the school is not ready to reach a decision, more discussion must be held.

The process of silencing the membership in order to give each member an opportunity to mediate the activity of the school, reduce the anxiety, etc. is known as the incubation period.

When every teacher feels a particular solution is wanted most or is best, unanimity is reached. Consensus is not unanimity; it is the best solution that can be reached at a particular time and under the present circumstances.

A situation in which each side gives up some demands or makes a concession to arrive at a decision is compromise. Compromise should never be mistaken for consensus.

There are some pleasant advantages to making decisions by consensus:

1. Consensus fosters a win-win philosophy as opposed to majority rule in which an individual or side loses.

2. It is a process of synthesizing and integrating ideas rather than selecting one idea over another.
3. Its thrust is to persuade rather than to coerce.
4. It provides a setting in which everyone contributes something to the discussion.
5. It provides adequate time for teachers to hash ideas over, rather than rushing into a vote.
6. It nurtures a precept that the integrity of the school is more important than a single issue.
7. It helps the school to function as a group rather than focusing on a teacher's idea, which leads to compromise.
8. It requires honesty, open communication, and a free exchange of ideas.
9. Every teacher gets "a piece of the action."
10. It enhances the probability that the decision will be implemented with little or no change.

A comparative analysis between the majority rule and consensus should further help you to understand why the latter is preferred over the former:

Majority Rule Consensus

A decision is reached by selecting a solution that is acceptable to more than half of the teachers. A decision is reached by selecting a solution acceptable to all members.

Quality decisions are sometimes not made because every teachers' ideas may not be heard.

Quality decisions are a by-product of the process, because every member's reservations and concerns are heard and responded to in a positive manner.Assumes competition where "sides" are identified with one side attempting to win over the other.

Assumes cooperation where teachers respect the rights of a member to disagree with the school; an individual's concerns and reservations are considered and everything is done to satisfy his or her needs. Thus, a win-win relationship is established.Decisions are usually arrived at rapidly by teachers. Implementation of a decision by teachers is slow to be realized and sometimes is changed during the implementation process, because every teacher may not be committed to the decisions of the other side. Decisions are usually arrived at very slowly. Implementation of a decision by teachers is realized very rapidly because all teachers have agreed to support it.

The opinions of principals, supervisors, experts, specialists, and dominant teachers may influence the other members of the team to reach a decision. The opinions of all teachers, regardless of their power status, have no influence on the decision because egalitarianism is practiced throughout the process. Acceptance of the decision is usually based on perceptions and judgments of facts. Acceptance of the decision is based on facts and feelings of teachers.

The Procedural Steps for Achieving Consensus Decision-Making

Although there are only a few major steps for implementing the consensus decision-making process, each is filled with essential points that must be mastered in order to produce united agreement on decisions:

Step I: Preparing for Discussion.

There are two basic ways to introduce something to the school for discussion purposes in order to arrive at a consensus. One, construct a proposal. Do this to inform teachers what must be achieved to fulfill their charge. Two, establish an agenda. The agenda can be established either prior to the discussion or during the meeting. In-school situations will usually require the agenda to be developed during the meeting so that everyone will agree on what should be discussed and in what sequence.

Step II: Introduce the Item for Discussion.

The principal introduces the goal or the item for the agenda. At times, particularly when an impromptu meeting has been called to agree to a solution to a problem, the introduction should contain a precise definition of the goal or item to be discussed and a clear statement of what has to be done to arrive at a consensus. This statement should focus on either what has to be accomplished, or what problem must be solved by the decision. When using a proposal for discussion purposes, the goal, if already given, should be considered in terms of identifying performance standards that need to be acquired to achieve the goal. Sometimes the goal, as well as performance standards, must be mutually agreed upon by the teachers. When using an agenda for discussion purposes, the school will need to mutually agree as to what the primary purpose of the meeting is and how it should be completed.

Step III: Present Background Information.

The principal, or a teacher introducing the goal or item for discussion, should give teachers as much background information as possible so that it has a beginning base to make decisions. When the discussion progresses, other essential information will emerge from among teachers.

Step IV: Discuss the Goal or Item.

The principal is responsible for helping the school build a united judgment that will lead to consensus. The following represents the essential actions that will take place by the principal and teachers during the discussion phase for reaching a consensus. First, the principal introduces the goal or item to the school, defines the problems, provides background information, and recommends an approach to the problem. An individual teacher may ask for clarification of the goal or item, and more specific background information. The teacher may use any or all of the clarifying material to supplement original ideas. A teacher responds to the idea of the principal, and includes his or her own ideas as it has been influenced by the teacher. Next, as long as the ideas and opinions presented are relevant to the original goal or item, the principal encourages the teachership for more. A teacher responds to the idea of the leader and includes his or her own ideas as they have been influenced by either another member or the leader. Several teachers then begin to respond to the earlier goal or item, offering their own ideas and opinions. Each statement builds on those of other teachers. As a result, each individual teacher's comment is unique and has been influenced by the ideas and opinions of other teachers.

Third, during discussion, the principal and individual teachers are responsible for conducting a smooth-operating meeting to reach a consensus by:

- keeping teachers from meandering;
- probing for more ideas and opinions;
- providing more ideas and opinions;
- summarizing where agreements and disagreements exist;
- citing new issues and problems when they occur;
- making certain all viewpoints, reservations, impressions, feelings, and concerns are heard and understood by the total teachership; and
- seeking process problems and working them through.

Finally, most viewpoints have been stated and teachers begin to repeat themselves.

The principal asks the teachers if anything new can be added to the discussion and then tests for a consensus by stating the position (solution) toward which the school seems to be moving.

Step V: Arriving at a Decision.

When all views have been heard, the principal orchestrates the activities necessary to aid the teachers to arrive at a decision. First, the school agrees or disagrees to the "consensus test" of the principal. The principal makes certain that all concerns and objections have been addressed by going from one teacher to another, and observing nonverbal and verbal responses from teachers.

Next, teachers listen and discuss each concern for the purpose of arriving at an agreement. At times, the decision that is arrived at may not entirely satisfy every teacher, but it may be the best decision that can be agreed to at that time under the existing circumstances. If one or more teachers continue to have a problem with the decision, it must be "worked through" the process.

The principal then continues to orchestrate the discussion of the school by encouraging each member to bring up and reflect on all ideas, concerns, and reservations.

If then it seems as though a consensus is reached among teachers, the principal states the consensus decision to determine if every teacher agrees and makes certain that specific responsibilities for carrying out the phases of the decisions are assigned to each teacher. If a proposal exists, every teacher responsible for completing a function or activity (which will have some impact on the decision) is required to sign the proposal as an indication of agreement. The signature is also used to indicate to the signers all the persons who have in one way or another been involved in the decision-making process.

Finally, if the principal realizes that a consensus cannot be reached at the present time, this usually means teachers do not have enough information to render a good decision. The decision will have to be deferred until more information is given to teachers, more discussion takes place, and the teachers digest the information.

Sometimes the teachers may feel that a decision must be made, perhaps because of a time constraint. Therefore, it will be necessary to continue the discussion, and for members to "stretch" themselves to reach a decision that may not be the best, but one all teachers can live with. The teachers should not be coerced or pressured into accepting a decision; vital by-products of consensus such as individual teacher's commitment, improved coordination, etc., would be seriously missing from the result.

What To Do When Blocking Occurs

It is the responsibility of the principal and facilitator to make certain that the individual rights of teachers to disagree is protected. There are several options to consider as indicated below:

1. Repeat what the other teachers have agreed to. Request the "blockers" to state their specific objections.
2. If the objection is reasonable, the principal can divide the school into mini-teams to consider the objection. The school may decide to meet as a whole to consider the objection; however, dividing the school into mini-teams is preferred.
3. If the objection seems to be inappropriate or far-fetched, the principal can state as objectively as possible that it is his or

her impression that the school has listened carefully, but the blockers' concerns are not appropriate at this time.

4. The principal should defer the decision for either ten to fifteen minutes or several days.

The Three Consensus Models

There are several different types of consensus models. Three of the most common, the Quaker consenus model, Filley's consensus model, and Panel consensus, can be useful in a school basis. Each one provides different step-by-step guidelines to achieve consensus. Which one you choose to use no doubt will be based on your individual preference.

The Quaker consensus model is based on a number of principles that are used as a code of behavior. It is employed at meetings scheduled to produce a consensus. It consists of the following steps:

1. Avoid arguing for your own point of view.
2. Avoid the win-lose approach.
3. Avoid changing your mind to avoid conflict.
4. Avoid majority voting and other conflict-reducing techniques.
5. View differences of opinions as healthy.
6. View initial agreement with skepticism.

Filley's consensus model is based on a set of prerequisites and prescriptions for arriving at the consensus. The prerequisites reinforce the prescriptions. These are:

1. Review and adjust the school size, constraints, spatial, arrangement and communication.
2. Review and adjust the perception of the teachers using reality testing to substantiate the facts.
3. Use reality testing to clarify and understand the attitudes and feelings of the teachers to one another.
4. Depersonalize the problem.

5. Search for a solution by generating alternate solutions.

If these prerequisites exist, the probability of reaching a consensus is enhanced when the following prescriptions have been met:

1. Narrow the range of solutions.
2. Evaluate the solutions in terms of quality and acceptability.
3. Allow teachers to justify preferences and feelings.
4. Agree on criteria of evaluation.
5. Use consensus when there is little expression of self-oriented need.
6. Review teachers' evaluations of alternatives periodically.
7. Don't use techniques that avoid conflict.
8. Divide problems into parts for evaluation purposes.
9. Resolve conflict before continuing with the evaluation process.

With panel consensus a variety of teams are set up in an inverted pyramid in order to winnow the various ideas offered as a solution to a given problem. There are five steps to this technique:

Step 1: Idea Generation.

Organize multiple teams to generate a large number of ideas to a given problem, using the nominal group process. This generates an improved quality of ideas and more variety than is produced during a brainstorming session.

Step 2: Screening Process.

Organize teachers into fifteen teams of twelve to fifteen members. Charge each team with the responsibility for generating five best ideas presented within the team.

Arriving at a Consensus

Step 3: Select Action.

Three teams of five experts with broad experience, selected from the cadre of principals, meet with a principal to write a justification for the best ideas from the seventy-five ideas that have been presented.

Step 4: Refinement.

Five central administrators (with expertise in the problem) meet with a principal to select the best ideas from the fifteen presented. They qualify, expand, and synthesize the ideas into five priority proposals without losing the unique character of the original ideas.

Step 5: Decision.

In this final step, five central administrators meet with a facilitator to select one or more of the ideas for implementation. If a consensus on an idea cannot be reached, the idea is sent to one of the preceding teams to reactivate previous ideas.

Consensus is the basis for arriving at all decisions at each step. If a consensus cannot be reached, the idea may be discarded and the next item of priority activated.

Attitudes That Support Consensus

There are two attitudes that will help the consensus decision-making process work well: a cooperative spirit and an acceptance of criticism. These will encourage a healthy psychological climate in order to arrive at a consensus and allow each team member to improve his or her relationship with other team members.

Consensus decision-making expects each teacher to cooperate. In a cooperative mood, teachers will:

1. Share information with others.
2. Trust and care for each other.
3. Accept individual differences as a value to the diversity of the team.
4. Welcome viewpoints from other perspectives.

5. Foster a win-win philosophy.
6. Capitalize on their individual strengths and minimize their weaknesses for the benefit of the school.
7. Recognize that there is not always a right solution, but one that may be a more appropriate solution.

Ideas developed during the consensus decision-making process become the property of the school; when a teacher brings forth an idea, it is usually because of his or her reservoir of knowledge, experience, etc., as well as the input of other teachers. At another time and place with different teachers, the idea may have been different. Once this is understood and accepted by all teachers, each of them should feel at ease to criticize ideas, to change ideas, or to add a residual idea. No teacher should take any suggestions or changes as a personal affront.

Conflict is neither good nor bad. It can be handled on a win-lose basis or on a win-win basis. When it is handled on a win-lose basis, one side competes against the other, and, although one side may win, neither side actually accomplishes much. However, when it is handled on a win-win basis, there are no sides; everybody works cooperatively, exchanging ideas and opinions until a decision is reached that is satisfactory to all teachers. Different points of view are catalysts. The strengths and weaknesses of each idea are examined in the crucible of interaction, through which a variable solution to issues emerges.

If the consensus decision-making process is working effectively, each teacher will value the feelings of the others; each teacher will approach an idea or decision in a healthy manner, caring for each other and considering the concerns of each teacher, until a workable and acceptable decision is reached.

Information is power and that power must be equalized. Equalize power and you provide each teacher with an equal access to information; therefore, no one teacher should have a monopoly on information, experience, skills, and ideas. When one teacher has information or anything else important to the school, all members should have equal access to that information. To determine if there is unequal power within the school, carefully consider the following questions:

Arriving at a Consensus

1. Does one teacher talk more than the others and tend to dominate the school?
2. Does one teacher tend to show off more than the others?
3. Does a teacher think more highly of one member than any of the others?
4. Does one teacher contribute more to the discussion than others?

If any of the above questions are answered in the affirmative, then make a critical observation and review to determine the power overload and what steps should be taken to equalize it.

Every human being can contribute something to a school. The contribution may be a person's analytical nature, the calm and relaxed manner in which a teacher asks or responds to a question, the inexperienced manner of relating to ideas, or the person's sensitivity. Consensus decision-making means that every teacher can contribute to the school performance in unique and different ways. When teachers feel that they are important, it is primarily because each member has demonstrated that he or she values other's contributions. Each teacher fosters within the school a sense of responsibility, a sense of competency, a sense of dignity and worth, and a sense of being useful and competent. All this helps to enhance their contributions to arriving at a decision.

Consensus decision-making also means that teachers must begin to trust each other. Trust can only result if teachers are honest with each other. Some guidelines to follow are:

1. Information will neither be destroyed nor concealed.
2. Teachers can depend on each other to abide by their agreements and to perform in a competent manner.
3. Teachers don't have to remind other members what they promised.
4. Teachers don't have to defend their positions or points of view continuously.
5. Teachers will not become defensive when other members attempt to influence them.
6. Teachers do not have to conceal their feelings.

7. Teachers don't have to change their models to emulate others.

The Attitudes That Hamper Consensus

Consensus is a powerful process for making decisions and getting teachers truly committed to their decisions. Certain attitudes like individualism and selfiishness can hamper the effect.

Consensus decision making encourages school competition as opposed to individual competition. When schools compete among themselves, the effectiveness of the school is based on how strongly teachers cooperate, how well they get along together, care for each other, and demonstrate concern over different points of view. This kind of competition is healthy.

Individual competition is unhealthy and does not promote effective decision making. It is evident when a teacher tries to achieve his or her personal gain at the expense of other teachers. For example, a teacher may try to withhold information and manipulate other teachers to get acceptance of his or her own ideas. Competition fosters mistrust and has no place when a school is striving to reach consensus.

Some Americans have been taught the value of individualistic competition in ways that cause teachers to exhibit selfishness. They may see their role in the school as one who merely contributes his or her own ideas, skills, talents, experience, and background to the discussion. Such an attitude prevents working out problems and arriving at solutions. It perpetuates an unhealthy relationship in a consensus-making situation because teachers think their personal goals and needs are superior to school goals.

As a result of individualistic orientation, teachers often think of their ideas as personal property; they sometimes become annoyed when a teacher is either critical or suggests changes. When this occurs, the defensive teacher may argue for his or her idea rather than accepting improvements.

Teachers may also hide their true feelings about an issue because they have learned that the best way to deal with conflict and disagreement is to suppress it or to compromise in order to get rid of it. However, by compromising a position, they fail to deal fully with their hidden emotions and have given up a great opportunity to arrive at a creative approach to the solution.

Sometimes teachers will allow specialists, experts, or consultants to think for them and to arrive at decisions. By giving in to

Arriving at a Consensus

authority, these same teachers surrender their power and defeat the purpose of consensus decision-making. When teachers surrender their power and limit their participation in discussion, they, in essence, are denying the other teachers a variety of viewpoints on an issue. Inactive teachers also create other problems for the school as a whole, including:

1. They may fail to take responsibility for a poor decision.
2. They may not fully understand the decision, or may not be willing to implement it.
3. They dilute the effectiveness of the consensus-making process. Teachers will have social problems such as bias, prejudices, and assumptions that tend to influence their thinking. Teachers who are not aware of these problems cannot deal effectively in the decision-making process. They will continue to exhibit these problems in one way or another during the discussion and when they arrive at solutions.

Alternate Forms of Consensus

Sometimes the pure form of consensus may not be possible or may not be worth the time and effort to devote to the decision-making process. Alternative ways to deal with these situations include semantic differential voting consensus, sufficient consensus, consensus decision with an exception, or consensus by committee.

With semantic differential voting consensus, members have agreed or not agreed on the decision based on one or more of the following:

- "I am strongly opposed to this idea but I would not exercise a veto to prevent a limited trial test."
- "I am not convinced this idea, is feasible, but I am willing to take a wait-and-see position by supporting a limited trial test."
- "I am weighing the advantages and disadvantages of this idea and believe it is worthy of a limited trial test."
- "I feel this idea has merit and support a limited trial test based on our criteria for success or failure."

- "I believe this is a good idea and I enthusiastically endorse a limited trial test of this idea based on our criteria for success or failure."

For sufficient consensus to work, the vast majority of teachers desire to take part in a particular action. If this fails, the principal or team leader can make an interim decision in order to satisfy the need to proceed, and to give the members sufficent time to continue dialogueing until a decision is reached.

In consensus decision with an exception, the principal presents a proposal to the school, which signifies an acceptance or rejection of the decision. The principal indicates those who favor the proposal, those who can live with the proposal, and those who are uncomfortable with it.

If no one is uncomfortable about the proposal, the decision is implemented, but if some teachers are uncomfortable about it, they are requested to state their reasons and a discussion ensues. After the discussion, the principal will ask the teachers if the idea should be implemented over the objections of the minority. An affirmative vote means majority rule. A negative vote means postponing the decision until a consensus is reached through a discussion.

The teachers reach a consensus on the proposal or item before discussing the solution through consensus by committee. Sufficient time is allocated for interaction and clarification. If a major objection is raised over the solution, the school breaks up into mini-teams for discussion and develops new proposals, amendments, etc. The mini-teams return to the school and determine if a consensus can be reached. Those objecting to the proposal are asked to stay aside and let the majority rule on the solution. If those objecting to the proposal refuse to step aside, a committee is established representing an equal number of varied opinions. The charge of this committee is to meet and to reach a mutually acceptable proposal. The proposal is brought back to the teachers for a final decision. If a consensus is not realized, then the school will vote to accept a majority rule, which is usually three-fourths of the membership, and then a three-fourth majority vote is conducted to accept the proposal.

The following guidelines should prove helpful in facilitating the consensus decision-making process:

Arriving at a Consensus

- Consensus meetings should be conducted as if they were friendly gatherings of friends rather than tense contests between opposing sides. Robert's Rules of Order and consensus tend to be incompatible, because of the former strict adherence to rules..

- Teachers must resist blindly arguing for their points of view, which often leads to confrontation. Instead, they must present their position in a clear and logical manner and listen actively to other positions, carefully considering what others have to offer.

- Teachers should refrain from changing their minds merely to avoid an argument or conflict. They should agree to a decision only when they are convinced that the reasons for it make good sense and are logical.

- The attitude among teachers should be "I win, you win." When a true consensus has been reached, everybody has a "share of the pie."

- All teachers must participate in the discussion, and they should encourage other members to participate.

- Each teacher should summarize the statement of the previous speaker before presenting his or her own point of view.

- From time to time, the principal should review the course of the discussion in order to clarify ideas and to point out similarities and differences in points of view.

- When teachers become emotional or tense, or when nothing is being said, the principal should call for a brief recess.

- If a tentative decision is reached, the consensus should be tested by bringing in an expert to discuss the decision or by leaving the final decision to a follow-up meeting.

- If a final decision is reached, the principal should review with the team what each member has agreed to do to implement the solution.

Remember: Consensus does not mean that everyone must be equally satisfied with the decision reached. However, everyone must be comfortable with the decision and should feel that it is the best that could be arrived at, given the time and circumstances. If anyone continues to have serious reservations, he or she has the right to block the decision, and the school must either continue to discuss it until the teacher finds it acceptable, or arrive at a new decision.

REVIEW

Key Points to Remember:

- Consensus is a decision-making process where teachers cooperatively aim at mutually acceptable decisions which all teachers will agree to support.
- Some of the advantages of consensus are: 1) it fosters a win-win philosophy; 2) it persuades rather than coerces; 3) it is a process of synthesizing and integrating ideas; 4) it provides a setting in which everyone contributes something to the discussion; 5) it helps the school function as a team.
- The procedural steps for consensus decision-making are: 1) prepare for the discussion; 2) introduce the item for discussion; 3) present background information; 4) discuss the goal or item; and 5) arrive at a decision.
- Three consensus models are: 1) Quaker consensus model; 2) Filley's consensus model; and 3) panel consensus.
- Attitudes that support consensus decision-making are: engendering a cooperative spirit and accepting criticism of ideas.
- The positive side of consensus involves valuing human feelings, equalizing power, respecting the contributions of others, and striving for trust.
- Attitudes that hamper consensus involve an individualistic philosophy, selfishness, psychology of owning ideas, not dealing with human emotions, and acquiescing to authority.
- Alternate forms of consensus consist of: 1) semantic differential voting consensus; 2) sufficient consensus; 3) consen-

sus decision with an exception; and 4) consensus by committee.

APPLICATION

To provide practical experience for the school to engage in consensus follow this exercise.

This exercise is an excellent means to give a school an opportunity to practice consensus. Although consensus decision-making will take longer than most decision-making models, it gets easier with practice. There are three steps to this exercise as indicated below:

1. Explain the consensus decision-making process by discussing the following points:

   - A unanimous agreement is not consensus. Consensus is a process by which elements of different views are heard and integrated into a final decision.

   - Everyone may not be totally satisfied with the decision, but it is the best decision that can be reached at that particular time.

   - Consensus means that everyone will agree to support the decision.

   - The goal is uniting rather than winning over the others, every member is considered important and the school tries to listen and respond to each other.

   - When a decision is not acceptable to the school as a whole, even though a majority may favor it, new options are explored and creative solutions that otherwise would be missed begin to blossom.

   - A climate of openness and support in which the concerns, feeling and ideas of each teacher are respected continues to grow and develop as the school becomes more proficient in using the process.

2. Pass out the "genie exercise" on the next page to all teachers.. Make certain everyone has a pencil. Divide the school either in dyads or triads. Consider groups with different demo-

graphics such as all males, all females, all school people, or all community people.

Once the exercise is distributed, respond to any questions of the teachers. Request the groups to reach a consensus.

3. When a group has reached consensus, ask it to take a break. When all of the groups have reached consensus, ask all groups to reconvene. Request someone from each group to write their choices on a flip chart and post it so that everyone can see it.

Ask the groups the following questions:
- Did the group select a leader?
- What method was used to arrive at consensus?
- How did the group feel when the other groups began to leave the room?
- If demographic grouping was used, did it affect the process of the final decision?
- Ask the teachers to comment about "values" heard when participating in the process.

The genie exercise: A genie is able to grant three wishes; however, only if the members of your school and community agree to the *same* three wishes. The wishes are as follows:

I want to be:
1. Guaranteed to live 125 years with the physical body of a 25-year-old person and the wisdom of a 250 year old person.
2. A winner of a $40 million lottery with no taxes.
3. The best person in the world in an area of my own choosing.
4. The winner of the Nobel Prize three separate times.
5. Able to heal people's physical ailments.
6. Rich, happy, and have many friends.
7. Able to bring back to life ten people of my own choice.
8. An Olympic star who has broken ten world records and is considered to be the best athlete ever.
9. Able to read people's minds with 100 percent accuracy.

10. Able to meet with God once.
11. The king or queen of the world.
12. The greatest doctor in the world.
13. The most attractive and richest person in the world.
14. In possession of a photographic memory and superior analytical skills.
15. Able to speak and understand all languages of the world.
16. The world's greatest mesmerist.
17. Able to fly.
18. In possession of super-human strength and intelligence.
19. Loved and respected by everybody.
20. A messenger from God.

CHAPTER **13**

Transforming Schools Through Success Emulation

LEARNING OBJECTIVE:

After reading and comprehending this chapter, you should be able to:

- Define success emulation.
- Identify the philosophical steps of success emulation.
- Describe the procedural steps for initiating a success emulation process.

What Every Principal Should Know About Implementing Success Emulation to Improve Schools

All principals should be able to search for the best-in-class (outstanding performing schools in one or more areas) schools and leading school practices that will lead to superior performance. The success emulation process of establishing goals and objectives based on best practices is being used increasingly by industries and some schools (though far too little). It is a positive, proactive, structured process that leads to changing operations and eventually attaining superior performance. To implement success emulation, you will need to structure and conduct investigations, and analyze and measure the opportunity for change

195

and how to install an active plan to achieve significant results. This chapter's format is a change from all the others. It has been designed to give the striving transformational principal directions and samples to enable a school design team to apply success emulation in areas to help transform the schools.

Defining Success Emulation

Success emulation is the continuous process of assessing school services, products, and practices against the best-in-class schools and other organizations or those schools recognized as the best in the country. Success emulation is a careful search for excellence in schools and other organizations, taking the absolute best as a standard for your school and trying to surpass it. The definition has further dimensions that deserves description: Success emulation is a self-improvement and management process that must be continuous to be effective. It should not be performed once and discontinued on the belief that the job is done. It must be a continuous practice because practices, processes, and performances constantly change. Best-in-class schools constantly get better and better. The search must continue to ensure that the best-in-class schools are uncovered. The transformational principal is well aware of this point and is obsessed with the principles of success emulation.

Success emulation can be applied to all facets of a school. It can be applied to the miscellaneous services and products provided for students. It can be applied to all processes, practices, and methods that are in support of getting the services and products effectively to meet the needs of students.

Success emulation is implied measurement. This measurement is accomplished in two forms. Internal and external practices can be compared and a statement of significant differences can be documented. The practices can be qualified to demonstrate the gap between practices. It also quantifies the size of the opportunity. Success emulation is not just a study of the best-in-class schools, but a process of determining the effectiveness of the leading school leaders of measuring results.

Success emulation should be directed at those schools and other organizations that are recognized as the best or as leaders in their specific areas. Best-in-class schools and other organizations may not always be appropriate. Careful investigation is

Transforming Schools Through Success Emulation

needed to determine which schools and other organizations to seek are worthy of emulation and why.

Success emulation is an ongoing investigation and learning experience that assures that the best practices, programs, and processes are uncovered analyzed, adopted, and implemented.

The Philosophical Steps of Success Emulation

The basic philosophical steps of success emulation are the key to success: know your objective, know the best-in-class or leaders in public education, incorporate the best and become great.

As the striving transformational principal you need to assess the strengths and weaknesses of your school. If you fail to determine your school's strengths and weaknesses, you will not know what to focus on to strengthen your school objectives.

Only when you compare your school with the best-in-class schools or the leaders in public education and how they got there will you be able to become a great school.

Learn from the best-in-school and the leading schools in the nation. If they are strong in any given areas, it will be important for you to uncover why they are and how they got that way. Locate those best practices wherever they exist and do not be reluctant to copy or modify and incorporate them in your own school. Emulate and improve on their strengths.

If careful investigations of the best-in-class school practices have been performed and if the best practices have been implemented, then you have capitalized on existing strengths to improve on your own weaknesses. Continue success emulation as a strategies focus and reach greatness.

The Benefits of Success Emulation

Success evaluation can benefit a school in several ways. It enables the best practices from any school or organization to be creatively incorporated into the processes of success emulation function. It can provide motivation and stimulation to the principal, teachers, and school people whose creativity is used to perform and implement best-in-class school findings. It has been determined that teachers are more receptive to new ideas and their creative adoption when those ideas did not necessarily originate in their own school. It identifies innovative programs and processes that would not have been recognized and thus not applied in schools for years to come. And, it promotes professional growth as a result of teachers' professional contacts and interactions with teachers and others in the best-in-class schools.

If you desire to gain the full benefit from success emulation to improve quality, it will be necessary for you to be guided by the following:

- Be determined and committed to becoming a transformational principal.
- Demonstrate an active commitment to success emulation.
- Maintain a clear and comprehensive understanding of how one's own school is organized as a basis for comparison to the best practices.
- Be willing to change and adapt to it based on success emulation findings.
- Be willing to share information with other success emulation schools, businesses, and industries.
- Focus first on best practices, and second, on performance.
- Focus on the leading schools and other organizations or other functionally best operations that are recognized leaders.
- Adhere to the nine-step success emulation process.
- Be open to new ideas, creativity, and innovativeness in application to existing processes.
- Continue success evaluation efforts.

There are nine detailed steps to achieving success evaluation. Each one contains guidelines for you to follow. These are listed below.

Step 1: Identify Success Emulation Subjects.

GUIDELINE 1: Identify the subjects to be emulated.
ITEM: Identify services your school provides.

Sample: * Instruction
           * Guidance
           * Counseling

ITEM: Identify services and products your school purchases or leases.
Sample:
- Payroll
- Scheduling
- Training
- Research and evaluation

ITEM: Identify practices/processes you use.
Sample:
- Total quality
- Site-based management
- Outcome-based education
- Accelerated learning
- Scientific method

ITEM: Identify critical success factors of your school.
Sample:
- Curriculum and instruction
- Research and evaluation
- Finance
- Human Resources

GUIDELINE 2: Brainstorm a list of subjects to be emulated.
ITEM: Review the emulation subjects that were developed during Guideline 1.
Sample: What are the most important subjects we should emulate at this time?
1. Staff development
2. Elementary reading
3. Elementary mathematics
4. Ninth- and tenth-grade geography
5. Total quality classroom
6. Site-based management
7. French
8. Computerized personnel records
9. Warehousing
10.. Painting and duplication

GUIDELINE 3: Select the subject(s) to be emulated.
ITEM: Now that you have generated a list of evaluation subjects, select one or more to be emulated.
Sample: * Ninth- and tenth-grade geography.

GUIDELINE 4: Determine the measurements
ITEM: Now that you have selected your subject(s) to be emulated, select measures that are true indicators of performance.
Sample:
* Number of students passing
* Time required to train teachers
* Number of students failing
* Cost per student
* Number of support staff needed to assist teachers

GUIDELINE 5: Summarize the purpose of your study
ITEM: Once you have determined all your measurements, develop a brief statement of the purpose of the study, emulating subject, and measurements. Also, indicate how the study will help you school in terms of what decisions will be made, actions to be taken, and strategies.
Sample: During the 1994-95 school year, 62 percent of the ninth grade and 48 percent of the tenth grade students failed the State Geography Examination. The purpose of the study is to evaluate our current level of teaching geography to ninth and tenth graders compared to in best-in-class schools. The results of this study will be the major factor to help us decide how to improve student achievement in geography.

GUIDELINE 6: Review study with teachers and administrators
ITEM: When appropriate, review the purpose of this study, the selected subject, and measurements for the study with the teachers and administrators. Reach a consensus on all items. Retain the list of the subjects you did not select for future planning.
Sample: After a thorough discussion of student needs in our school, we finally reached a consensus to conduct an emulation study in the subject of geography. We were all in favor of basing it on the following measures, of which the last was suggested by the principal.

* Number of students passing
* Time to train teachers
* Number of students failing
* Number of support staff needed

STEP 2: *Identify Sucess Emulation Partners.*

GUIDELINE 1: Select success emulation partners
ITEM: Prepare a list of schools or companies to be emulated. Those that may be able to help you are the following.

- Teachers
- Other school people
- Professors
- Professional associations
- You may also refer to the following:
- Educational journals, magazines, books
- Newspapers, newsletters
- Superintendent's annual reports

Sample
* Transforming Schools Through Success Emulation
* Springstead High School, Hernando County, Florida
* Garfield High School, Los Angeles, California
* Yselta High School, El Paso, Texas

GUIDELINE 2: Select the school or company to conduct your study
* Garfield High School, Los Angeles, California

STEP 3: *Determine How to Collect Data*

GUIDELINE 1: Prepare a list of questions for success emulation
ITEM: After you review the purpose, subject(s), and measurements for success emulation, prepare a list of questions to gather data. Make certain your questions are clear.

Sample: Gather data questions:
1. How did you come across your geography program?

3. How much more funds did it cost?
4. Was the community involved? How?
5. How do the students feel about the program?
6. What makes this program better than any others?
7. What was the most difficult thing to do to implement the program?

GUIDELINE 2: Answer the questions for your school.
ITEM: Respond to all the questions on the list for your school. After doing this, you may find it necessary to modify either your questions or measurements.
Sample:
1. Our program evolved around the textbook.
2. We used no outside professional help.
3. No additional funds were spent outside the textbook cost.
4. The community was not involved in our program.
5. Teachers report that most students feel that the program was not oriented to them.
6. No comment.
7. The most difficult thing about the program was to get the students' attention.

GUIDELINE 3: Searching for other sources related to your study
ITEM: Search for sources within your district related to your study, and speak to the following:

- Teachers
- Support staff
- Principals
- Central school administrators
- Librarians

Other sources of information that should be considered are indicated below:

- Magazines and newspapers
- Annual reports
- Professional organizations
- Research papers

- Government documents
- Conference materials
- Professional books
- Consultants

Sample: The librarian gave us a copy of a report she received from a friend in California indicating the outstanding achievements of students in the best-in-class school in the subject of geography. The search revealed nothing else.

GUIDELINE 4: Review the method for conducting original research
ITEM: Now that you have completed the research of the subject of your study, you need to consider how you are going to conduct your research.
Sample: We reviewed the following channels for collecting information for the survey:

- Mail survey
- Telephone interview
- Focus groups
- Quotations
- School visitation
- Personal interview

GUIDELINE 5: Determine the method for continuing research
ITEM: When selecting the method to conduct your research, consider the following:

- Availability of time
- Complexity of the information to be gathered
- Funds available
- Other who are participants in the study
- Need for probing skills

Sample:

A consensus was reached that a school visitation followed up with telephone interviews would be the best approach to conduct this study.

GUIDELINE 6: Determine who will conduct the research
ITEM: Some alternatives you should consider are the following:

- A design team
- Quality coordinator
- Principal
- Consultant
- Quality improvement team
- A central school administrator
- Quality improvement team leader

Sample: We decided to organize a design team to conduct the study and report back to the team. The design team has the option to use a consultant.

STEP 4: Compare Current Gaps With Best-In-Class Schools.

GUIDELINE 1: Tabulate the data
ITEM: Now that the data has been collected, it should be reviewed to determine if it is appropriate for the questions that were asked during the data-gathering process. At times, it may be necessary to use basic statistics to tabulate your results or to develop groups. Xerox uses the following to tabulate its data:

- Averages
- Maximum value
- Minimum value
- Ranges

Sample: We use the following to tabulate our data:
1. Student achievement levels
2. Rate of students' progress during the previous school years.
3. Social/economic levels of the students
4. Kind and duration of training received by teachers.

GUIDELINE 2: Analyze the data
ITEM: When analyzing the results of your tabulation, identify those statistics and factors that are related to the purpose of the study. When analyzing the data, be mindful of environmental factors—internal and external—in which the school is situated.
Sample: All questions that were posed before the host school people were critical to the purpose of the study.

GUIDELINE 3: Determine the benchmark
ITEM: After you have analyzed the data and reviewed the purpose of the study, determine the desired performance measurement.
Sample: The benchmark design was determined based on the report of the excellent achievement level of students in the visiting school.

GUIDELINE 4: Determine the gap
ITEM: Compare the results of your own measurement data to the best-in-class. Make certain it is consistent with the data for the study. One method is to perform this is as follows:

$$\text{Gap 1} = \frac{\text{Our school}}{\text{Best-in-class}}$$

Sample: The analysis indicated the following gaps:
- Poor: Gap 1 (student achievement level)

$$\frac{45\%}{98\%}$$

- Poor: Gap 2 (time devoted to training):

$$\frac{2 \text{ hrs}}{35 \text{ hrs}} = 94\%$$

- Poor: Gap 3 (program expense):

$$\frac{3,150}{15,000} = 79\%$$

GUIDELINE 5: Determine reasons for gaps
ITEM: After you have formulated the gaps, use the information to determine the reasons.
Sample: The analysis indicated the following gaps:
GAP 1: Poor.
The gap of 46 percent between our school and the best-in-class is due to their program and the process by which teachers instruct their students.

GAP 2: Poor.
The gap of 94 percent between our school and the best-in-class is because the district is more serious about training and developing their teachers than we are. While we consider the cost as an expense to our school, the best-in-class considers it an investment.

GAP 3: Poor.
The gap of 79 percent between our school and the best-in-class is due to program expense.

GUIDELINE 6: Develop a list of emulation drivers
ITEM: Based on the collected information and the visitation at the school, develop a list of factors that are driving the best-in-class school performance. Consider the following:

- School culture
- School administration
- Standards
- School environment
- Finance

Sample: The design team identified several factors that appear to be driving the best-in-class school.

1. The superiority of the geography program.
2. All teachers received the same training in the geography program.
3. The principal is highly committed to the program.
4. The community is heavily involved in the program.
5. Students enjoy the program because it is interesting and reality-oriented.

STEP 5: *Project Future Performance*

GUIDELINE 1: Project the future gap between our school and the best-in-class school

ITEM:Review Step 4 to determine if data is available to project performance to two, three, or five years. Look for trends. If data are not available, use your best judgment. Discount any assumptions you may make in developing your projections. Determine if the gap will close or widen.

> Sample: We developed a run chart of student achievement in geography for the past three years. The results indicated that our students had retrogressed by 4 percent, 10 percent, and 11 percent over the past three years. The likelihood is that the gap between our school and the best-in-class will continue to be high.

STEP 6: *Communicate Results of the Study and Gain Acceptance*

GUIDELINE 1: Determining the audience for communicating and the study and results

ITEM: Prior to preparing your communication, develop a list of those people who must accept the results of your study. School people who should be considered are as follows:

- Superintendent
- Central school administrators
- Support people
- Principal
- Teachers
- Unions/associations
- Team

> Sample: We decided that the principal, team, and the school as a whole should receive a copy of our study and findings, and that same would be submitted to the assistant superintendent for curriculum and instruction.

GUIDELINE 2: Deterimine the method for communicating the results of the study
ITEM: Consider the following methods for communicating the results of the study:

- Memo
- Presentation
- Final report

Sample: A memo of the conclusions and findings was submitted to the superintendent and all central school administrators. In addition, send a memo to the principal, teachers, and support people inviting them to a formal presentation. The results of the study were disseminated to other high school teachers via the district-wide newsletter.

GUIDELINE 3: Organize your analysis
ITEM: Consider the following when organizing your analysis:

- Key results
- Conclusions
- Recommendations

Study Process:

- Respondent selections
- Methods employed to collect data:
- Analysis techniques

Sample: Three high schools were considered as best-in-class choices. The Garfield High School was selected because its community resembled ours. Data was collected on the best-in-class through visitation and followed up with two telephone interviews. A list of questions was prepared prior to the visitation and used as the basis for generating pertinent information regarding the study. Several classrooms were visited, examined, and discussed, and several students were interviewed by members of the design team.

Members of the design team reached the conclusion that best-in-school geography program was superior to ours and recommended the following:
1. Adopt the geography program implemented by the best-in-class school by presenting the study and analysis to the school as a whole to reach consensus on its adaptation.
2. Retain personnel in the best-in-class school to train turn-key trainers of the program in our school.
3. Organize another design team to plan and develop other curriculum and instruction aids and launch the program using professional assistants from the best-in-class school.

A copy of the list of questions is attached to this report. A letter from the superintendent of schools of the best-in-class school is also included attesting to the outstanding results of the best-in-class in geography.

GUIDELINE 4: Obtain approval
ITEM: Do not be surprised if there is negative feedback about your presentation. The real intent of your presentation is to get the central school administration acceptance and buy-in the analysis and implementation strategy.
Sample: The design team met with the central school administration and gave a formal presentation on the study and findings. After responding to several questions, all central school administrators enthusiastically agreed to support the project. The superintendent was very delighted and personally thanked each design team member for the study and findings. She indicated that she would like the design team to conduct this presentation to the other two high schools. After obtaining approval from the central school administrators, the results of the study were cascaded within the school.

STEP 7: Establish a List of Functional Goals

GUIDELINE 1: Develop a list of current goals
ITEM: Prior to determining your functional goals, review your current goals by referring to the following:
- School quality improvement plan

- Strategic quality plan

Sample: Current Goals:
- Increase student achievement in English from 17 percent to 50 percent by June 30, 199X.
- Increase the number of parents satisfied with their school from 29 percent to 75 percent by June 30, 199X.
- Increase student achievement in mathematics from 38 percent to 75 percent in June 15, 199X.
- Reduce student absenteeism from 61 percent to 96 percent by June 15, 199X.

After reviewing the current goals, the team decided to add the following goals to the strategic plan:
- Increase student achievement in ninth- and tenth- grade geography from 0 percent to 90 percent by June 30, 199X.

GUIDELINE 2: Determine what changes should be made
ITEM: You will need to determine what changes in your goals are needed to achieve or exceed the results of the best-in-class school. Review the current plans and make modifications. Regardless of the extent of your changes from your goal, you should assess your study based on the following:
- How much will it cost?
- What training will be required?
- What resources are needed?
- How difficult will the change be?

Sample: After reviewing the current goals, the team decided to add the following goals to the strategic plan.
- Increase study achievement in the ninth- and tenth- grade geography from 0 percent to 90 percent by June 30, 199X.

GUIDELINE 3: Review the gap between your school and the best-in-class
ITEM: Review and revise your original performance gap projection.
Sample:

The team revised its performance gap projection to 85 percent - 95 percent by June 30, 1998.

GUIDELINE 4: Obtain commitment for your goal(s)
Sample: The principal as well as the geography teachers voiced commitment to fulfilling the goal.

STEP 8: Set Short-Range Objectives

GUIDELINE 1: Establish short-range objectives (one year or less) to attain long-range goal.
ITEM: Once you have established your long-range goals, set one or more short range objectives to incrementally achieve your long-range goals.
Sample: Short-range objectives (one year or less) to increase

- Student achievement in English from 17 percent to 30 percent by June 10, 199X
- Number of parents satisfied with their school from 29 percent to 50 percent by June 30, 199X
- Student Achievement in mathematics from 38 percent to 60 percent by June 15, 199X.
- Reduce student absenteeism in mathematics from 61 percent to 40 percent by June 15, 199X.

STEP 9: Develop an Action Plan

ITEM: Prior to developing your detailed action plan, obtain approval from your principal. Sometimes it is advisable to get central school administrators to approve the action plan. However, this is not always required.
Sample: The action plan was submitted to the principal and team leader for her review and approval.

GUIDELINE 1: Develop action plans to attain your short-range objective
ITEM: After you have completed your short-range objective, you need to develop gap-closing activities to achieve your objec-

tive(s). Brainstorm a list of actions to achieve your objective. Use force-field analysis to weigh each action to determine its impact on the objective.

Sample: Gap-Closing Activity: Training and Development

- Reallocate a budget to retrain teachers and substitute teachers and to produce instructional materials.

- Meet with the principal of the best-in-class school to select two teacher to train our teachers.

- Organize curriculum and instruction design team to work with trainer/consultant to prepare appropriate classroom materials.

- Train teachers and monitor their performance.

STEP 9: *Implement Plans and Monitor Results*

GUIDELINE 1: Implement your action plans

ITEM: Once the action plans have been developed, make certain all parties understand and carry out their activities on the date indicated.

Sample: Review your action plan to construct a Gant chart or Pert chart to monitor each activity.

GUIDELINE 2: Monitor results

ITEM: Keep track of your progress to determine if corrective action is necessary, and act accordingly.

Sample: Every four weeks, give students a test to determine the rate of passing and failure (P&F). If the rate of failure is high, bring in a trainer/consultant to review the teaching process. Use a control chart if necessary.

$$\text{1st month: P\&F rate} = \frac{41}{210}$$

$$\text{2nd month: P\&F rate} = \frac{35}{209}$$

3rd month: P&F rate = $\frac{30}{206}$

4th month: P&F rate = $\frac{20}{208}$

GUIDELINE 3: Develop your action plans
ITEM: After you develop your gap-closing activities, you may need to develop an action plan. If you have only a few activities, this step may not be necessary. If there are a large number of activities, consider using a Gant or Pert chart. The action plan should contain the following:

- Activities
- Date
- By whom

SAMPLE: Action Plan:

Activity	Date	By whom
1. Reallocate budget for program	12/01	Principal
2. Select and retrain teachers	12/04	Best-in-class school teachers
3. Organize a curriculum and instruction design team	12/05	Quality improvement team
4. Change curriculum and instruction design team	12/06	Quality improvement team
5. Monitor teacher's performance and retrain selected teachers	12/07-08	Turnkey trainers

GUIDELINE 4: Obtain approval for your plans
ITEM: Once you have developed your short-range objective and action plan, obtain approval from your principal or team leader.

Sample: The team conducted a presentation on the action plan to the principal

GUIDELINE 5: Develop a plan to recalibrate your benchmark
ITEM: In order for success emulation to be effective, you will need to recalibrate the benchmark. Recalibration is the process of reevaluating your plan to determine if it is still valid. Recalibration should be done on an annual basis.
Sample: The design team developed a plan to recalibrate during 19XX. The only change considered important is to search for other similar urban schools to conduct school visits.

GUIDELINE 6: Recaliibrate
ITEM: Review each of the nine steps and update them as necessary. Review each activity and try to add other activities to improve on your success emulation plan.
Sample: A questionnaire has been developed and disseminated throughout the nation. The results will be used for recalibration if required.

Identify a subject in your school to be improved. Develop a list of questions to collect data from the best-in-class school.
1._____
2._____
3._____
4._____
5._____
6._____
7._____
8._____

Source for this chapter: Benchmarking for Quality Improvement, 1989; Stanford, Conn.: Xerox Corporation

Success emulation is one of the most effective methods for transforming schools through identifying outstanding practices, principles, processes and programs, improving on them and implementing those pertinent to your school needs. Basically, success emulation is building and improving on the best of others and making your school better than the best.

REVIEW

KEY POINTS TO REMEMBER:

1. Success emulation is the continuous process of assessing school services, products, and practices against the best-in-class school and other organization or those schools recognized as the best in the country.
2. Some important dimensions of success emulation are continuous processes, service, products and practices, measuring, and learning from schools and other organizations renowned as leaders.
3. Philosophical steps of success emulation are to know your school objective, know the best-in-class or leaders in public education, incorporate the best, and become great.
4. The procedural steps for implementing success emulation are: 1) identify success emulation subjects: 2) identify success emulation partners; 3) determine how to collect data; 4) compare current gaps with best-in-class schools; 5) project future performance; 6) communicate results of the study and gain acceptance; 7) establish a list of functional goals; 8) develop an action plan; and 9) implement plans and monitor results.

APPLICATION

Convene a meeting with all your teachers and get a consensus as to the most pressing problems besetting the school. Ask for volunteers to serve on a success emulation design team. Request the team to use this chapter as an approach to arrive at a success emulation plan to solve the problem cited by the teachers.

CHAPTER 14

Transforming Schools Through Participative Management

LEARNING OBJECTIVES

After studying and comprehending this chapter, you should be able to:

- Define participative management.
- Identify forms of participative management.
- Describe the benefits associated with participative management.
- Explain how participation works.
- Identify when participative management works best.

What Every Principal Should Know About Participative Management

Authority must give way to participation if our schools are to improve. A quiet revolution is taking place, not in the streets or on the campuses, but in some of our enlightened schools. It began during the latter end of the twentieth century, and will gain more momentum in the future. As it progresses, more and more teachers are rebelling against authority-oriented principals. The revolutionaries are not just teachers, but some are principals, directors, supervisors, and a few superintendents. They are tired of the authoritarian behavior of their supervisors. They are tired of the way decisions are made without meaningfully involving those who will be directly affected by the decision. They are tired of the inbred, traditional, hierarchical management structure that excluded them as a vital component in the decision-making network.

There is a wide spread thrust to change the manner in which decisions are made and how jobs should be restructured to consider seriously the people in those jobs. In the twenty-first century, the transformational principal will take an optimistic view of their teachers' potential, and will push decision making along all levels of the school to encourage the upward flow of fresh and creative ideas. These principals will give new responsibilities and opportunities to all of their teachers because they are aware that when teachers have something meaningful to which to commit themselves, they can help make their school more effective educationally, economically, and humanly. This chapter should put you on the journey to participative management.

Defining Participative Management

Although participative management is not a new idea, it is expected to blossom throughout most schools today. It appears even to this day to be a style of management that releases the human potential allowing teachers to grow in the school environment and to make a significant contribution to the attainment of goals and objectives. It has been found to positively affect teachers' attitudes, commitment, quality, and productivity.

Participative management is a process of getting things done in a school by creating an environment wherein teachers are encouraged to become mentally, emotionally, and actively involved in problem-solving situations that will help realize the philosophy, goals, and objectives of the school.

Any act on the part of school administrators that allows mental and emotional involvement qualifies as participatory management. The transformational principal communicates not only what teachers have to know in order to perform their jobs, but also the types and kinds of information that they desire to know.

He or she also gives them a greater sense of identity, self-respect, self-esteem, and self-fulfillment. Performance is more likely to improve when specific objectives and standards are set. Participation in setting objectives that improves subsequent performance is acting out this type of management. In addition, the transformational principal informs teachers as to where they fit in the school, that what they do is important to the success of the school, and that they mean something special individually, and will reap benefits of mental and emotional involvement. Finally, by delegating responsibilities, and providing performance feedback and positive reinforcements, they become an active party in the participative management movement.

The Forms of Participative Management

Participative management is the process by which teachers are involved in planning, controlling and performing varied activities in order to do their jobs. It will not be enough for the teacher to teach. He or she must also become involved in planning what is to be taught and how, in monitoring the progress of students and using the results to strengthen the instructional program, and in the actual teaching of content to students. Similarly, it will not be enough for the custodian to clear out the bathrooms or sweep the floors. He or she must be involved in planning and determining the work to be performed and in developing and using check sheets to make certain his or her responsibilities have been performed. The key element here is that genuine participative management only occurs when school people are part of the planning and controlling of their work.

Basically, there are at least four major types of planning and controlling activities in which teachers and other school people can participate and make a difference: participation in setting objectives, participation in the decision-making process, participation in solving problems, and participation in effectuating change. Each is discussed below.

Participation in Setting Objectives

When teachers and other school people set objectives for themselves, they are more likely to achieve them than if the principal sets them. There is a time for individuals to set their own objectives, for a principal and teacher to set objectives together, and for teams to set objectives. Regardless of the method of setting objectives, the activity tends to help teachers gain better control over their performance efforts by identifying the specific end results of these activities. A common approach to setting objectives is strategic planning.

Usually strategic planning is initiated by the board and superintendent agreeing to some long-range goals for the district. These goals are sequentially integrated with other long-range goals developed by various other school administrators within the district. The principal receives and forwards these goals to his or her teachers who then either individually or collectively have an opportunity to participate in a conference to develop their own short-range objectives, performance standards, and action plans to help realize the long-range goals. When strategic planning is implemented, far too often it is fraught with problems. Principals and supervisors have not been properly trained in executing the process. For example, many of them are inept at counseling and coaching teachers in attaining objectives and inducing motivation. They are not clear as to the philosophical posture of the concept. Teachers sometimes are rushed into the program without proper training. As a result, they write unclear objectives, fail to identify proper performance standards, set unrealistic and unchallenging objectives, and set too many objectives. Care must be taken to prevent these problems from eroding the participatory process.

Setting objectives includes other areas of participation that should be understood and encouraged. They are:

- Establishing performance standards.
- Developing an action plan for achieving objectives.
- Monitoring the attainment of objectives.

Participation in the Decision-Making Process

To understand decision making, it is necessary to understand the difference between decision making and problem solving. Problem solving is the process by which a problem has been identified, alternative solutions to the problem have been generated, and the most appropriate solution has been selected. As a result, problem solving involves usually more training, more skill, and more effort than decision-making. Usually, traditional principals speak of problem solving and decision making as though they were the same thing. They aren't. This section will dwell on participation through decision making and the next section will enable you to learn of the difference between the two.

Basically, there are two forms of participation through decision-making: consultative participation and direct participation. Consultative participation was the initial form of participation in that it originated at the onset of the human relations management era that began back in the 1960s. Although teachers under this approach felt that they were merely being manipulated by school administrators into believing that they were actively involved in the decision-making process, and in many cases they were initially, this approach to participation gave the process a "dirty" name. In many instances, principals got teachers involved in a decision-making process, but in the final analysis, the decision had already been made. Today, transformational principals understand and appreciate what teachers can contribute to the decision-making process. Consultative participation in its real form involves getting their input to change prior to executing it and using that information to help arrive at a decision.

Direct participation got its momentum in the 1980s. Although many of the best-run companies in America realized the benefits of direct participation, it was the Japanese management style that really threw this form of participation into high gear. The Japanese realized that when people were given the opportunity to make decisions for themselves, or were directly involved in decisions that affected them, then the people were more committed to these decisions. William Ouchi quite comprehensively discussed direct participation in his best-selling book *Theory Z*.

In most cases, direct participation is realized more effectively when consensus is the manner in which decisions are reached. Consensus means that everybody within a team has cooperatively arrived at a mutually acceptable decision that all members will agree to support.

Activities that involve consultative participation may include the following; however, many of these could also involve direct participation:

- The preparation of the curriculum guide.

- The revision of a student absence policy.
- The preparation of a team or department's budget.
- The setting of goals.

Activities that are appropriate for using direct participation are as follows:

- Arriving at an agreement on the philosophy of the school.
- The selection of a standard course text.
- Deciding on the format of the report card.
- Permitting the secretarial pool to decide on a specific word processor.
- Allowing the maintenance people to decide on the brand of a piece of equipment.

Both forms of participation should be more extensively used with greater emphasis on direct participation. Each can play an effective role in strengthening the management of schools.

Participation in Problem Solving

When teachers' acceptance of a solution to a problem is not an issue, then there is really no need to initiate their participation in solving the problem. On the other hand, if acceptance is an issue, it is extremely important to provide teachers with opportunities for participation in solving the problem so that they can influence or "control" the chosen solution. This will enhance teachers' commitment to acceptance of the solution because they will get a sense of ownership of the solution. When quality is of little importance, however, teachers' acceptance is important. It is extremely crucial to organize a team or group to solve the problem. Yet again, if quality is important, but teachers' acceptance is not, then nothing is wrong with the principal solving the problem himself or herself without team participation. In addition, if the principal needs additional information in order to render a solution, he or she should provide an opportunity for a teacher to assist him or her in reaching a decision.

When both teachers' acceptance and the quality of the solution are important, then problem solving through participation is not only crucial, but will be difficult. To accomplish this feat,

Transforming Schools Through Participative Management

the team leader should be trained as a facilitator so that he or she can facilitate, integrate, and enhance the problem and solution discussion by considering both the personal goals and needs of teachers and the goals of the school. As a result, the following are necessary for effectuating problem-solving teams:

- Ability to use brainstorming or nominal group process to identify and select problems and ideas.
- Ability to analyze the problem by gathering data and information, then arranging it to depict peculiarities of the problem.
- Ability to analyze the data by assembling it into graphs and charts.
- Ability to solve the problem by selecting the most appropriate solution.
- Ability to use others to help verify the solution to the problem.
- Ability to present the solution to the principal to obtain his or her approval.
- Ability to implement the solution to the problem when appropriate.

Participation in decision-making has several benefits as indicated below:

- Provides teachers with increased control over their school environment and activities.
- Leads to greater commitment and acceptance regarding a solution.
- Provides teachers with an added dimension to their job, which adds new meaning to work.
- Enables teachers to be actively involved in all activities related to the job, giving them a greater sense of ownership of the solution to the problem.
- Provides, at times, an opportunity for teachers to carry out the solution, thereby giving them a sense of completing the total task, beginning with identifying the problem and ending with implementing the solution.

Participation in Effectuating Change

When teachers' economic security, orientation, status, social, and physical maintenance needs are met, they receive a sense of psychological and physical satisfaction. However, if any one of these conditions is changed without their participation, that satisfaction will tend to become a dissatisfaction. This occurs primarily because all human beings tend to be highly addictive to security, and when change is imposed on them, they tend to believe the worst and will resist or reject it. Sometimes, the insecurity that may envelop teachers can be so great that they may even resort to violence or other destructive measures to resist change. The real point is that teachers don't resist change; they resist being changed - unless they are active members in planning and controlling the change. It appears that the psychological affect of participation in the change creates a sense of ownership, which in most instances completely wipes out any insecurity that teachers may have had at the onset of the change.

Participation in change is perhaps the most time-consuming and complex of all forms of participation. It will normally require the principal and teachers to participate in collaborating, generating, analyzing, and interpreting school data and information in an effort to develop specific creative and innovative change solutions to complex problems.

Activities related to participation in change are as follows:

- Developing and implementing a new reading program.
- Adopting a twelve month school year.
- Implementing modular-scheduling.

The Benefits Associated With Participative Management

Participative management can benefit the prime movers in school because of the following:

- It enables the principal to feel that they are helping the district administrations' team in making higher-level decisions. Therefore, principals obtain an enhanced perception of their own self-worth and the contribution they make to the school.

- It allows the principal to learn more about the management of the district, because they gain access to large amounts of information that hitherto was reserved for district administrators. As a result, they are able to use this information in a meaningful manner in their own building.
- It helps the principal to be honest by speaking what is on their minds without being intimidated or penalized. From this climate is generated a high level of insight and more ideas.
- It enables the principal to allow all teachers who feel that they have something to offer or who know something about the issue to get involved.
- It provides an excellent opportunity for principals to build a consensus regarding controversial matters.
- It allows those who will be affected by a decision to participate in its deliberation for the purpose of influencing decisions and building commitment to them.
- It provides a collaborative opportunity that multiplies teachers' efforts by providing support, assistance, and stimulation of performance.
- It is a method that develops and educates the principal during the process of participation.
- It allows for more wide-range higher quality and creative discussions/solutions than would normally be generated.
- It is an effort to balance or confront vested groups when change is badly needed.
- It avoids participative action and provides a means to explore multiple options.
- It enables teachers to acquire new skills, new information, and new acquaintances.

Although participation will be growing management practice in the twenty-first century, there are a large number of problems, dilemmas, and decisions that must be addressed in order to get maximum results. Basically, these evolve around teamwork and team building: how teams are organized; how issues are selected;

how the inner workings of teams relate to the rest of the school; and how teams should be evaluated, recognized, and rewarded.

The Problems of Participative Management

When participation is operating smoothly there are numerous benefits as discussed above; however, success does not occur overnight, or ever, in some instances. The transformational principal is mindful of the problems associated with participation and does everything possible to avoid them, or if they do occur, to solve them. One of the most common problems in participative management is the principal's failure to properly train, develop, and educate teachers in the process. Sponsoring a comprehensive training program in schools will be one of the most pressing problems confronting the principal. The success or failure of participation rests solely on the shoulders of the principal. His or her first move is to get the superintendent to approve a certain percentage of the budget for training and development activities. A figure of from one half of one percent to one percent would be a strong indication that the superintendent is serious about training "its own." Training for teamwork and team building should most likely involve courses in group dynamics, conflict resolution, problem-solving techniques, consensus decision-making, etc.

Another problem associated with participation is failure of the principal to listen to the ideas of the teachers. Participative management will certainly fail if he or she does not accept the suggestions, ideas, and action plans of its teachers. The principal does not have to approve everything the team may present, but he or she should not ignore them.

Another problem associated with participation is the refusal of some principals to share power with their teachers. Transformational principals will do less of telling teachers what to do and more of letting them decide what they should do. This will require him or her to explain the objectives, to provide guidance, and to assist teachers in achieving these objectives. It is only natural that some principals will be threatened by participative management. In fact, if experience is any judge, the demise of differentiated staffing was the result of teachers being threatened by this innovation. Times have changed. Even though principals may be threatened with participation, those teachers who are striving for self-fulfillment through the school environment will not permit the principal to return to the traditional, nonparticipative approach to managing schools.

Participative management requires that a leader be either appointed or selected to head a team. When participation is carried to the extreme, the team becomes leaderless because no one wants to assume the power position. When this occurs, it becomes very difficult to get anything accomplished because on one is available to make the final decision or organize the ideas of the team so that it can make a decision.

A problem that is also associated with participation is the fact that teachers have a natural thirst for information when they are involved in participative management. To this end, they feel that they have to know everything about a problem or situation. This thirst for knowledge puts a tremendous strain on the principal and team leaders to maintain a sense of order and to arrive at decisions in a timely manner. When a lot of ideas are generated, it is difficult to focus on significant factors—even the smallest thing may result in hours upon hours of discussion. The principal and team leader must keep the team focus on the issue so as to avoid wandering from the main issue.

Participation is not something to be practiced all the time. There are degrees of participative management and there are some times when participation is neither desirable nor appropriate. When participation should and should not be used is a problem that is expected to confront numerous principals throughout their tenure.

How Participation Should Work?

Participative management requires hard work, patience, and persistence. Two things must take place in order to make it work effectively: freedom with structure and nurturing trust.

Inherent in participative management is freedom, however; freedom must have structure. To provide structure, the transformational principal establishes for teachers at the outset ground rules and boundary conditions to guide their behavior and performance on the job-what they can decide for themselves and what others must decide for them. Without structure, participative management is doomed to fail; teams flounder, and team members become demoralized with the process. Much of the original idea of participative management produced no guidelines, or those that were produced were vague, unclear, contradictory, and subject to a great deal of guesswork. As a result, these quasi- participative teams stumbled badly before they learned the true meaning of participative management. In many instances, they spent most of the time deciding how to decide rather than actually making decisions.

Thus, implementing participative management without guidelines, objectives, constraints, or boundaries can be devastating. The transformational principal, as well as teachers, understand that responsible leaders do not surrender all of their responsibility just because they are involving a large number of teachers in the decision-making process, nor should they let teams flounder without performance and behavior guidelines. The principals must provide assistance.

A participatory process for solving problems in Japan was the quality control circle. A key element in the quality control circle concept is a steering committee. The purpose of this committee is to set guidelines and monitor the implementation of this participatory process. The steering committee is one of the main reasons for some ten million quality control circles that are flourishing in Japan.

Trust is also a key element in participative management. Teachers must learn to trust the principal, and the principal must realize that teachers can make a meaningful contribution to the well-being of the school, if only given the chance. This will not be an easy task. In general, the principal and teachers have mistrusted each other for too many years for this problem to be easily solved.

What is the best way to nurture trust when implementing participative management? Trust won't appear merely by wishing it. Several prerequisites must be met if it is to be nurtured throughout the school. Principals must be the prime movers, but teachers must be patient with the principal and give him or her time to change or modify their behavior in order to implement participative management. Some ways to do this is as follows:

- Reduce external controls by giving teachers the opportunity to monitor and correct their own performance.

- Allow teachers to perform tasks, chores, or activities without fear of the outcome.
- Give more responsibilities to teachers.
- Provide teachers with more power and authority to perform their jobs.
- Provide teachers with more freedom to use their own discretion in performing a job.
- Ask teachers to identify trust indicators, and then use the results to determine how proficient the principal is in this humanistic competency.
- Keep working at it; trust will not occur overnight. Attitudes, once acquired, are difficult to change, and this will only occur when the principal is consistent in his or her behavior.
- Personal and school goals must be compatible. The actions of the teachers and schools are not intended to do damage to either party.

In order for mutual trust to be realized between teachers and the principal, several conditions must be met. You must become flexible with teachers. Let up on policies and procedures that restrict them. Give them more authority to act without close supervision, and bend the strict adherence to time.

Initiate more frequent and longer contact with teachers. Make an effort to become more familiar with them on and off the job through numerous social, personal, and recreational activities. By doing this, principals will transform an unknown and indifferent relationship into one that is close. The closeness will reap trust, in addition to other benefits. The contacts with teachers must be over a long period of time in order to diminish many undesirable practices that were previously nurtured by teachers.

Provide opportunities that will expand trust. Although principals may become more flexible with teachers and meet with them more frequently and for a longer duration, there will be more need for them to become involved in a number of job-related and personal activities that will reveal evidence of trust.

When Participative Management Works Best

Experience has shown that participation works best when team members are strong-minded and there is effective leadership in the school organization. Increased participation is generally associated with better communications, improved performance, interteam cooperation, superintendent support, reduced cost, and less stress associated with the job. In essence, participation works best within a well-organized school environment with strong and capable school administrators. When participation is coupled with egalitarianism, that is, when teachers are able to share and equalize power with school administrators, then the benefits associated with participation are usually excellent. This strong leadership of principals who have the ability to mobilize school people and set guidelines is an essential ingredient in effectuating a strong participative program.

The transformational leader knows how to delegate responsibilities to teachers. This does not mean the transformational principal is obviating his or her responsibilities for monitoring and supporting team efforts. Far too many traditional principals took an either-or point of view. However, delegation performed by team members means that principals not only set the basic parameters, but are also involved available to support teams and team members, to review and monitor performance results, and to redirect and recounsel the team when necessary. Strong principals also help coordinate activities, maintain and centralize trends, and function as a point of contact with other teams and schools. The impression teachers feel when they see that the principal is concerned about performance results is a good reason for the prncipal to stay involved with teams, even when he or she has delegated responsibility. Teachers sense that the transformational principal cares about what they are doing and that he or she cares for them. If the principal slowly walks away after delegating responsibility and never requests reports or monitors or evaluates performance, then sooner or later, teachers will begin to wonder if anybody really cares about them and if what they are doing is worthwhile. The strong principal who makes a practice of holding teams accountable and indicating reporting relationships is also demonstrating he or she does care for them and the value of their performance.

REVIEW

KEY POINTS TO REMEMBER:

Participative management is a process of getting things done in schools by creating an environment wherein teachers are encouraged to become mentally, emotionally, and actively involved in problem-solving solutions that will help realize the philosophy, goals, and objectives of the school.

Some of the various forms of participative management are: participation in setting objectives, participation in the decision-making process, participation in problem-solving, and participation in effectuating change.

The benefits of participative management allow the principal to feel that he or she is helping the district administrators; allows the principal to learn more about the district; allows the principal to be honest about his or her feelings without being intimidated; allows teachers to contribute something to the school; allows the principal an excellent opportunity to reach consensus on decisions; allows those affected by the decision to have some influences on it; multiplies teachers efforts by providing support, methods that educate the principal during the process; allows for more creative and high-quality decisions; allows for balance or confront vested groups; precipitate actions and provides a means to explore multiple options; and enable teachers to acquire more skills.

Some of the problems inherent with participative management are: 1) failing to train teachers; 2) failure of the principal to listen to teachers; 3) refusal of the principal to share power with teachers; 4) no one desiring to become the team leader; 5) team members not staying focused; 6) knowing when teachers should participate in the decision-making process.

Freedom with structure and nurturing trust are the two things that *must* take place to make participative management work.

APPLICATION

Call in union officials and inform them of your desire to involve teachers more in the school decision-making process. On the other hand, don't call the union officials in, but to invite them to a lunch or dinner, a setting in which both parties will be on an equal basis. Convey to them how changing times and conditions require changes in the management of schools. Discuss with them the grand scheme of transforming the school and how the process of the transformation is involving teachers in decision making, as well as the number of other changes you are seeking. State that you will be looking for their assistance and cooperation. Mention how the union will benefit from these changes and what they can look forward to during the transition. Solicit from them their own ideas for change and how they see their role. Before meeting with the union, you might put members of your staff to work researching information regarding the contemporary practices of some of the national school union officials.

CHAPTER **15**

Implementing Total Quality in Schools

LEARNING OBJECTIVES

After studying and comprehending this chapter, you should be able to:

- Define total quality education.
- Identify customer-provider interface.
- Describe the privatized practices of total quality.
- Identify the steps for implementing total quality in schools.
- Define moments of truth.
- Describe cycles of service.

What Every Principal Should Know About Implementing Total Quality In Schools

Total quality education is the vehicle for focusing the energy and resources of the school toward a common goal: continuous improvement of products and services to students. When the total quality philosophy has been fully inculcated throughout the school, students become more conscious of quality, not only in the school, but throughout their daily lives. Their progress in school is improved as well as their self-esteem because they are no longer failures. Much more content is learned because they don't proceed to another lesson until they master the present lesson. Teachers are happy not only because students are learning more, but also because they are absent less from school and are not overwhelmed with discipline problems that affect non-total quality schools.

Defining Total Quality Education

Total quality or TQ education is a cooperative form of educating students that relies on the talents and capabilities of all people within the school to continuously improve quality and productivity using teams. Embodied in this definition are the major ingredients necessary for total quality education to flourish in the school: 1) participative management; 2) continuous process improvement; 3) consensus decision making; and 4) the use of participative management recognizes that all people have something to offer to the school improvement process if only given the chance. This will take time, however, as the principal listens to them and provides a process for them to be initially involved with the developing of the process. Continuous process improvement means acceptance of small, incremental gains as steps in the right direction for reaching total quality. It, in essence, means that substantial gains can be reached by the accumulation of seemingly minor improvements, yielding tremendous gains in the long run. This applies to teachers in terms of their incremental improvement efforts and students in terms of their repeated attempts to master subject content they have not mastered on the first attempt. Consensus decision making is an attempt to get everyone who will be affected by the decision to agree on the decision. The best way to implement total quality in education is through teams, either through teacher teams or cooperative student teams. Teacher teams involves a cross section of the teachers in the school and members of the community. This approach empowers teachers and other people directly involved in the day-to-day operations of the school to improve the school environment. Student cooperative teams allow students to team up in small groups to assist other students in the educational process.

Customer-Provider Interface

Because we are discussing the steps for implementing TQ in school, it is important for the principal to define the customer-provider interface to teachers as well as enforce it in the school.

Since TQ relates to the customer-provider relationship, which is relatively new in education, attention should be given to how the customer relates to the provider and what services are provided by the provider. Figure 15.1 below illustrates the interface between the customer and provider. Customer and provider are further defined as "I" for internal and "E" for external. The terms customers and providers are discussed below.

A provider is any person or group on which teachers depend for input that is used to deliver a service to satisfy its customer or to produce a product. Input includes things like resources, materials, information, equipment, services, and products. An internal provider is any person or group that works in the district to satisfy a customer. For example, the staff development department of the district inputs data from various persons and groups within (and sometimes outside) the district about staff development needs, and it receives advice about its budget from the business department. These two sources are internal providers.

At the same time, the staff development department might decide to bring in consultants and prepare training materials from a publisher. These sources are considered external providers.

A customer is any person or group to which teachers deliver either a service or a product in order to meet and exceed a need, requirement, or expectation. There are two types of customers: internal and external. An internal customer is a person or group located within the district who receives a service or product. Most school people are aware that students are internal customers. However, a few do not relate to teachers as customers. When a member of the staff development department provides some service in terms of training to a group of teachers, the teachers become internal customers, and the staff development people become internal providers. Parents are also external and internal customers. For example, when parents send their children to school, they become external customers. When they participate in school affairs, they become internal providers.

Figure 15-1 Interface Between the Customer and the Provider

Customer	Type	Provider	Type	Services
Studets	I	Teachers	I	Instructions, counseling, guidance, leadership, materials, supplies, space, technology, equipment, safe and secure environment
Teachers	I	School administrators and all support staff	I	Multiple support
School administrators	I	Board of Education	I	Multiple support
Parents	E	District	E	Knowledge, experience, wisdom skills, character
Community	E	District	E	Knowledge, experience, wisdom skills, character
Colleges and Universities	E	District	E	Minimum Academic skills, character
District	E	Vendors	E	Materials, supplies, equipment technology

I= Internal, E=External

The Principles and Practices of Total Quality

TQ operating principles and practices are consistent with criteria from the Malcolm Baldrige National Quality Award. The Baldrige criteria identify a complete and "nondenominational" framework of what it takes to become a total quality school. The three principles of TQ to maximize customer satisfaction are to:

1. Focus on achieving customer satisfaction.
2. Seek continuous and long-term improvement in all the school processes and outputs.
3. Take steps to assure the full involvement of all teachers improving quality.

Put another way, the essence of TQ is involving and empowering all teachers (and all school people) to improve the quality of services and products continuously in order to satisfy and even delight the customer. To achieve this goal requires identifying

Implementing Total Quality in Schools

customers and their needs; having a clear idea of how the school plans to go about meeting expectations; and making sure that everyone in the school understands the customers' needs and is empowered to act on their behalf. There are a few quick fixes for improving quality. Experience shows that it takes years to create a new environment or culture that places a premium on greatness; to build structures that will sustain and manage change; and to provide education to drive the effort.

How does a school achieve a commitment to TQ that meets the above description? This approach to TQ emphasizes several elements or practices that, when integrated as a strategy for quality improvement, result in the fundamental changes required. These include school administration leadership and support, planning, customer focus, measurement and analysis, commitment to training, teacher empowerment and teamwork, and quality assurance.

The Essential Steps for Implementing Total Quality in Schools

There are a number of ways to implement TQ in education. The most preferred way is to implement TQ district-wide. However, if the superintendent is reluctant to do so, individual principals should consider the following steps:

Step 1: Create Vision and Values Statements.

This factor assumes that a mission has already been developed by the schools and units. Every school attempting to implement an effective total quality process has prepared vision and values statements. These statements provide the spiritual direction and guidance that are major factors in energizing schools. (See chapter six.)

Each statement should reflect school needs, cultures, the nature of customers, and other environmental factors. In some schools, the principal develops the vision and values statements, and in others, he or she involves all school people. In both cases, a deliberate attempt was initiated to communicate the final documents to all their people. Every school organization must make attempts to determine if its values are being inculcated throughout all units.

Step 2: Integrate Strategic Quality Goals With Action Plans.

Develop strategic quality goals to communicate to the entire school family that total quality is an important thrust toward the success of the school. In addition, the development and implementation of action plans provide the basis for demonstrating how total quality initiatives will be implemented.

Some strategic quality goals include the following:

- 100 percent accuracy of all textbooks.
- Elimination of fear in the schools.
- All services will meet customer expectation the first time and every time.
- Once strategic quality goals have been set, their deployment within the school organization should begin immediately.
- School quality improvement plans will be developed by each school.
- Unit quality improvement plans will dovetail with quality school improvement plans.
- Unit quality improvement plans will be based on cycles of service and moments of truth.

The following is a sample action plan:

1. School quality improvement plans will be developed by each school in support of district quality strategic goals.
2. A plan will be developed and executed to reduce fear in the school, unit, and classrooms. Each year, a survey will be used to assess the degree to which fear has been eliminated in the school.
3. Internal and external assessment of customers' satisfaction levels will be conducted on a regular basis for continuous improvement.
4. All school people will be required to undergo sixty hours of training annually.

Implementing Total Quality in Schools

5. An annual assessment using the Malcolm Baldrige National Quality Award Criteria will be performed to measure principles of total quality.
6. Teams will begin working through the summer to build the school's quality service measurement system.
7. A formal communication plan will be created to convey strategies, efforts, events, activities, and results of the district.

Step 3: Select a Total Quality Model.

A piecemeal approach for implementing total quality will not work. Selecting an appropriate TQ model is one of the most essential points for achieving greatness in a school. There are several available models that schools can review and select from to establish a TQ process. Some of them are listed below:

- Deming model
- Juran model
- Crosby model
- ISO 9000 model
- Malcolm Baldrige model
- Various state models such as the Sterling model in Florida and the Excelsior model in New York.

Perhaps the most comprehensive model is that of the Malcolm Baldrige Award Criteria, which has a unique and effective scoring component that enables a school to measure its present level of quality detainment and then evaluate its progress over a period of time.

Step 4: Organize a Design Team to Match the School's Culture to Its Total Quality Process.

Regardless of whether a school is issuing its own people or a consultant to implement the total quality process, it has been determined that it is essential that a design team be organized at the outset. The design team should be composed of all major departments of the school. Its charge is to assist the principal to develop his or her total quality model; coordinate quality implementation efforts with other programs to ensure the availability of resources; and evaluate the effectiveness of all implementation steps. Operating through informal personal networks within the school, the design team is expected to diminish any fear others may have regarding the total quality process.

Step 5: Develop a School Structure to Implement Total Quality.

The implementation of total quality requires six elements, as illustrated in Figure 15-1. First, create a quality steering committee to guide and direct the planning, development, launch, and evaluation of the total quality process. Sometimes the superintendent is the chairperson of the committee, which is comprised of a cross section of school and community people. Next, select a quality coordinator. The quality coordinator is a member of the quality steering committee and orchestrates all the activities of the committee. Third, create a quality service support team. This team consists of directors and supervisors, and its purpose is to support all quality initiatives of the quality steering committee, quality improvement teams, and quality action teams.

Organize education process analysis teams. These teams consist of cross-functional members of the school organization. They are formed to improve the operating effectiveness of both line and staff functions.

Fifth, create quality improvement teams. Each school is required to establish quality improvement teams to identify and analyze quality improvement approaches and to solve them. Quality improvement teams consist of ten to twelve members, who may include the principal, teachers, students, parents, and other school people. Unlike education process analysis teams, the focus of quality improvement teams is usually confined to their respective schools. A facilitator is utilized to facilitate effective quality improvement meetings.

Finally, select quality action teams. Quality action teams are organized by quality improvement teams to assist them in conducting research, collecting data, analyzing and solving problems, or tracing quality improvement applications.

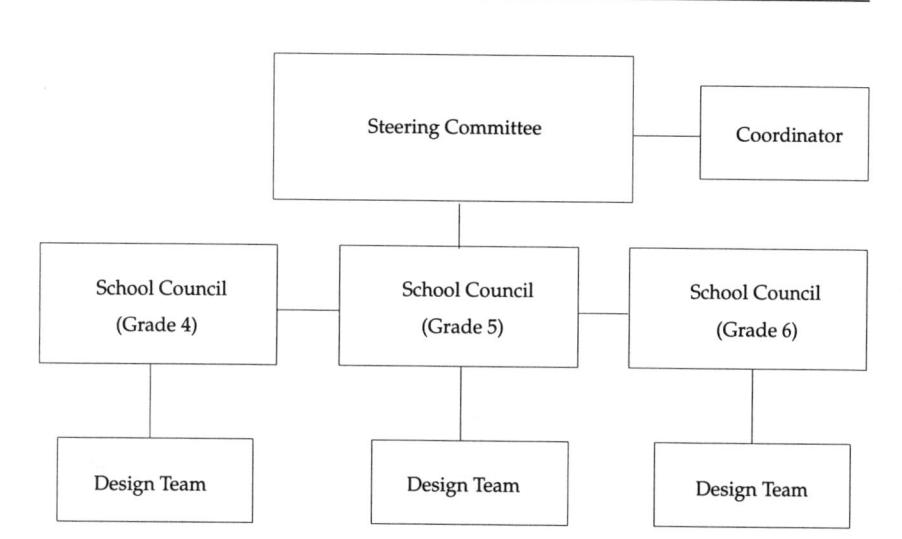

Figure 15-2 School Structure in Implement Total Quality

```
                    Steering Committee ─── Coordinator

   School Council      School Council      School Council
    (Grade 4)           (Grade 5)           (Grade 6)

   Design Team         Design Team         Design Team
```

Step 6: Design Total Quality Training.

Specific total quality training falls into two major categories: general TQ awareness, training and results-oriented TQ training. General total quality awareness training requires:

- Building quality improvement teams.
- Focusing on the customer.
- Creating a guidance system for total quality.
- Organizing a quality steering committee.
- Conducting education process analysis sessions.
- Creating the quality service measurement system.
- Forming quality improvement teams.
- Conveying the school master plan for implementing total quality.

Results-oriented total quality training requires:

- Conducting decision-making analysis.
- Executing project planning and critical techniques.
- Implementing success emulation.

- Constructing flow charts and Pareto charts.
- Preparing cause-and-effect analysis.
- Develop customer perception surveys.
- Constructing run charts and control charts.
- Developing scatter diagrams and histograms.

Step 7: Prepare an Effective Communication Plan.

An effective communication plan is necessary to support the implementation of total quality. Its purposes are as follows:

- To convey the message to the entire school that the total quality process is a team effort.
- To recognize and reward school people for their quality initiatives.
- To create a common understanding and language for quality.

Although schools are not known to plan the various ways in which they will communicate the particulars of their TQ process, successful manufacturing and service organizations do. It is high time that schools do the same. The following is an example of a communication plan:

- ❑ Establish a quality steering committee. Communicate throughout the school the mission, membership, and functions of this committee. Use videotapes to do so.
- ❑ Create strategic quality goals and incorporate them into the school improvement plan. All schools and units should prepare quality school improvement plans to support these goals. The plans should be stated in writing and presented personally by the school and unit leaders in quarterly updates to the quality steering committee.
- ❑ Organize education process analysis to enhance cross-functional communication. Develop education process analysis educational materials and conduct meetings whereby participants work on processes of their choice and a short videotape of actual sessions to teacher and school people. Use internal news media to present interviews of education process analysis workshops to the entire school.

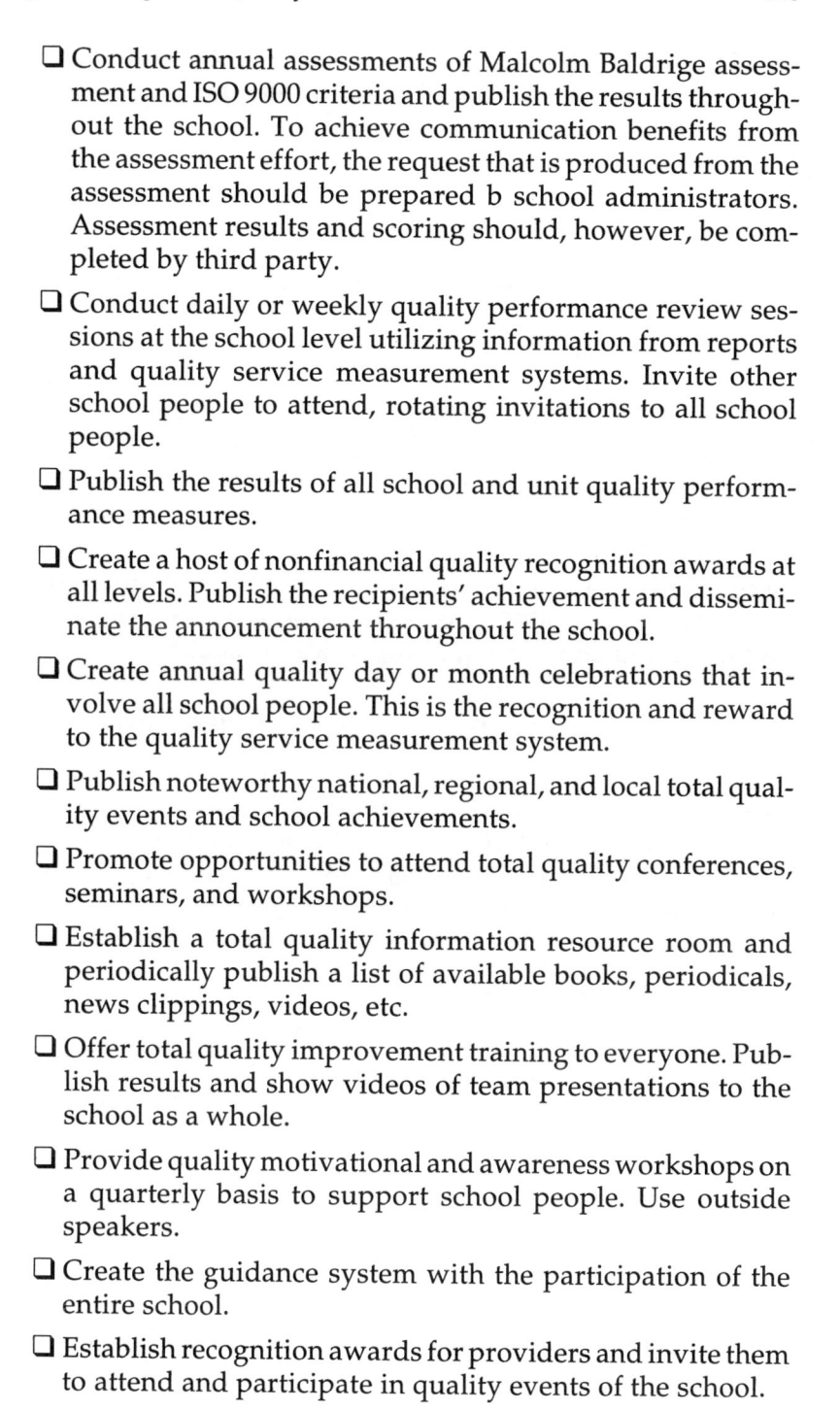

Implementing Total Quality in Schools 243

- ❏ Conduct annual assessments of Malcolm Baldrige assessment and ISO 9000 criteria and publish the results throughout the school. To achieve communication benefits from the assessment effort, the request that is produced from the assessment should be prepared b school administrators. Assessment results and scoring should, however, be completed by third party.
- ❏ Conduct daily or weekly quality performance review sessions at the school level utilizing information from reports and quality service measurement systems. Invite other school people to attend, rotating invitations to all school people.
- ❏ Publish the results of all school and unit quality performance measures.
- ❏ Create a host of nonfinancial quality recognition awards at all levels. Publish the recipients' achievement and disseminate the announcement throughout the school.
- ❏ Create annual quality day or month celebrations that involve all school people. This is the recognition and reward to the quality service measurement system.
- ❏ Publish noteworthy national, regional, and local total quality events and school achievements.
- ❏ Promote opportunities to attend total quality conferences, seminars, and workshops.
- ❏ Establish a total quality information resource room and periodically publish a list of available books, periodicals, news clippings, videos, etc.
- ❏ Offer total quality improvement training to everyone. Publish results and show videos of team presentations to the school as a whole.
- ❏ Provide quality motivational and awareness workshops on a quarterly basis to support school people. Use outside speakers.
- ❏ Create the guidance system with the participation of the entire school.
- ❏ Establish recognition awards for providers and invite them to attend and participate in quality events of the school.

❑ Educate all school administrators in the Malcolm Baldrige National Quality Award Criteria and other quality models and explain how they apply to schools. Conduct workshops, videos presentations, and seminars.

Step 8: Determine Education Processes.

Education process analysis is one of the best analytical and action tools for achieving quality improvement. School people who participate in education process analysis team efforts gain a better understanding of their own operation and that of other schools so they can encourage team members from other schools and units to implement actions to improve quality and productivity, and so they may receive recognition and support for their ideas from school administrators. The education process analysis team uses flowcharts to illustrate education processes across schools and departments, and applies the concept of internal and external customer satisfaction as the basis for identifying opportunities and establishing quality service measurement.

Step 9: Develop a Quality Service Measurement System.

Any school that wishes to achieve a total quality environment is required to develop the heart of total quality; that is, the quality service measurement system. Quality performance measures should cover a multitude of characteristics based on the needs, requirements, and expectations of the customer.

Step 10: Implement Success Emulation.

Organizations such as Motorola and Xerox maintain that the key to their success is due to their emphasis on total quality and success emulation. In fact, Motorola has been cited as one of the top Total Quality Organizations in the United States. Emulation is a process that involves determining the critical success factors of an organization; identifying those schools that are the best-in-class in these critical success factors; and emulating the strategies, tactics, and techniques of those schools.

Published data sources:
- Annual reports

- Professional journals
- Periodicals
- Newsletters
- Conference proceedings
- Local newspapers
- Union agreements
- Association publications

Unpublished data sources:

- Site visits
- School people of schools being emulated
- Provider interviews

Interviews with observers and experts for the following information:

- Product technology
- Products and processes under development
- Product and service cost
- Internal synergy
- Organizational structure
- Areas of new breakthroughs

Customer interviews for information on:

- Purchase price of products and services
- Purchase terms and conditions
- Quality of customer service
- Product quality
- Delivery practices
- Strategy
- Strengths/weaknesses of your school's products and services

Step 11: Develop a Recognition and Reward Program.

Recognizing and rewarding quality efforts, expressing gratitude for quality accomplishments, and celebrating quality successes must be performed in a timely and sincere fashion. This can vary from a handshake to giving those who earned them lavish gifts. It must be reflective of the involvement and gratitude of central school administrators, and it must be engaged. A recognition and reward program for those who produce quality is essential. Develop a recognition and reward program by engaging in the following activities:

- Allocate a budget for a recognition and reward program.
- Develop a recognition and reward program.
- Obtain feedback from appropriate teachers on the program.
- Celebrate quality success.

The Customer Experience

Karl Albrecht, a noted total quality consultant maintains that we need to adopt a slightly different vocabulary to discuss the customers in schools. He said that in the past we learned to equate value with objective characteristics of tangible products. For example, the car has overdrive, the camera had multifocus, the suit is wrinkle-free, etc. He says that these characteristics are easily measurable, observable, and therefore, easily quantifiable. However, when the quality issue is a service, the element of quality changes profoundly.

The following are some of the differences between service quality and product quality:

- Pure service is intangible.
- There are few, if any, specific criteria for service quality.
- Service providers are perceived to be the service.
- The customer participates in the creation and delivery of the service.
- Service variability is inevitable.

Implementing Total Quality in Schools

- Trust between the customer and service provider is a key element.
- Service quality is consumed as it is produced.

Pure service quality is intangible. When a teacher conducts a class, the customers—the students—are "buying" his or her education, skills, and experience, even though it is paid for by the district, since they feel the results of the teacher's service. There are few, if any, specific criteria for service quality. How do you measure service quality? If you create a measurement scale, how can you be sure that your measurements are accurate and realistic? You need to be certain of who is making the measurement and what kind of comparisons they are using. What are your alternatives to measure? These are important considerations.

Quality is not a tangible item, but it is a "customer's reaction to an experience." Albrecht says that "...even if the experience includes a physical "delivery" of some sort, the essence of total quality delivered depends solely on the customer's mental and emotional state resulting from the experience. He also says that quality experience is all about a person's feelings, beliefs, values, commitment, concepts, and philosophy.

Schools implementing total quality must become service-focused schools by:

- Becoming obsessive about listening to, understanding, and responding to customer's changing needs, requirements, and expectations.
- Creating and communicating a well-defined, customer-based service strategy.
- Developing and maintaining a customer-friendly quality service measurement system.
- Hiring, inspiring, and developing customer-oriented teachers and other school people.

A quick and effective way to introduce the concept of Total quality, in schools is the introductionoftheconceptofmomentsoftruth.

Moments of Truth

Early in the 1980s, Jan Carlzon, CEO of Scandinavian Airlines System, determined how to bring the intangible aspects of service into sharp focus so they can be identified, thus allowing organizations to manage their operations on behalf of the customer. He originated the concept of "moments of truth." Carlzon maintains that there are points in all organizations at which the customer comes in contact with the provider and something "fundamental and memorable takes place." The occasions may be favorable or unfavorable. What the customer sees and feels about the school organization occurs as a result of these encounters. Moments of truth are defined as any episode in which a customer comes into contact with the school and gets an impression of its services and products.

Moments of truth come in a variety of forms and result in a mixture of impressions that may be favorable or unfavorable, some examples are cited below:

- Customer registers her child in school. Resulting impression: "It took me only ten minutes to register John for school. I met his teachers, who seem nice. If this is an indication of the efficiency of this school, then I will not transfer John to a private school."

- Customer speaks to a receptionist about why her child could not come to school today. Resulting impression: "The school receptionist was rude and discourteous. I sure gave her a piece of my mind. Who does she think she is? I pay her salary."

- Customer receives information from the school. Resulting impression: "The school has its act together, the guidance counselor was able to retrieve the information I requested in no time."

- Customer notices poor condition of restroom facilities in school. Resulting impression: "This school does not care about the health of its students, nor does it teach students good health habits."

- Customer asks to address the board. Resulting impressions: "The board has been courteous and helpful. I am able

Implementing Total Quality in Schools 249

to contribute to and have an effect on the education of my child."

- Customer receives information from the school. Resulting impression: "I should have received this information last week. The school should have its act together. We certainly pay enough for its services."
- Customer receives notice that her child was struck with a dirty needle while in school. Resulting impression: "Couldn't the school think of a better way to inform me of this incident than merely sending me a notice? What kind of security do they have in that school? Now what is the probability that my child will get AIDS? Just wait until I go up to that school."

Once you begin to relate to the customer in terms of moments of truth, you will begin to reinvent your philosophy about how you think about quality. When you select and analyze your moments of truth, particularly on the most important ones, you will begin to see things as the customer sees them. The moments of truth, once selected and analyzed, require you to focus on defining, delivering, measuring quality, and doing something to improve it.

Periodically, each school must identify and critically analyze those moments of truth that will have a major impact within a cycles of service. The following are the procedural steps for completing a moment of truth: First, indicate the critical moments of truth. Then, cite the things that can happen or fail to happen that will make the moment of truth unsatisfactory. Third, list the customer's expected standards at that moment of truth, as verified by customer research. Fourth, indicate the factors that add value to the service, as seen in the eyes of the customer. Finally, describe a proposed strategy to add value to the moment of truth.

Identifying and Analyzing Your Cycles of Service

Cycles of service are comprised of a number of interrelated moments of truth. Here is a quality improvement concept that allows you to diagram and analyze school services from the perspective of the customer. Each cycle of service forces you to deal with those moments of truth from which the customer forms impressions and opinions of the quality of service of the school or unit.

Thousand of cycles of service occur all over the school all of the time. To deal with the quality of service of these cycles, which comprised multiple moments of truth, each must be identified, analyzed, and improved. The following are example of cycles of service:

- Hiring new teachers
- Processing a purchase order
- Shipping a package
- Reimbursing teachers for travel expenses.
- Assigning homework to students.
- Administering a test to students.
- Delivering a lesson to students.

Let's examine the cycle of sequence for delivering a lesson to students. The moments of truth for this cycle could include the following:

- Introducing the lesson
- Presenting the lesson
- Asking students questions
- Assigning homework
- Critiquing the lesson
- Concluding the lesson

Now let us reveiw the presentation of the lesson. The lesson was presented on a thirty minute lecture to fifth grade students. The reaction of the students: most students found it boring, seven students feel asleep, no students took notes, and all but four students of twenty five passed a test regarding the presentation. What was the outcome of this particular moment of truth: poor quality.

REVIEW

Key Points to Remember:

Total quality in education is the vehicle for focusing the energy and resources of the school toward a common good, continuous improvement of products and services to students.

A provider is any person or group on which teachers depend for input that is used to deliver a service to satisfy its customer or to produce a product input. A customer is any person or group to which the QI team delivers either a service or product in order to meet and exceed a need, requirement, or expectation.

Some principles and practices of total quality are to focus on satisfying the customer, strive for continuous and long-term improvement, and involve teachers in improving quality.

The following are essential steps for implementing total quality in education:

1. Create vision and values statements.
2. Integrate strategic quality goals with action plans.
3. Select a total quality model.
4. Organize a design team to match the school's culture to its total quality process.
5. Develop a school structure to implement total quality.
6. Design total quality training.
7. Prepare an effective communication plan.
8. Determine education processes.
9. Analyze a quality service measurement system.
10. Implement success emulation.
11. Develop a recognition and reward program.

Moments of truth are defined as any episode in which a customer comes into contact with the schools and gets an impression of its services and products.

Cycles of service are comprised of a number of interrelated moments of truth.

Application

Based on the needs of your school, develop a communication plan to transform your school, using the communication plan included in this chapter. Assess your plans in three months by interviewing teachers by grade to ascertain areas where the plan could be improved.

CHAPTER 16

Installing School-Based Management

LEARNING OBJECTIVES

After studying and comprehending this chapter, you should be able to :

- Identify the essential stages for installing school-based management.
- Realize that similar to the implementation plan of total quality, school-based management is a systematic process.

What Every Principal Should Know About Implementing School-Based Management

School-based management does not just happen. It is not something that is done with a snap of the principal's finger. Rather, it comes about as a result of a well thought-out and carefully executed plan. It takes time, perhaps more than is desirable, but in the long run, students, teachers and administrators stand to benefit. All principals should know the steps involved for implementing school-based management. Some schools have installed their school-based management programs by jumping erratically back and forth between these steps. When this happens, it builds doubts and creates obstacles in the minds of administrators and teachers alike. It is better to have a program course charted out carefully. Careful planning helps avoid problems, inspires confidence, and lays the foundation for continual forward momentum.

If your superintendent has already given a commitment to school-based management, most of this chapter may not pertain to you. However, you may benefit from this chapter by assessing your school-based management thrust by organizing what presently exists in your program compared to what this chapter discusses. If, on the other hand, your district has not implemented school-based management, you have two options. You may ask your superintendent to use your school as a trial study to determine if the program should be implemented districtwide or you can get permission from your superintendent to implement the program without its being a trial study. If you accept the second option, it is taken for granted that you, the principal, have done your homework and are already connected to the program.

The Phases for Implementing School-Based Management

Comprehensive implementation is divided into five phases: preliminary, training, installation, maturation, and evaluation.

Preparation of the implementation plan necessitates the identifying and prioritizing of all required activities. A time frame for implementation, statement of staff responsibilities, and budget must also be developed, based on the needs of your school.

Preliminary Stage

The preliminary stage involves the preparatory work necessary to get the process into forward motion. It consists of the initial training by the principal, the appointment of a coordinator, the organization of a steering committee, and the preparation of material used to implement the program.

Once the principal develops an interest in school-based management, he or she should select a coordinator to explore the viability of implementing the program. The principal can either appoint someone directly, take responsibility for this position himself or herself, or organize a steering committee and require the committee to select a coordinator.

Assisted by the principal, the coordinator performs the following activities to establish a steering committee:

- Prepares operational guidelines for the steering committee.
- Selects members of the steering committee either through the union or teachers themselves.
- Sends a letter to each person congratulating these individuals on their selection. (Included in the letter are the time, date, and location of the first meeting.)
- Convenes the meeting, introduces the coordinator, explains guidelines, and engages the membership in selecting or electing a chairperson.
- Turns the meeting over to the chairperson.
- Has the coordinator deliver a brief overview of school-based management to give the membership a better perspective of the program and their responsibilities.
- Meets with the chairperson to establish an agenda for the next meeting.

In some instances, the newly appointed coordinator may have little or no knowledge about school-based management. He or she should, therefore, bring an expert along to furnish information on the program and its requirements. Some districts, such as Hammond School District in Hammond, Indiana, and Dade County School District in Dade County, Florida, conduct workshops on school-based management.

You should collect and read books and articles on school-based management. The National Center to Save Our Schools in Westbury, New York, distributes resource packets, directory, books, and a journal on school-based management.

Visit at least two districts and two companies that have implemented either school-based or team-based management. Assess the school's needs and readiness for implementing school-based management.

The following questions should be asked to determine needs and readiness for school-based management:

- Are we maximizing the skills and talents of our teachers?
- Do teachers have a voice in the decision-making process?

- What does the union want from the principal?
- Are we, as a school, capable of doing more?
- Do we have a number of prevailing problems that have gone unsolved for years?
- Does the principal manage by Theory X or Theory Y? Will the principal be willing to share his or her power with teachers?
- Does the collective bargaining agreement allow us to implement school-based management? If not, what can be done to get the union to cooperate?
- How high is the trust level between the principal and teachers?
- How do teachers relate to one another?
- How do they function as a group?
- How are problems identified within the school?
- How are problems solved?
- To what extent are teachers' needs being met in the schools?
- Are teachers committed to achieving common goals?
- What is the quantity and quality of service provided to students?
- What is adequate recognition for good performance?

The primary purpose for assessing the needs and readiness of the school is to determine what type of empowerment activities are most appropriate for the school. This assessment need not be overly formal or structured. The main point is that teachers should give their conscious attention to an open assessment of those factors that have an impact on school-based management. The assessment may involve collecting relevant information from teachers about the school environment. This is done through discussion, interviews, opinion surveys, and an analysis of performance indicators. The results of the assessment can serve as the basis for implementation of specific projects and solutions to problems, along with providing information that can be used to evaluate school-based management.

Installing School-Based Management

Once the needs and readiness problems have been addressed, an outline should be prepared with responses to the above questions. These should be discussed with the superintendent. Some superintendents may request a formal write-up so that they can have time to react to it. Other superintendents may need little or no time to discuss reasons why the district should go forward with using your school as a pilot study because they are already convinced of its importance.

Once the superintendent gives the green light for the pilot study, the coordinator must plan the training agenda so as to obtain the most comprehensive training in all critical areas of school-based management. You should attend workshops to obtain intensified training. Training should encompass the following:

- Enrollment in a three-day course in school-based management.

- Acquire resource packets on school-based management and other literature and make arrangements to attend training activities.

- Spend two weeks visiting districts that have a successful program in place. Dade County School District and Hammond School District are recommended.

- Invite experts and guest lecturers to appear in the school to deliver presentations on school-based management.

- Collect and study all materials obtained from other schools, consultants, and companies that have implemented either school-based or team-based management.

- Retain a consultant to assist training and development efforts and other important functions, such as proposal preparation, analysis of the implementation plan, execution of the implementation plan, evaluation of the pilot plan, and preparation of the annual report.

To determine the appropriate model for the program, it will be necessary to consider the following questions in addition to others that may arise:

- Should the entire school be restructured into teams?

- How should the professional and nonprofessional support staffs be used in school-based management?
- Should there be one council or multiple councils in the school? Why?
- What should be the composition of these councils? How should the membership be selected or elected?
- What other groups should be created, and why?

The model should be thought out very carefully. One way to do this is to study models adopted by other schools and determine which one best meets the needs of the school. At times, the principal may want to involve all of the teachers in deciding on the model. This is a wise move and should be practiced by the principal. Figure 16-1 illustrates a school-based management model.

Collect proposals on either school-based management from

Figure 16-1 A School Based Management Model

```
        ┌─────────────────────┐   ┌─────────────┐
        │ Steering Committee  │───│ Coordinator │
        └─────────────────────┘   └─────────────┘
                   │
     ┌─────────────┼─────────────┐
┌──────────┐  ┌──────────┐  ┌──────────┐
│  School  │  │  School  │  │  School  │
│ Council  │  │ Council  │  │ Council  │
│ (Grade 4)│  │ (Grade 5)│  │ (Grade 6)│
└──────────┘  └──────────┘  └──────────┘
     │             │             │
┌──────────┐  ┌──────────┐  ┌──────────┐
│  Design  │  │  Design  │  │  Design  │
│   Team   │  │   Team   │  │   Team   │
└──────────┘  └──────────┘  └──────────┘
```

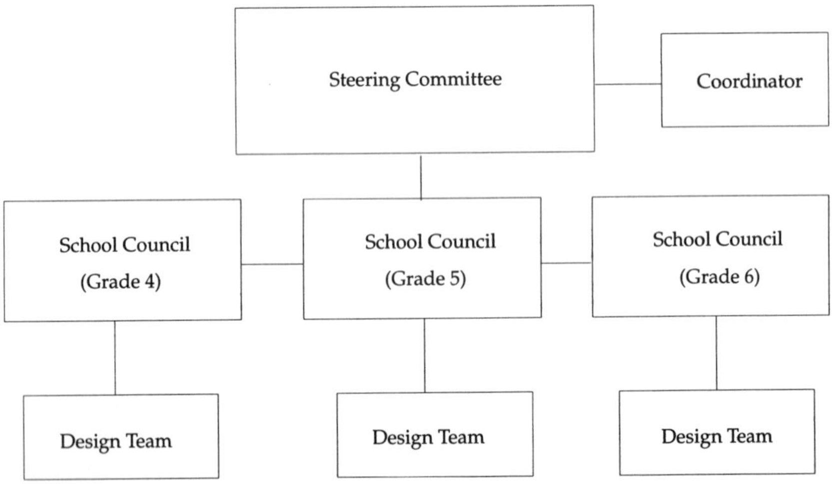

other schools. These materials are useful in helping to develop an outline for preparing the implementation proposal. In addition, they may afford an opportunity to do some creative swiping to strengthen the program.

Installing School-Based Management

Once the coordinator becomes fortified with knowledge and training, the next step involves the preparation of the school-based proposal. Before executing this step, the coordinator should review his or her notes and discuss the proposal with the principal and/or steering committee so as to obtain initial approval for the various elements it includes. The elements that should be discussed for the proposal are as follows:

- Pertinent terms such as school-based management, empowerment, self-management, school council, team, etc.
- Purpose, goals, and objectives of school-based management.
- Philosophy of the school..
- Expectations of school-based management.
- Approach and structure of school-based management program.
- Functions of each component of the structure.
- Allocation of the school budgets.
- How decisions will be reached.
- The training program.
- How councils and teams will be organized and who will comprise them.
- Responsibilities of each level of the school as it pertains to school-based management
- How membership will be determined.
- The parameters of the councils and teams.
- The statement of agreement between the principal, administration, and union reaction to the collective bargaining agreement and school-based management.
- Describe how school-based management will evaluated.
- How the community will be included.
- A time frame for the implementation of school-based management.
- The implementation plan.

In developing the proposal, the coordinator should do the following:

- Identify the needs of the school.
- Request schools to share their materials on school based management.
- Develop a proposal outline and obtain approval from the principal or superintendent.
- Complete the proposal and discuss with the entire school faculty.
- Make changes as discussed and agreed.
- Obtain approval from the superintendent.

To construct an implementation plan, use the explanation immediately preceding each activity to complete your implementation plan by indicating responsibility areas, time frame, and cost. Cost is important because it gives you some idea as to what should be allocated as an initial budget.

Submit the proposal with the implementation plan to the superintendent and steering committee for discussion and approval. Make sufficient copies for the superintendent and the school's steering committee. Give them a few days to review the materials and arrange to discuss every aspect of the proposal and plan with them. As a result of the discussion, revisions, deletions, and additions may be necessary. Make the changes and obtain approval for the proposal and plan. Obviously, these two documents cannot receive final approval until the superintendent acts on them.

The superintendent teamed with the principal, coordinator, and union president should meet with all teachers to officially launch the program. Usually, important aspects of school-based management are included in a brief document that is submitted to each. An agenda should be prepared and given to the participants. The agenda should include:

- Remarks about the benefits of school-based management from the superintendent and/or principal.
- Introduction and remarks from the coordinator of school-based management.

Installing School-Based Management

- Introduction and remarks from the president of the union.
- Additional remarks from the principal as to the schedule of events.

Hire a consultant to assist with the implementation plan. Names of consultants who can be retained for this purpose are contained in the directory on school-based management and can be obtained from the National Center to Save Our Schools.

Hold a meeting with the principal, teachers, and coordinator. The intent of this meeting is multifold:

- To demonstrate through his or her attendance and remarks at this meeting, the principal's commitment to school-based management.
- To formally introduce the coordinator, and, if possible, the consultant, and describe their functions.
- To establish a sense of the cooperation between the principal and union through the appearance and remarks of the president of the union.
- To conduct an awareness session on school-based management.
- To address the needs, concerns, and aspirations of teachers.
- To discuss the overall approach of school-based management, its structure, and other details contained in the proposal.

Institute the school improvement plan for the school as a structure to supplement the school-based management program. This requires the following activities. First, establish the council (or councils) and effect the plan for either electing or selecting the full membership. Inform those who have been elected or selected and convene an organization meeting. At this meeting, either the principal or another member is elected or selected as the council leader. The principal describes the responsibilities, introduces the coordinator, and describes activities individuals will perform. The charge of the council is made clear. One copy of the proposal is given to the council leader, and individual members receive a copy of the implementation plan. The meeting concludes and time is established for the next council meeting.

Second, other groups within the structure must be organized. These groups should meet in a fashion consistent with the description contained in the proposal. These meetings are similar to the council meetings with the exception that the training received by these groups is not as comprehensive and intense.

Once the structure is put in place, the coordinator meets with the steering committee to deliver a list of the membership in the council and other groups. In addition, he or she also discusses other matters with the superintendent or steering committee and delivers a report on the progress of the school-based management structure.

Provide intensified training and development to each council member. This entails the following activities:

- Visiting two districts that have implemented school-based management.

- Attending a national conference on school-based management.

- Attending an intensified training course held outside the district over a minimum of three days.

Announce the pilot study. Under the direction of the superintendent and principal the coordinator disseminates a memo to school and community people that the school-based management program may be inaugurated. Then, assisted by the coordinator, the council leader prepares the agenda for the second meeting and convenes this and other meetings.

Training Stage

The training stage consists of collecting, developing, and evaluating training materials, along with selecting the appropriate personnel to be trained. You should start by establishing a resource center on school-based management. Purchase an adequate assortment of training materials. Obtain a copy of a training resource to receive copies of their training materials. Once this material is reviewed, a determination should be made as to whether or not the material is feasible for use in the training program. Training materials should include audiotapes, video tapes, books, 16 millimeter film, and games.

Although a great deal of material can be acquired through visitations, training courses, consultants, organizations, and vendors, these should be supplemented with materials that address the needs of your school. It will be necessary for the coordinator and the consultant to prepare an adequate number of "homemade" training materials so that the council leader can establish a relevant and ongoing training program for members.

You need to train all council members. There are three ways to accommodate this activity:

1. Use a portion of every council meeting to train members;
2. Dedicate three full days for training, and a portion of every council meeting thereafter to continue the training; or
3. Use as many council meetings as necessary exclusively for training.

Regardless of the manner in which training of council members is conducted, one or more of the following activities should occur during these meetings:

- The council should select a simple problem to work on first in order to achieve success quickly.
- Use specialists within the district to help collect and gather information on problem areas.
- Use a consensus (with or without modifications) to arrive at solutions.
- Brainstorm or use the nominal group process to identify and solve problems.
- Use the Delphi technique to survey experts on situations, issues, problems, and solutions.
- Use force field analysis to determine a solution.
- Use the cause-and-effect diagram to arrive at solutions to problems.
- Use all of the interpersonal skills learned during the training to conduct effective meetings.
- Conduct council meetings.

Although the proposal usually spells how frequently the council should meet, the council can elect to meet less or more frequently depending on its needs. However, no council should meet less than once a month. The coordinator is expected to attend all meetings and to assist the council leader with training.

Continue the training of the council leaders. While training is conducted primarily by the coordinator, other persons within and outside the district can and should be used if their expertise in a given area exceeds that of the coordinator.

Arrange for council members to attend specific training events. There are several ways to do this.. Let the council as a whole attend a national conference or workshop on school-based management. Arrange for the council as a whole to visit other districts with successful programs that employ the practice so that they can learn how school-based management is implemented. Or, send out invitations to administrators, teachers, and community members to attend council meetings. But these invitations should not be sent out until council members feel comfortable solving problems.

Evaluate the effectiveness of the training program and make necessary adjustments. The best way to do this is to request that the coordinator attend council meetings to identify strengths and weaknesses, review materials, and make suggestions for improvement. It is also advisable for the coordinator to interview council members to obtain relevant information.

Training should be viewed as an integral part of school-based management. Yet, it is the most underfunded area in most, if not all, district budgets. Therefore, it is necessary to get the superintendent to allocate a percentage of teachers' salaries for training and development purposes.

Hold regularly-scheduled meetings. This activity by the council leader and members will begin to become a way of life throughout the school as the process begins to "blossom" and solutions to problems begin to emerge. The principal should attend council meetings, provide information when necessary, and meet with leaders to provide his or her encouragement and support.

Maturation Stage

During the maturation stage, the program has been expanded and the council is holding regular meetings. At this point, continue steering committee meetings. At this stage, the steering committee has ironed out most of the problems associated with school-based management and is acting as an overseer, making certain that nothing goes astray with the program.

You should continue to promote the program. To establish a comprehensive program, a comprehensive recognition plan is developed, approved by the steering committee, and systematically executed. When this phase has been implemented, it provides for a more orderly and timely method for promoting school-based management.

An essential feature of the program is to keep the superintendent informed of the progress of the program. To ensure that the superintendent is informed continually, the following should always be done:

- Disseminate progress reports.
- Contact the superintendent by telephone to discuss program results.
- Distribute appropriate written articles.
- Hold conferences with nonparticipating teachers.

In an effort to observe the progress of the program, individual members of the steering committee should request an invitation to attend one of the meetings. This meeting should not take place until the teachers and coordinator believe that the council members are ready. Attendance at meetings provides an excellent opportunity to congratulate members for their outstanding efforts. It should be seen as a way to keep the meetings operating smoothly.

Evaluation Stage

The evaluation stage involves the collection and evaluation of data to determine the impact of the program. Collect post-assessment data. This activity involves the collection of post-assessment data, comparing it with the baseline data and preparing an impact study. In order to avoid "leaks," persons working on the report should be advised not to discuss the findings with anyone. Review impact study with steering committee. Prior to disseminating the results of the impact study, the coordinator discusses the study with the steering committee to determine how it should be disseminated to others within the school.

Publicize the impact study. The impact study may be prepared in outline form with illustrations. It should be distributed and then discussed, first with the superintendent and then, others in the district. Upon direction from the steering committee, the principal or coordinator reports the results in the local newspapers and prepares articles for publication.

Based upon the impact report, the principal, coordinator and steering committee discuss and analyze how the program can be improved. Afterward, the implementation plan is updated to implement the recommendations. A subsequent status report is prepared within a reasonable period of time to keep the steering committee informed.

One of the most effective methods to promote school-based management as well as to recognize individual council members is to conduct an annual conference, involving teachers, school people, and community members. The purpose of this conference is to bring together people from the school and the community and to inform them as to what the councils have achieved during the school year.

Develop an annual report. An annual report describes the origin of school-based management, its progress, and its impact and benefits. It should be submitted to the Sterring Committee for approval and then distributed to the council members, the school staff, and community members. The annual report should consist of the following:

- Rationale for school-based management.
- Description of school-based management structure.
- Outline of expansion plan.
- Description of the impact of school-based management on the school.
- Outline of problems encountered by the councils and how they came about.

Installing School-Based Management

- Delineation of what problems were solved and what problems remain to be solved.
- Description of what can be expected in the future.
- Details on what changes have occurred to make school-based management more effective.
- Description of how councils were recognized and rewarded.
- Brief comments on the outcome of the annual conference.

School-based management is an outstanding program for introducing teachers to the shared decision making process. It is also an ideal prerequiste for launching a total quality process that requires more steps.

REVIEW

Key points to remember:

School-based management does not just happen, it comes about as a result of a well thought out, carefully executed plan.

A comprehensive implementation plan consists of the following five phases: preliminary, training, installation, maturation, and emulation.

Preparation of the plan for implementing school-based management will entail identifying and prioritizing all of the required activities and executing the plan in a certain time frame.

Although the steering committee is responsible for the success of school-based management, it is the coordinator who carries out the activities of the steering committee.

Application

1. Seek out a school-based management consultant. Submit your school-based management implementation plan to him or her and request and assessment of your plan with a detailed report.

2. Based on the report indicated in item one, revise your implementation plan if necessary and submit it to the steering committee for approval. It may be necessary for either the

principal, coordinator, and/or steering committee to request an appearance with the consultant to discuss his or her assessment and recommendations.

CHAPTER 17

Implementing Total Quality in the Classroom

LEARNING OBJECTIVES

After reading and comprehending this chapter you should be able to:

Implement Total Quality in the school by hrlping teachers to perform the following:

- Select appropriate Total Quality principles for classroom observance.

- Understand the System of Profound Theory of Knowledge as it relates to the classroom.

- Teach classroom use of the Shewhart/Deming Plan-Do-Check-Act Cycle.

- Identify Total Quality expectations of principals, teachers, and students.

- Discuss Dr. W. Edwards Deming's Triangle of Interaction.

- Identify classroom activities for implementing Total Quality.

What Every Principal Should Know About Implementing Total Quality in the Classroom

Principals should not be satisfied with excellent schools. Excellence refers to the best traditional school administration, principles, and practices that have produced some positive results in schools. However, these traditional principles and practices are no longer adequate to accommodate the needs of our students. The school environment has changed drastically, and so have students. What is required is a transformational change. The only well thought-out, field-tested alternative available today for us to elevate from excellent to *great* schools is to begin the journey to total quality or the journey toward achieving greatness in schools is predicated not by merely implementing it on a school level, but also on a classroom level. It is at this level that the transformation must take hold, thereby transforming the teachers and students, along with parents. It is also at this level at which principals find it very difficult to relate TQ principles and practices for classroom use.

The Steps for Implementing TQ in Classrooms

Although the contents of this chapter is written for teachers, it should be the basis for principals to train teachers to implement TQ and guidelines for teachers to stay on course for maintaining the TQ journey.

Although there are multiple steps for helping teachers to implement TQ in the classroom, the following are the most important.

Select Appropriate TQ Principles.

The first step for implementing TQ in the classroom involves reviewing the principles of the three gurus of quality, Drs. W. Edwards Deming, Joseph M. Juran and Philip B. Crosby and selecting those principles that are appropriate for classroom observance. Some revisions may be necessary. The following have been chosen for your review:

1. Make it clear that teachers are committed to quality (Dr. Crosby).

2. Create constancy of purpose toward improvement of service and product (Dr. Deming).

3. Drive out fear to maximize student efforts (Dr. Deming).

4. Raise the quality awareness and personal concern of all students (Dr. Crosby).

5. Replace competition with cooperation (Dr. Deming).

6. Cease dependence on grades and ranking. Require statistical evidence of quality (Dr. Deming) instead.

7. Organize to attain quality (Dr. Juran).

8. Train teachers to actively carry out their part of the quality improvement process (Dr. Crosby).

9. Encourage students to communicate to teachers the obstacles they face in attaining quality improvement (Dr. Crosby).

10. Report classroom quality progress (Dr. Juran).

11. Recognize and appreciate students for their quality initiatives (Dr. Crosby).

12. Do it all over again to demonstrate that quality improvement never ends (Dr. Deming).

Some schools may wish to confine themselves to the principles of a specific guru, such as Dr. Deming. This is certainly all right; however, are teachers certain that all beliefs about TQ should be covered by a single set of TQ principles? For example, Dr. Deming's principles are devoid of recognition; Dr. Juran's principles are devoid of commitment (although implied); and Dr. Crosby's principles are devoid of constancy of purpose. In essence, teachers should study each set of principles carefully before developing their own or adopting one specific set.

The principles, techniques, and activities of TQ should be integrated with everything the teacher does in the classroom. For example, according to Theresa May Hicks, an elementary school teacher who practices Dr. Deming's philosophy in the classroom: The System of Profound Theory of Knowledge can be taught with social students, science, math, etc. The Shewhart/Deming plan-Do-Check-Act Cycle can be taught to students to produce a product in social studies, to write a report, etc. The fish bone diagram can be used to help students to see the relationship between cause and effect; between what they do and its effect. In fact, TQ principles and practices can be used in conjunction with any academic subject matter to make learning fun and enjoyable.

The first action that must take place is to produce a TQ classroom for students to understand what quality is; who is responsible for quality; what is expected of students in a TQ classroom; and how students can produce quality. The principal should make certain that teachers make it clear to students where the staff stands on quality. Teachers should talk to students about quality not only as it pertains to school, but also as it pertains to their personal lives. During this meeting with students, the teacher should demonstrate a deep passion for TQ. Through his or her words, actions, and deeds, students should get the sense that the quality of their lives is interwoven and bent on how well they embrace the TQ concept and pursue the quality journey. The principal should make certain that all teachers discuss the following and adhere to the substance of this chapter:

- What is quality?
- Who are customers and providers?
- Who are internal and external customers?
- Who are internal and external providers?
- What do students have to do to put forth quality work?
- What are learning characteristics, measures, and standards?
- What does it take to have a quality experience?
- Who defines quality?
- How is quality traditionally defined?
- Where does quality happen?
- Who should produce quality?
- Why should students be convinced about quality?
- How does a class implement quality?
- What are the activities of quality?
- What are the different ways to produce quality?

Implementing Total Quality in the Classroom

- What role do teams play in quality?
- Why are teams essential for improving processes?
- Why is team building important?
- Discuss the role of team leaders and members.
- Discuss how the team will solve problems.

After the teacher demonstrates a strong commitment to TQ, the teacher's next step involves the creation of a mission, vision, and shared values statements. Techniques to develop each are described below.

Prepare a Mission Statement

First, teacher's shoud indicate to students that a mission statement identifies the aim or purpose of the class; that is, Why does the class exist? Whom does it serve? Engage students in a discussion of questions, such as: Why are you here? What are you trying to do?

What does it mean to you to do well? What does the teacher have to do so you can do well? How will we know if we are doing it well together? Ask students to independently write their versions of the class mission on a sheet of paper.

Go around the room looking for excellent examples of student-prepared mission statements, and request them to write their creations on a flipchart sheet or blackboard. Discuss each mission statement. Ask students to decide on the best two examples. Use the examples to reach a consensus about a mission statement that is acceptable to the classroom. Communicate the mission statement by reaching an agreement on how it should be communicated (i.e., printed on school stationery, etc.).(For more about the mission, see chapter five.)

Create a Vision Statement

Next, indicate to students that it is insufficient just to prepare a mission statement, and that a vision statement must also be prepared and communicated. Explain that a vision statement identifies the future direction of the classroom; that is, the vision statement describes what the classroom wants to become. (See chapter six for more information.)

Ask students to take a pencil or crayon and a sheet of paper, and to draw a picture of how their classroom should look in the future. Then, ask students to respond to the following statement to write a vision statement: My parents want our class to prepare me for the future by. . .

Ask students to imagine that they are journalists and have been assigned the responsibility of writing an article. They are to describe the successes the classroom will have achieved at a future time (five or ten years from the present).

Ask students to think about what they value most about the classroom. Then, have them list five ways to complete the following stem statement: In our classroom, we really care about. .

Once the above steps have been completed, develop a worksheet as described below to discover key items that should be associated with the vision statement. For instance, use a five-whys worksheet to illuminate the vision statement, such as:

- Why should our class implement TQ? Because TQ makes learning fun and enjoyable.

- Why does TQ make learning fun and enjoyable? Because emphasis is on continuous improvement, cooperation, quality effort, and no failure.

- Why is the emphasis on continuous improvement, cooperation, quality effort, and no failure? Because every student is given an opportunity to be more productive.

- Why is every student given an opportunity to be more productive? Because school should be designed to maximize learning on the part of every student in school.

- Why should school be designed to maximize learning on the part of every student? So that every student can become more than they ever hoped to be.

Use all that has been discussed, and assign a group of students to draft a vision statement. Discuss the draft version of the vision statement with the entire class and agree on a final version.

Create a Shared Values Statement

Now that the mission and vision statements have been completely spelled out, the next step involves preparing a shared values statement for students, teachers, and principals. Shared values statements in essence describe specific behaviors desired from students, teachers, and the principal. This can be carried out simply by having students brainstorm those beliefs they feel are important to ensure a smoothly operating TQ classroom.

The following stem statement is an example of one that can be used to generate acceptable behavior in a TQ classroom: How should students conduct themselves in a TQ classroom? This statement can also be used with minor revisions to generate acceptable beliefs for both teachers and the principal. (For more information about shared values, see chapter seven.)

Drive Out Fear in the Classroom

Discuss with students the term fear. Ask them to describe what happens to them emotionally when they are fearful. Tell of an incident when the teacher experienced fear either in school, at home, or in some other situation. Also discuss what he or she did to dissolve that fear. In an effort to reduce fear in the classroom, request students to generate a list of practices that produce fear. Depict these items by producing a Pareto chart. In addition, consider the following other activities to reduce fear in the classroom.

Request students to conduct a force field-analysis to identify the major forces to reduce fear in the classroom. Ask students to execute a cause-and-effect analysis to identify the major causes of fear in the classroom, and to perform another to eliminate those causes. Have students produce a list of activities through brainstorming to make learning fun and enjoyable.

Create Quality Awareness

Raise the quality awareness and personal concern of all students in the classroom by implementing the following activities:

- On the first day of the week, convene a meeting of all students and discuss where each individual and the class are in terms of quality.

- Use appropriate quality terminology throughout the school day everyday, and expect students to do the same.

- Prepare T-shirts with "quality" imprinted on them for students.
- Send quality progress reports home with students.
- Invite Malcolm Baldrige National Quality Award winners in to talk quality to students.
- Train parents to embrace quality philosophy, principles, and practices.
- Celebrate quality victories.
- Nurture a classroom environment whereby every student demonstrates a genuine concern for each other.
- Be on call for all students twenty-four hours a day.

Replace Competition With Cooperation

Schools are set up to be competitive for both teachers and students. Explain to students what competition produces. Indicate the following:

- A victim is required.
- Results will produce a winner and a loser.
- It places blame on others.
- Change is resisted.
- Self-esteem is affected.

Ask students to identify examples of competition, such as merit program for teachers; tracking of students; competing for grades; teacher evaluation; ranking of schools; and ranking of classes.

Inform students that when they compete, some fear is realized, even by those who are winners, because they are fearful of losing. Emphasize that everybody within a system is interrelated; what happens to one component has an effect on another. In fact, the Theory of Systems-Knowledge of the interrelationships between all the companies and the school people within that system-implies that in a win-lose situation, there are no winners. Everybody loses.

Cooperation should replace competition. TQ requires the formulation of teams to work on projects in which results are shared, and each team member's success is linked to another.

Cooperation is engaged when the following is instituted: peer tutoring; cooperative learning; articulation between junior and senior high school; mentioning (when an experimental teacher assists a new teacher needing assistance); learning groups; teacher-administrator planning; team teaching; and the network system.

Change Focus of the Grading System

Meet with parents to explain improved techniques of evaluating student learning and growth with less of an emphasis on traditional testing and grading and more on statistical evidence and authentic testing. Reach an agreement to either replace the traditional testing and grading with authentic testing and statistical evidence, or use both with the former on an experimental basis. Consider the following:

- Eliminate Fs and Ds.
- Eliminate all grades and establish a B for minimum quality acceptance.
- Agree on minimum standards such as eighty percent and increase that standard on an annual basis.
- Give students A-pluses for extra work.
- Solve a problem.
- Use a video portfolio.
- Evaluate work based on five indices, but without a failing index.
- Design a proposal and mock-up.
- Assemble a portfolio.

Organize to Attain Quality

Organize the classroom for quality by first organizing quality improvement teams of students and turning them loose on the classroom or school to locate and solve problems. Create cooperative learning teams to facilitate the learning process from time to time. Identify problems by creating and initiating a variety of ways to listen to the customers. Use the teacher as a facilitator, coach, problem solver, manager, mentor, or chief executive officer to arouse and maintain the quality interest of students.

Organize one or more quality improvement teams to work on either classroom or school problems. Require students to meet and manage their quality meetings similar to how quality improvement teams conduct their meetings. At times, the team may need the service of other students from within or without the school. In certain situations, an adult school person may need to be on the team. The teacher should serve as a facilitator.

Familiarize teams with the three different projects in which they will work on throughout the school year:

- Research project (to collect data)
- Problem-solving project (to arrive at a solution)
- Implementation project (to implement the solution to problems)

Require all teams to develop a set of rules or guidelines with associated consequences to monitor the rules that are broken in their teams. Instruct students to maintain a histogram with each infraction receiving a colored dot corresponding to the rule. The left axis should be labeled "number of broken rules," and the right axis should be labeled, "date."

Teach students how to use consensus to arrive at team decisions. Encourage teams to search for opportunities to initiate quality improvement, to innovate, and to grow. Encourage teams (as a group) to prepare a newsletter summarizing progress toward achieving either the mission or vision. Promote team learning. The teacher should choose one team member at random to demonstrate what he or she has learned. Advocate the team on that basis.

Assign complementary roles by requesting one team member to record items, another to encourage full participation, another to be a devil's advocate to challenge common views, and the fourth to observe and provide feedback to help the team reflect on how well it is operating.

Encourage the team to devise and publicize their own name and symbol. Encourage teams to unite with other teams to con-

Implementing Total Quality in the Classroom

tribute to each other's successes. Strengthen the teams' skills at evaluating alternatives by assessing each alternative on four criteria:

- The tangible gains and losses for the team or class.
- The tangible gains and losses for the customer.
- Intangible gains and losses in the self-approval of team members and other students.
- Intangible gains and losses in the self-approval of teachers, school administrators, and parents.

Require teams to develop a balance sheet. On one side of the balance sheet the team identifies the tangible gains and losses for the class and school, and on the other side, the intangible consequences. Then they, rate each item on a scale from one to ten, and from no importance to extreme importance, and then discuss them.

Train Teachers to Implement Total Quality

The effectiveness of the class and student as teams is predicated on how committed and fortified with knowledge and know-how the teachers are in implementing TQ in the classroom.

Teachers must be educated and trained in the following areas:

- History of quality;
- Drs. Deming, Juran, and Crosby and their quality principles;
- The System of Profound Knowledge;
- Shewhart/Deming Plan-Do-Check-Act cycle;
- Dr. Deming's Triangle of Interaction;
- Basis of quality improvement concepts;
- Scientific approach;
- Decision-making tools;
- Cooperative learning;
- Team-building skills;
- Consensus;

- Strategies for integrating course of study with quality concepts;
- Program strategies;
- Customers and providers interface; and
- Cooperative learning.

Encourage Students to Communicate With Teachers

From time to time, students will be faced with a number of obstacles that may prevent them from attaining quality. Initially, students should generate through brainstorming a list of obstacles that will hamper their attempts to achieve quality, and they should develop a strategy for preventing them. Periodically throughout the school year, the teacher should convene an obstacle meeting, and discuss with students those problems, either in schools or at home, that prevent them from producing quality. It may also be an excellent idea to establish a suggestion program in the classroom or school whereby students, parents, and teachers can contribute problems and ideas. Early in the school year, have them generate through brainstorming a list of obstacles that may hamper their attempts to achieve quality, and develop a strategy for removing these obstacles.

Report Classroom Quality Progress

Even though the teacher may be the only person implementing TQ in the school, he or she should make it a point to communicate TQ results either on an individual, classroom, or school level. This should not be an opportunity for the teacher to brag that his or her students are using statistics, but to engage school people in a conversation as to what their students did the previous year (before quality initiatives), and what is being accomplished this year. Perhaps the best way to approach this is to involve the principal and students in these exercises.

The following are a number of other activities to report student quality efforts:

- Invite Baldrige winners to the class and have the students show off their quality initiatives.

- Assist the class to produce a quality newsletter using the Shewhart/Deming cycle, and distribute it throughout the school district.
- Invite local newspapers to visit the classroom to report on the students' quality efforts.
- Schedule students to go to community groups to present their quality initiatives.

Recognize and Appreciate Students

Although Dr. Deming is not much for recognizing quality efforts, the other two gurus are. However, the recognition and reward programs in TQ in education must change to include the following:

1. Don't have anymore losers. The 1 to 2 percent who are winning and are recognized for their achievement in school in the traditional approach are abandoned for 100 percent winners in the TQ approach.
2. Establish a peer-to-peer award. This award is activated by a student when another student desires to recognize that peer with an award. A process is initiated by the teacher to enable the student to do so.
3. Create quality recognition activities. All members of quality teams are given T-shirts or sweaters with the imprint of "Unnatural Elementary School Quality Team." Food is served as a celebration event when some extraordinary feat of quality is performed.
4. Team efforts are recognized, as well as individual efforts.
5. Recognize and reward parents for their quality efforts also.
6. Give students an opportunity to attend board meetings to give a presentation on quality.
7. nvite teachers, students, and parents to attend presentations given by quality teams.
8. Give students certificates for completing training in quality.

9. Establish a quality recognition program whereby students are given quality booklets. Whenever a student produces something of quality, the teacher stamps the booklet. At the end of the term, students turn in their booklets and receive prizes for the number of stamps of quality they have received.
10. Take the class to a Baldrige National Quality Award-winning company and have the recipients "talk quality."

TQ is a continuous process. Get other teachers and students turned on to quality. Request to appear at a meeting of the board of education to get the members excited about quality. Further, locate a teacher to help him of her become a champion of quality. Finally, get parents involved in the quality movement. Give them T-shirts with the imprint "I am a quality mother/ father helping to produce a quality child. Join me."

The System of Profound Knowledge

In order to make the transformation to TQ in the classroom, both teachers and students must make the journey. Dr. Deming maintained that the journey must be guided by a System of Profound Knowledge, and that the teacher must become the leader. Everything accomplished by the teacher for students (classroom management, teaching strategies, curriculum, and instruction, etc.) is done with the notion that the primary purpose of TQ in the classroom is to educate students about the System of Profound Knowledge. The system has four interrelated parts or components: theory of systems, theory of variation, theory of knowledge, and theory of psychology.

Theory of Systems

The principal should explain the theory of systems to teachers so they are able to demonstrate to students the relationship between process and system. Indicate that a process is the grouping in sequence of the tasks required to produce something. Give a personal example, such as the number of tasks a student must accomplish when he or she arises in the morning to go to school. Ask them to identify some processes in school and at their homes.

Once teachers feel that students are aware of processes, introduce them to a system. Indicate to them that if a series of related

Implementing Total Quality in the Classroom

tasks can be called a process, then a group of interrelated processes can then be seen as a system. For example, a school system includes all the people in the school performing numerous tasks to educate students. Give students some examples of thought-provoking systems, and ask them to explain how the following are systems: a vacation, wildlife, and a book. Inform students that a system includes the following:

- It must have an aim or purpose.
- The aim must be clear to everyone in the system.
- All parts or components must be interconnected and interrelated.
- All parts or components cooperate rather than compete.

Tell the class that you are going to introduce them to a new word. Cite the syllables of the word optimization. See if any of the students can define the word. If not, define the word for them.

Optimization is defined as a process of orchestrating the efforts of all components toward the achievement of a single aim. Indicate to students that a system that is not optimized is at suboptimization level. To reinforce comprehension of the term, ask students questions such as the following:

- How is a system optimized?
- What can you do to optimize the education you are receiving?
- What are problems that can cause suboptimization of a system?
- Can a system be optimized if one component is not achieving its aim? Why?
- Why is competition harmful to a system?

Theory of Variation

The principal should introduce teachers to the Theory of Variation so that teachers are able to explain the concept of variation to students by explaining that everything—all systems, processes, people, performers, products, etc.—vary over time. Explain that whenever a problem occurs in a system, it is due to either a common or a special cause. A problem due to a large number of small sources of variation results in a large number of defects or mistakes due to common causes. The sum of these common causes determines the variation of the system, and therefore its limits and capabilities.

On the other hand, special causes of variation are not due to the system. They occur because of specific circumstances. For example, a delay in delivery of textbooks to the school may be a special cause of why a large number of students did not pass the course. Discuss the two types of mistakes people make when analyzing such variation, and explain the following:

People sometimes mistake the cause of variation as being special, when in fact the variation is caused by the system (common cause). People sometimes mistake the cause of variation as being common, when in fact it is special in nature, and should be analyzed further and eliminated.

Discuss with students the following questions on variation:

- What two steps can be taken when dealing with a stable system (common cause)?
- What steps should be taken to deal with special causes that are above control limits? Below control limits?
- Why is it important for students to comprehend the theory of variation?
- Is it fair to blame people for variations in the system? Why, or why not?
- Identify when you are confronted with a common or special cause of a system. What do you do about it?
- Request students to identify steps that can be taken to eliminate special causes that fall below the control limits. Explain that understanding the Theory of Variation is important, because most of our problems rest not in the people, but in the system in which the people are involved. Therefore, charting whether or not the problem is within or without the system is important in order to solve system problems.

Engage students in the following activities to reinforce their learning of variation in the system. Have students play jacks and record how many jacks a student catches every time he or she drops the ball while playing the game. Depict the vertical axis with a scale of 0 to 5 and the horizontal axis with a scale of 0 to 20. Have a student jump rope twenty separate times before missing a jump. In this case, the horizontal axis would be numbered 0 to 20 to indicate the number of repetitions.

Encourage students to determine what can be done to improve the process if the fault lies within the process or outside the process.

Theory of Knowledge

Indicate to students that according to Myron Tribus, a consultant on quality, quality education has four dimensions: knowledge, know-how, wisdom, and character. Explain that the first dimension of a quality education is knowledge that enables students to understand what they learn and how to relate it to other things that they learned.

Indicate that knowledge provides them with the ability to generalize from their experience.

The second dimension of a quality education is know-how. Know-how enables students to put to work the knowledge that they have learned. Although knowledge can be gained from many sources, such as reading, listening, and discussion, know-how can only be acquired through doing.

The third dimension of quality education is wisdom. This is the ability of students to understand what is important and what is not important. Indicate that wisdom enables students to establish priorities, and helps them to determine what is worthy of their focused attention.

The fourth dimension of quality education is character. Students should be taught to see character as a combination of knowledge, know-how, and wisdom, coupled with motivation. Ask students to relate the four dimensions of quality education to a process. Some examples of questions are as follows:

- Are the dimensions interrelated?
- What would happen if one component was missing?
- What is the product?
- What is the cumulative effect?
- Identify a special cause that could impact this process.

Theory of Psychology

Nevertheless, the principal may desire to reread some of his or her books on psychology before introducing this action to teachers. Explain the Theory of Psychology to students by indicating that in order to help them to understand themselves and people, they must appreciate how people differ and behave. They must understand that people learn differently and at different speeds, have similar and dissimilar likes and dislikes, and have different needs and expectations.

Some of the theories students should be introduced to are the theory of personal goal fulfillment, the theory of expectancy, the theory of human zones, and the theory of human addictions.

Inform students that all human beings fulfill their personal goals before fulfilling other people's goals. Ask them to explain this theory to you, and to cite when it occurred for them. Tell them that if they are not sensitive to the needs of others, and do not integrate their goals with those of others, people will think they are selfish.

Explain the theory of expectancy to students by asking them to define the term expectancy. Emphasize that if they want something bad enough, they will need to have high expectations for it. Indicate that "you get what you expect."

All human beings have three zones: the goal of acceptance; the goal of indifference; and the goal of rejection. Usually, to get people to accept anything, their zone of acceptance has to be increased, causing a corresponding decrease in the zone of rejection. To widen the zone of acceptance, other theories may need to be applied appropriately. For example, you may need to entice them with something they hold valuable to encourage them to widen their zone of acceptance.

All human beings are endowed with three basic addictions: security, sensation, and power. The security addiction is related to food, shelter, clothing, or whatever you equate with your personal security. The sensation addiction is concerned with finding happiness in school and in life by providing you with more and better measurable sensations and activities. The power addiction is concerned with dominating people and situations, and increasing your prestige, wealth, status, and pride, in addition to other subtle forms of manipulation and control.

Implementing Total Quality in the Classroom

When initiating change, all three addictions must be taken into consideration, particularly the security addiction. Thoroughly discuss these theories with students. Bring this discussion up to date from time to time. There are a number of theories of psychology that are appropriate for the teacher to discuss with students. These can be found in any book on psychology.

The Shewhart/Deming Plan-Do-Check-Act Cycle

Although this phase of the may sounds easy, many teachers have experienced problems when presenting this cycle to students. Teach students that the Shewhart/Deming Plan-Do-Check-Act Cycle or scientific planning model, as illustrated under Figure 17-1 and as described below.

Figure 17-1 Shewhart/Deming Cycle

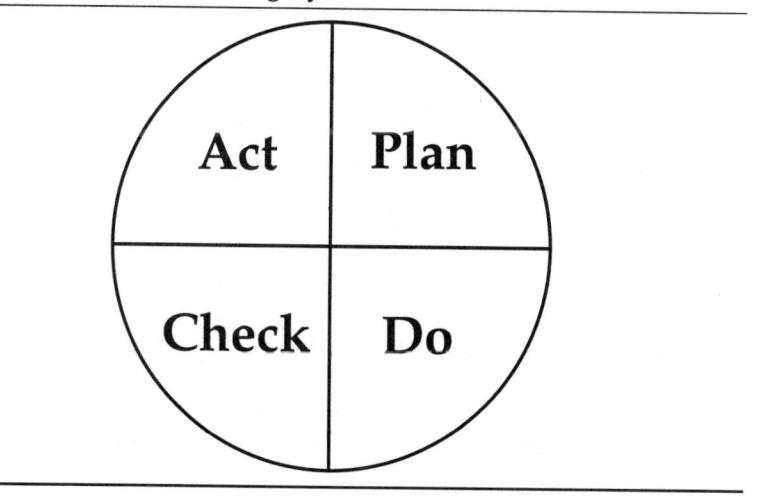

PLAN:

1. Identify the problem or opportunity for improvement; define it as a process to be improved (usually a single objective will suffice).

2. Find the possible reasons (causes of variation) for the problem or situation. Determine only major causes.

3. Analyze the major causes to determine the effect they have on the process in order to ascertain the major causes.

DO:

4. Take corrective action of the process by developing a well thought-out plan with clear objectives.

CHECK:

5. Evaluate the impact of the corrective action, and compare results to objectives. If improvement results, proceed with steps six and seven; if not, go back to step one, and continue the process.
6. Standardize; otherwise, go back to step two.

ACT:

7. Standardize the proposed change to prevent problems from recurring, and plan the next improvement initiative.

There are a variety of ways in which teachers can use the Shewhart/Deming cycle in the classroom. The following are a few examples:

- Request teams of students to interview either a teacher or principal to determine the most pressing problems confronting the school, and solve these.
- Ask students to request that their parents to give them a problem around the house that has not been solved, and solve it using the Shewhart/Deming cycle.
- Use appropriate course content, and request students to produce a product using the Shewhart/Deming cycle.
- Ask students to plan a vacation with their families using the Shewhart/Deming cycle.
- Request the class to use the Shewhart/Deming cycle to develop a school conference on TQ.
- Ask students to develop a plan for implementing TQ in the school using the Shewhart/Deming cycle. Show the plan to the principal and get his or her reaction. If approved, give the plan to teachers and students for their comments and suggestions. Create a flowchart for the plan.

Implementing Total Quality in the Classroom

- Request students to develop a comprehensive plan using the Shewhart/Deming cycle to research information on what parents' needs, requirements, and expectations are concerning the school.

Deming's Triangle of Interaction

Lastly, explain the Triangle of Interaction to teachers by requesting them to follow the same seven steps for students at the end of this section. Dr. Deming maintained that neither the creation nor the testing of a product and how it will perform or be accepted are sufficient to describe it as quality. He said that quality can only be measured by the interaction among these participants, as shown in Figure 17.2 and discussed below.

Figure 17-2 Dr. Deming's Triangle of Interaction

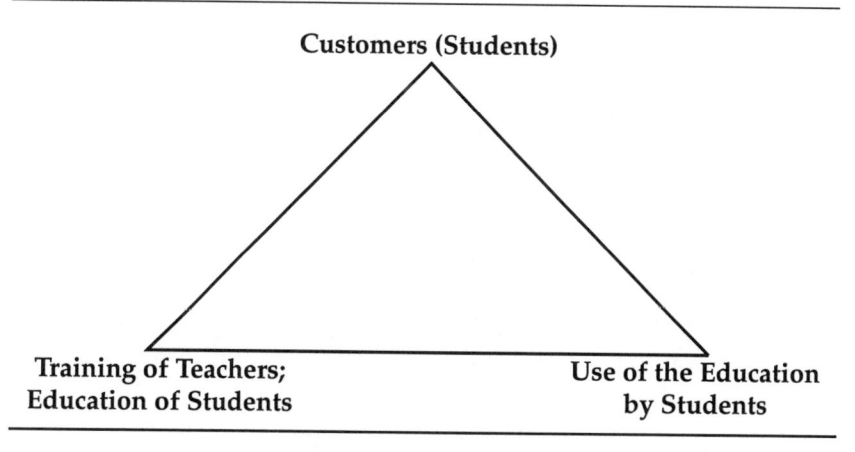

```
                  Customers (Students)
                         /\
                        /  \
                       /    \
                      /      \
                     /        \
                    /          \
                   /            \
                  /_____\
   Training of Teachers;        Use of the Education
   Education of Students              by Students
```

The top of the vertex of the triangle refers to the product; that is, the education received by the student, testing of the education in actual use, and steps taken by students to improve or enhance their education. The right vertex of the triangle refers not only to the way the student makes use of his or her education, but what he or she thinks about the education they have received. The left vertex of the triangle refers to the actual education received by students; additional education engaged in by students to enhance their knowledge; additional assistance given to students when they experienced difficulty in grasping topics; what subject matter is available to them; as well as the training received by teachers.

According to Dr. Deming, a student can receive the best education in the country, but if he or she uses that education for destructive means, then he or she has not received a quality education.

Explain Dr. Deming's Triangle of Interaction by doing the following seven steps:

1. Request students to arrive at a list of "bad" and "good" uses of the knowledge they gain from education.

2. Request students to generate a list of ways in which they can use their education now and in the future.

3. Have students use the nominal group process to silently generate a list to identify ways in which they can improve their education.

4. Ask students to see if there are ways in which they can "take care" of their learning.

5. Request students to suggest ways the teacher can continue his or her education, even though he or she has finished formal education.

6. Ask students to relate Dr. Deming's Triangle of Interaction to their experiences in the classroom.

7. Use Dr. Deming's interaction triangle to demonstrate how it can be put to use to operate the classroom as a small business.

Some Activities for Helping Teachers to Implement Total Quality in the Classroom

There are a countless number of activities that can be used to implement the principles and practices of TQ in the classroom, while at the same time making learning fun. The following are the three basic steps for accomplishing this feat:

1. Fortify the teacher with knowledge and experience in the various tools, such as brainstorming, fishbone diagram, force-field analysis, etc.

2. When the teacher feels comfortable with the knowledge and experience he or she has received in using the various tools

in TQ, they should look for opportunities to use the tools in the classroom to reinforce and make the learning process fun.
3. Require teachers to teach TQ tools to students, with or without integrating them into classroom work, starting with the easiest tool, such as brainstorming, and ending with the control chart.

The following are some activities that can be used to strengthen student use of TQ tools:

- Drive out fear in the classroom by having students brainstorm ideas, select the top six to nine, and develop an action plan or the Shewhart/Deming cycle to drive out the fearful activities.
- Determine why students are not doing homework in a timely manner by having them do a cause-and-effect analysis to determine the major causes, and eliminate these by performing the Shewhart/Deming cycle.
- Ask students to assess the teaching process using a control chart to ascertain why a large number of students are not passing a particular course or subject.
- Have students track student lateness to class using a run chart.
- Ask students to use force-field analysis to identify the main reasons why parents are not involved in their children's homework.
- Request students to use cause-and-effect analysis to determine the root causes for students who are experiencing difficulty passing a course.
- Give students experience in developing the Pareto chart by having them prioritize problems in the classroom or school
- Ask students to conduct an analysis to determine problems affecting the reputation of the school.
- Request students to measure the effect of a process change using a histogram.
- Ask students to determine the relationship between time spent on a task and student achievement. (Is there a rela-

tionship between the time students spend on learning and level of achievement?)

- Request the class to conduct the nominal group process to generate and prioritize a list of things that destroy quality.
- Have students collect information on problems, either in the classroom or school, and show them the many ways the information can be illustrated in charts and graphs.
- Ask students to develop a fishbone diagram to determine why there has been a loss of or increase in joy in learning.
- Request students to develop a flowchart regarding brushing their teeth.
- Ask each student to develop a flowchart on a process of their own choosing.
- Request students to develop a flowchart to conduct a quality improvement meeting.
- Ask mini-teams of students to use the nominal group process to develop a fishbone diagram to determine the cause of discipline problems in the school, without prior explanation of the nominal group process.
- Explain to students three behavioral lifestyles as they pertain to the classroom. Delineate win-win, win-lose, and lose-lose styles, and give some examples of these. Indicate that the orientation needed to make TQ work in a classroom is win-win. This means that everyone—individuals and the school system—benefit from advancing TQ. Stress that this means that all students in the class have a clear understanding of what they can do to support and contribute to nurturing not only their own success, but also that of the class and school.
- Ask students to create a master list of what win-win would mean to the class. Begin by asking the class to break down into small groups or teams and brainstorm: "What does win-win mean for our class in finding quality services and products?" Record responses on a flipchart sheet for all to see. The master list should contain from one to twenty-five key actions.

Implementing Total Quality in the Classroom

When the master list has been completed, the teacher should ask the class if they are really committed to this list, and if they will take every action listed to support the win-win requirements. Ask each student to sign his or her name on the master list, indicating support for building a TQ classroom through win-win requirements.

The class should schedule another meeting within sixty to ninety days to reinforce their commitment to win-win relationships. Situations or actions in which win-win is not working should be discussed and reworked.

Checklist For Making The Transition To Total Quality

Get teachers to use the following checklist to monitor their individual progress in implementing TQ in the classroom. The following activities have been designed to facilitate the implementation of TQ in the classroom:

1. Review the principles of quality of the three gurus and select those that you think are appropriate for the classroom.

2. Draw an illustration of the System of Profound Knowledge and post it in classrooms. Request that teachers refer to this illustration throughout the school year and incorporate it into coursework.

3. Illustrate the Shewhart/Deming cycle, and fortify all students with the procedure. Make certain the cycle is used by teachers and students.

4. Generate a code of behavior for principals, teachers, and students, and have the parties sign it.

5. Request teachers to discuss at length the participants in the Triangle of Interaction.

6. Have teachers meet as a group and develop appropriate TQ activities to incorporate in the classroom.

REVIEW

Key points to remember:

The steps for implementing TQ in classrooms consists of the following:

1. Select appropriate TQ principles
2. Prepare a mission statement
3. Create a vision statement
4. Create a shared values statement
5. Drive out fear in the classroom
6. Create quality awareness
7. Replace competition with cooperation
8. Change focus of the grading system
9. Organize to attain quality
10. Train teachers to implement TQ
11. Encourage students to communicate with teachers
12. Report classroom quality progress
13. Recognize appropriate students

The System of Profound Knowledge has four interrelated components: Theory of Systems, Theory of Variation, Theory of Knowledge, and Theory of Psychology.

The Shewhart/Deming Plan-Do-Check-Act Cycle is a scientific planning model.

Dr. Deming's Triangle of Interaction maintains that quality can only be measured by the interaction of students and teachers.

Some activities for implementing TQ in the classroom are as follows:
1. Fortify teachers with knowledge and experience in various TQ efforts.
2. Request teachers for opportunities for opportunities to use TQ tools.
3. Teach TQ tools to students.

Application

Convene a team of teachers to examine the list of TQ principles that the three gurus have identified. Request the team to select those principles that they think are appropriate for classroom use. Use the checklist in this chapter and compare the lists. Mutually agree on a list to be used in your school.

CHAPTER 18

Implementing Outcomes-Based Education

LEARNING OBJECTIVES

After reading and comprehending this chapter you should be able to:

- Define outcomes-based education.
- Identify some assumptions of outcomes-based education.
- Cite essential tenets of outcomes-based education.
- Identify difference between traditional and transformational education.
- Explain the procedural steps for installing outcomes-based education.
- Discuss problems related to outcomes-based education.

What Every Principal Should Know About Outcomes-Based Education

Outcomes-based education is perhaps the most revolutionary and powerful classroom program ever conceived to transform not only the school, but the individual classes. If you don't believe me, go to the Johnson City Central School District in Johnson City, New York, for yourself. Teachers are actually teaching and students are learning much more then they did in yesteryears. Even if you as a principal are not interested in installing an outcomes-based education program today, you will later so prepare yourself today to gain everything you can about the process. Also, strive to achieve greatness in your school through the transformational process by amalgamizing outcomes-based education and total quality education to maximize the education process and make learning fun and enjoyable for students.

Defining Outcomes-Based Education

Outcomes-based education is a student-focused, results-oriented educational process based on the belief that all students can learn. In most traditional schools, it is assumed that students have been educated when they have taken the prescribed subjects and spend a specified period of time in the classroom. Outcomes-based education is a process of transforming the school's curriculum and introducing programs to determine the skills, knowledge, and ways of thinking that students need to function in the world. As a result of this transformation, specific and desired outcomes are identified and students work on realizing these outcomes at a certain level of performance. More specifically, outcomes-based education is:

- The success of every student as a learner is of primary importance.
- Continuous improvement is a common thread that is woven through the education program.
- A philosophy that focuses on education and assessment based on the needs of each student.
- The basic strategy associated with outcomes-based education implies that:
- What a student learns is already identified.
- Each student's progress in school is based on demonstrated achievement.
- Each student's needs are accommodated through multiple instructional strategies and assessment tools.
- Each student is provided with sufficient time and support to realize his or her potential.

The Essential Tenets of Outcomes-Based Education

Outcomes-based education is based on the premise that all students can and must be successful learners. It mandates that there is no limitation to human potential if all stakeholders participate in this instructional process. To ensure success for all students, the following tenants provide a process for meeting the needs of all students.

What is expected of the student must be clearly identified. As a result, outcomes must be: future-oriented; student-centered; publicity defined; focused in lifetime skills; based on high expectations; and based on sources from which all other educational decisions flow.

Learning is:

- Monitored carefully toward attainment of outcomes.
- Characterized by each student's needs, interests, and developmental level.
- Activity and reality-based for maximum application of knowledge, skills, and orientation required for the student to realize success.

Each student's education plan is geared to his or her demonstrated achievement and progress.

- Focus is on attainment of outcomes and the application of learning rather than on covering materials.
- Examination of the learning process is appropriate to the realities of the student.
- Movement to the next learning is based on achievement, rather than time.
- Achievement is demonstrated by the student and recorded based on criteria reference tests, rather than a standardized norm reference instrument.
- Students move to the next level because they have demonstrated an acceptable level achievement geared to future success in life.

Each student's needs are accommodated through multiple assessment strategies.

- Instrumental deliveries are based on each students' needs, desires, interests and readiness for learning.
- Instruction design is based on continuous progress and assessment that is focused on students' needs.
- Teachers improve the learning process through instruction and coaching based on theory, research, interest, and analysis.
- Assessments are used to substantiate learning and provide the basis for additional learning decisions.
- Students eventually become more adept at designing their own learning options and assessments.

Each student is provided ample time and assistance to reach their own potential. All students strive to become more responsible for their own learning, advised in making appropriate learning decisions, independent in learning and thinking, and self-assessing.

Time is used as a variable based on the needs of students. It is also managed more effectively by students and teachers to achieve increasing levels of accomplishments.

Assistance is sought from all school people to maximize the learning process. It is devoted to all types of assistance as used by both traditional and nontraditional schools.

The chart below explains the variations between traditional and transformational education.

Traditional Education	Transformational Education
1. Fosters permanent failure	1. If students performance does not reach an acceptable level, he or she is given several opportunities to do so.
2. Standards of performance are compromised.	2. Students are expected to complete one standard before proceeding to the next one.

Traditional Education	Transformational Education
3. Rote learning is prevalent; absorption of facts and learning to receive knowledge.	3. Students are taught to appreciate and deal with real-life situations that they will encounter later in life.
4. Tracking is practiced.	4. Tracking is eliminated because all students are required to achieve the same outcomes, although at different times.
5. Limited time to achieve.	5. Multiple time to achieve.
6. Simple assessment instrument to test proficiency.	6. Multiple assessment tools to evaluate achievement.

Outcomes-Based Education Installation

Dr. William Glasser, author of *Quality School* indicated that the Johnson City Central Schools are probably the best model in the United States of what could be called quality schools. Since the Johnson City Central School District received a grant from the Federal Department of Education to develop a booklet on procedures, it was used to describe how their outcomes-based education program was developed. It is an excellent opportunity for a principal to use success emulation to copy the procedure Johnson City Central School District used to reflect its program. In addition, this same district has organized teams of trainers from its district to assist other schools to implement outcomes-based education. In fact, numerous districts have already used the expertise of the Johnson City Central staff. Please contact the district for more information.

The following is an account of how the Johnson City School district implemented its outcomes-based education program and is contained in a book entitled *The Outcomes-Driven Developmental Model*.

Johnson City School Model

Step 1: Review Its Uniqueness or Characteristics and Arrive at Your Own. Outcomes-based education is different from all other school improvement programs because it is:

- *Holistic and Comprehensive*
  It addresses all facets of school operation from instruction to leadership.

- *Systematic*
  It uses logical and systematic methods for achieving its objectives.

- *Research-based*
  It operates on the premise that all decisions should be based on the research literature.

- *Practical*
  It always takes into account the realities and needs of schools and people as it translates research into practice.

- *Integrative*
  It draws upon research and knowledge from all relevant disciplines and fields of knowledge.

- *A decision-making process*
  It is a process for making daily and long-term decision about school operations.

- *Realistic*
  It is always mindful of the realities of personal and organizational change and improvement.

- *Empowering, participatory, and noncoercive*
  It provides participatory, rather than coercive ways of working with people and students.

- *Long-term oriented*
  It assumes that significant and enduring change must avoid the "quick-fix" mentality.

- *Operational*
  It emphasizes what to do and how to do it, and it avoids "get tough" solutions that rely on dictates and mandates.

Implementing Outcomes-Based Education

- *Constantly Renewing*
  It includes many mechanisms to ensure ongoing individual and school examination and renewal.

- *Culture changing*
  It provides the means to change the entire culture of a school so that objectives can be more effectively achieved.

- *Sensitive to affective needs*
  It creates the conditions that enable all school people and students to meet their social and emotional needs.

- *A practitioner-to-practitioner model*
  Teachers and administrators train their counterparts in schools that adopt outcomes-based education. We do what we train others in - everyday.

- *Ongoing in assistance*
  Training always extends through at least two or three years and contact is normally maintained far beyond that time.

- *Respectful of what already exists*
  It builds upon the positive things that already exist in a school and provides a tailored process that helps each school achieve its goals in its own way.

- *Control theory-oriented*
  It provides a theory of human needs and behavior that is highly predictable, prescriptive, and realistic.

Step 2: Address Their Success Connections. Outcomes-based education is essentially a process, rather than a program, for increasing the capacity of a school or entire district to achieve its goals more fully. Training should help schools to identify the critical questions that must be addressed regarding school improvement and to arrive at responses to these questions that are extensive in scope, mutually compatible, and grounded in the research literature. The following four questions are addressed:

1. What do we want?
2. What do we know?
3. What do we believe?
4. What do we do?

When you are clear and consistent in your responses to these four "success connection" questions, you will find that your goals, knowledge, beliefs, and actions produce a synergy that empowers everyone in your school.

Through outcomes-based education training, schools or entire districts are helped to arrive at consistent responses to the success connection questions. This consistency guides the daily decision-making of everyone involved in outcomes-based education. Both teachers and administrators must ask themselves questions such as, "Is what I'm doing based on valid knowledge and is it going to help me get what I want?" and "Are my beliefs helping or hindering me in achieving what I want?" These are where wants, beliefs, knowledge, and actions come together paves to the ways for success and excellence.

Dr. Glasser's work in control theory demonstrates quite clearly that all people have needs for connectedness (love and belonging), power, freedom, fun, and survival. Connectedness is the need to have a sense of belonging to those people, places, and things that are important to the individual. Power is the feeling that you are the primary cause of what happens in your life. Freedom is the opportunity to make decisions from an array of alternatives, and fun refers to the need for enjoyment, recreation and newness in your life.

A school's pursuit of its goals must also help school people to meet their basic human needs so that both the school and the people in it can pursue their goals in a mutually reinforcing fashion. Outcomes-based education is a process for increasing the probability that such a blending of individual and school needs will occur.

Consider the following question. When outcomes-based education and the success connections are in place, who can influence the school's responses to the four previous questions? The answer is anyone at anytime. A leader, according to outcomes-based education, is someone who influences what the school wants, knows, believes, and does. Outcomes-based education provides the framework that empowers anyone to exert such influence and function as a leader. In outcomes-based education, positional power counts for much less than the power that comes from knowledge and the ability to respond effectively to the four questions.

Step 3: Study Their Model of Outcomes-Based Education Components But Describe and Produce Your Own. The mission of outcomes-based education asserts that all students can and will learn well. Through examination and discussion of the research literature the Johnson City staff arrived at a consensus about its mission and the five *student exit behaviors*. This process helped the staff achieve clarity about what kind of student they wanted to produce.

No decision or action is taken without validation by appropriate research literature. An outcomes-based educator is a professional who makes his or her decisions in accordance with the best research literature. This mode of operation has unfortunately not been the norm in education. When research is referred to it must be effectively translated into practice. Any effective school, therefore, requires a transformational principal - one who can create a compelling vision of what can and should be and who can empower and enable others to realize the vision. These leaders help others discover and develop their unique potential to serve the mission of the school as well as themselves.

Outcomes-based education also requires a school to get very clear on what it believes about a wide range of factors related to academic excellence. These beliefs constitute the philosophical base. Specific beliefs about learning rates and styles are developed. The research stated that the probability of high achievement is greatly increased if students have the prerequisites for a given set of objectives. The important of ensuring, rather than guessing or assuming, that students have the prerequisites became, therefore, a guiding belief about good instruction. Emphasis should be on the perception, rather than remediation, or learning errors. These and many other beliefs, which are rooted in the research literature, provide a living belief system for outcomes-based education.

The psychological base provides a knowledge base and viable set of beliefs about human behavior. Why do human beings do what they do? How do they learn? What psychological needs do they have? What motivated them? How can they be helped to become more effective learners and people in general? What conditions do they need to make progress in all areas of human endeavors? A sound psychological base of knowledge and beliefs enables a school to deal with these questions.

Six administrative supports ensure effective management of the entire process of school improvement. A *Staff Development Model* provides a vehicle for continuously renewing the staff. Regardless of what is being learned, the staff proceeds through four sequential stages of development: basic knowledge, comprehension, application, and creativity. Since change is contact, the entire administrative team must understand how people and schools change and execute a change process for bringing about effective change. Problems constantly arise; therefore, a *Problem-Solving Model* ensures that problems are readily identified and resolved. Students and staff pursue their goals more effectively in a good climate; therefore, outcomes-based education includes a model for monitoring and improving the climate.

Outcomes-based education also includes a *Management Model* which ensures that adopters develop and implement management practices that are based on the best management research and literature. Finally, all the administrative support would be relatively ineffective without a communications network that involves all staff in the flow of information, ideas, and in decision making. In outcomes-based education, expertise rather than position yields the greatest power to influence the program . The communication network tapes the expertise of all school people and creates a genuine sense of ownership and participation. The network empowers them.

Outcomes-based education requires the nurturing of community support. The superintendent sets policy to achieve the mission and it serves a vital role in helping the community to remain committed to the program. To fulfill its function, the superintendent must establish a clear board policy (a statement regarding courses of action) and provide superintendent support (the deeds or actions that support the courses of action) in many and varied ways. The superintendent, in collaboration with teachers and administrators, must have a plan to nurture public support. One of outcomes-based education's strengths is that it systematically draws upon the resources of other schools and educators across the nation that are also intent upon outcomes-based change. These resources and colleges constitute a process of networking. All of the community support helps to build the trust level in the school and this trust becomes the foundation for further progress.

Implementing Outcomes-Based Education 307

The classroom support directly serves instruction. The research on learning leads to specifications for instructional and curriculum processes and school and classroom practices. These instructional and curriculum specifications guide the staff and administrators in implementing what they know about the art and science of teaching and it results in a basic instruction procedure that is used by all. This procedure specifies how teachers should proceed with planning and instruction to maximize student achievement. School structures provide the rationale for different students grouping practices within and across grades.

Mission: All Students Will Learn Well

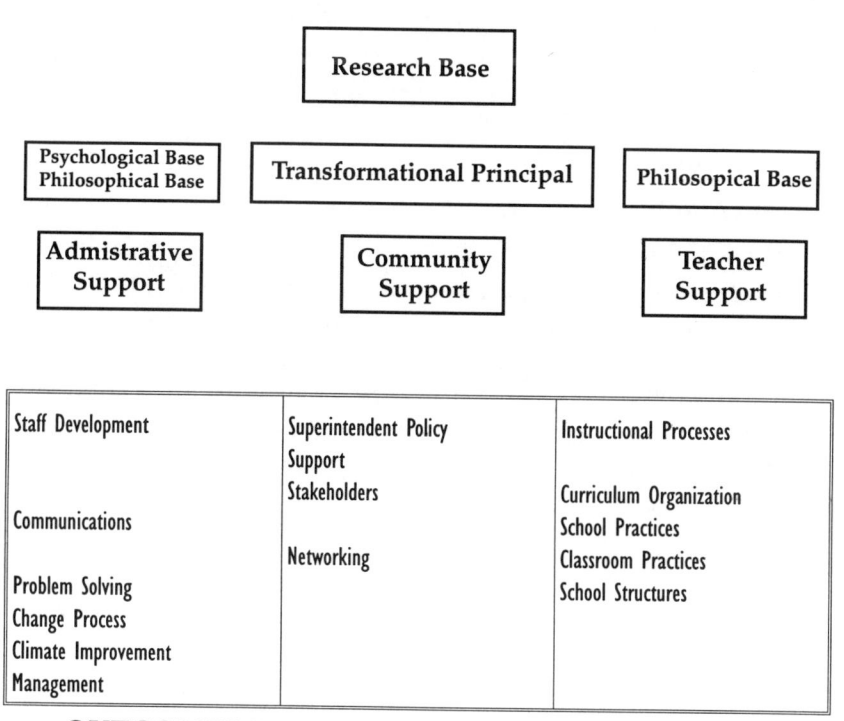

	Research Base	
Psychological Base / Philosophical Base	Transformational Principal	Philosopical Base
Admistrative Support	Community Support	Teacher Support

Staff Development	Superintendent Policy Support	Instructional Processes
	Stakeholders	Curriculum Organization
Communications		School Practices
	Networking	Classroom Practices
Problem Solving		School Structures
Change Process		
Climate Improvement		
Management		

OUTCOMES-DRIVEN DEVELOPMENTAL MODEL

DESIRED STUDENT EXIT BEHAVIORS

1. Self-esteem as learner and person.
2. Cognitive levels low to high.
3. Self-directed learner.
4. Concern for others.
5. Process Skills: problem solving, communication, decision making, accountability, and group process..

A driven developement model is the basic requirement for each of the components described below.

General Components

1. *Research Literature*: Agree to make all decisions in accordance with the best research literature. Establish and maintain a significant and continuing involvement with the research literature.

2. *Mission:* Arrive at a simple, clear, and brief statement of its mission. They must ensure that all members of the school community, including students and parents, understand the mission and agree with it.

3. *Students' Outcomes:* Identify the outcomes or exit behaviors it wants for each and every student. The statement must be detailed enough so that the behaviors are clear. The exit behaviors or outcomes must also serve as a guide for all members of the school community when they make decisions that affect these outcomes. The statement must be published, understood, and endorsed by all.

4. *Philosophical Base:* Arrive at a set of philosophical principles that will guide all actions and decisions. This philosophical base must be published and endorsed by nearly all members of the school. It will, of course, be arrived at through discussion, deliberation, and participation by all members of the school community. All can influence this base, but those opinions that have validity in the research literature will wield the greatest weight.

5.

Implementing Outcomes-Based Education

Psychological Base: Arrive at an understanding of human behavior and needs. This understanding will be published and adhered to by all members of the school community.

6. *Transformational Principal:* All administrators must receive training in transformational leadership, understand its concepts, and engage in specific leadership behaviors.

Administrative Supports

1. *Staff Development Model:* Develop and implement a systematic staff development model that incorporates training and change processes and a plan for program diffusion.

2. *Communications Network:* Establish a communications network that promotes the flow of information and ideas throughout the school community and into the community.

3. *Problem-Solving Process:* Adopt a problem-solving process that is understood and endorsed by all. All members of the school community must know how to use and participate in the problem-solving process.

4. *Change Process:* Know how to proceed with effective change.

5. *Climate Improvement Model:* Arrive at a model for climate improvement that deals with the critical climate factors.

6. *Management Model:* Develop a management model that satisfies the requirements of modern management practices and the psychology of human needs and behavior.

Classroom Supports

1. *Instructional Process:* Arrive at an instructional process that incorporates the essential elements of good teaching and learning. The process will be used by all teachers and administrators.

2. *Curriculum Organization:* Organize their curriculum in a manner that supports the instructional process.

3. *School Practices:* Arrive at an agreement regarding three critical school practices: the certification of students learning, the use of time, and the assignment of students to groups.
4. *Classroom Practices:* Arrive at a set of regulation for ten critical classroom practices: testing, retesting, homework, incompletes, discipline, correctives, attendance, review, and enrichment. These practices will be arrived at, endorsed, and practiced by all members of the school community.
5. *School Structures:* Receive information on various approaches to grouping students.

Community Supports

1. *Superintendent Supports:* The superintendent must arrive at a concise statement of policy that guides the actions of all members of the school community. The statement of policy will insist that all decisions be made in accordance with the best research literature.

   For outcomes-based education to be successful, the superintendent must provide support in many and varied ways. He or she must, for example, be fully informed about outcomes-based education, their mission statement, the student outcomes, and the philosophical base. He or she does not have to be an expert, but should know enough to ask the right questions and to understand the responses. The superintendent must engage in actions that support their policy.

2. *Stakeholders:* All school people must receive training on how to establish and maintain the support of the various elements of the public. The public consists of many elements and the support of each must be cultivated.

3. *Networking:* Receive training in how to engage in effective networking that consists of maintaining contact with other outcomes-based management uses and the research literature.

Implementing Outcomes-Based Education

The Adoption Procedure

The following Adoption procedure is the one implemented by the Johnson City School District and is the implementation process it uses for disticts interested in adopting their model.

Phase I: The Design Team

Objective 1: Establish a Design Team

If, after an awareness experience, your school is still interested in outcomes-based education, it should establish a design team consisting of

1. The principal of the building involved.

2. A central office instructional leader.

3. A minimum of three teachers from each grade or department involved.

4. If a middle school is involved, the instructional leaders from each major discipline.

5. More participants are desirable on the design team.

Objective 2:

The design team will prepare for a one-day visit to Johnson City School District. The preparative will consist of examining literature and reading about outcomes-based education.

Objective 3:

The design team should visit Johnson City School District for one day to become familiar with outcomes-based education requirements. The visit will enable the design team to talk with teachers, administrators, students, and possibly parents. It serves mainly as an opportunity to see how the program really works on a daily basis.

Phase II: The Design Team Completes Its Tasks

During this phase, the design team will make the final decision on proceeding with outcomes-based education based on observation and research. A "go" decision will commit them to one year of training.

Phase III: Entry Training

The design team will begin its training by receiving two days of training in the leadership and management of school improvement.

Phase IV: Basic Training

The design team and as many teachers and administrators will achieve a fundamental understanding of selected outcomes-based education components. Administrators will build their leadership and management skills and knowledge. Teachers will specialize in improving their skills and knowledge regarding the five classroom supports.

Phase V: First-Year Implementation

All trainees will continue to implement what they have learned with on-site technical assistance, monitoring, and evaluation.

Phase VI: Intermediate Training

All trainees will receive the highest level of training regarding all outcomes-based education.

Phase VII: Advanced Training

All outcomes-based trainees will receive the highest level of training regarding all outcomes-based education components.

Phase VIII: Second-Year Implementation and Diffusion

In this phase, the outcomes-based trainees will achieve self-direction in the operation of outcomes-based education, diffuse outcomes-based education throughout their school, and develop a plan for future action.

Outline of the Outcome-Based Education Training Plan

Prepatory Stage

Phase I: The Design Team

    Objective 1: Establish a design team.

    Objective 2: Prepare for a one-day visit to Johnson City School District.

    Objective 3: Visit Johnson City School District.

Phase II: The Design Team Completes Its Tasks

    Objective 1: Design team completes its task.

    Objective 2: Make a go/no-go decision.

    Objective 3: Negotiates an adoption agreement.

Phase III: Entry Training (2 Days)

Implementing Outcomes-Based Education

Objective 1: Design team prepares for entry training by expanding its knowledge base.

Objective 2: Design team develops a detailed action plan for the implementation of outcomes-based education.

Implementation Stage

Phase IV: Basic Training

Design team, principal and teachers achieve a fundamental understanding of selected outcomes-based education components.

Phase V: First-Year Implementation

Design team implements on-site technical assistance, monitoring, and evaluation.

Phase VI: Intermediate Training

Design team, principal, and teachers achieve a higher level of understanding of selected outcomes-based education components.

Self-Direction Stage

Phase VII: Advanced Training

Design team, principal, and teachers achieve the highest level of understanding of all outcomes-based education components

Phase VIII: Second-Year Implementation and Diffusion (five days during second academic year)

Design teams diffuse outcomes-based education training throughout the school, achieves self-direction in school improvement and develops a plan for future action.

Step 4: Agree to Adopt Their Key Component and Add Others to Meet Your Own School Needs.

Step 5: Review Their Adaptation Procedure, But Develop Your Own.

Step 6: Consider Their Training and Developing Program. However, arrive at your own to meet the needs of your teachers.

Step 7: **Study Their Instructional Process Model and Devise a Better One for Your School.** Prior to effecting changes in the Johnson City School District's model, learn to effect their model—and then engage the entire school in arriving at a consensus in terms of what changes should be made in the model to accommodate your school needs.

How to Deal With Critics of Outcomes-Based Education

Outcomes-based education, similar to most transformational processes, is not without its enemies. Disgruntled stakeholders have been vivacious in blaming the current ills in public education, such as increasing school crimes, offensive text books, increasing taxes, etc. In addition, these negative parents and community members tend to blame all the ills of the school on reforms, regardless of any success received or traditional education. One source cites the following objections to outcomes-based education:

- Outcomes-Based education is essentially a more advanced version of professor Benjamin Bloom's Mastery Learning, which is pure Skinnerian, behaviorist, stimulus-response conditioning and indoctrination.

- The American Association for Supervision and Curriculum Development (ASCD), which publishes *Educational Leadership*, a major promoter of OBE, is a spin-off of the left wing National Education Association.

- Rather than being taught facts, information, concepts, and essential skills in reading, writing, and arithmetic, children are engaged in supposed "higher order thinking skills," ignoring the self-evident truth that it is impossible to employ "higher order thinking" without a base of factual knowledge.

- The curriculum is tilted heavily to the affective domain in order to manipulate and change feelings, attitudes, and values.

- Behavioral objectives are loaded with vague terms geared toward "politically correct" outcomes.

Implementing Outcomes-Based Education 315

- Cooperative learning is stressed by organizing virtually all learning activities into group activities.
- Parents are required to take "effective parenting" classes.
- In high schools, the "Carnegie Units" required for graduation are abandoned . . . and students are required to demonstrate ambiguous and subjective "learning outcomes" that cannot be objectively measured.
- Training for "global citizenship" is established as the primary purpose of all education.

To prepare for critics who oppose the transformation and to get them on your side, you should do the following:

1. Identify all stakeholders, those who oppose the transformation to outcomes-based education and those who don't.
2. Make an analysis as to what their attitudes and expectations are and try to accommodate them.
3. Get the most vicious one to become a mentor on the design team to plan and implement the transformation.
4. Keep all stakeholders informed of the transformation.
5. Go throughout the community and discuss the results of outcomes-based education.
6. Take stakeholders to other outcomes-based education schools and have them discuss their models.
7. Learn from the experiences of other schools.
8. Retain an expert in outcomes-based education and have him or her to assist you with disenchanted parents.
9. If all else fails, reduce the pace that you are using to implement outcomes-based education.

Review

Key points to remember:

Outcomes-based education is a transformational process that is students-focused, results-oriented, all based on the belief that all students can learn.

The procedural steps for implementing outcomes-based education consists of the following steps:

1. Review process uniqueness and create your own.
2. Assess the process success connection and develop your own.
3. Study the process model and develop your own.
4. Agree to adopt the process key components and add others to meet your own needs.
5. Review the process adaptation procedure, but develop your own.
6. Study the instructional process model and devise a better one for your school.
7. Consider their training and developing program, but arrive at your own.

Application

Based on the chapter entitled, "Implementing Success Emulation," use the guidelines to establish an outcomes-based education in your school. Make certain that a communication plan is included in your program, such as that denoted in chapter fifteen, entitled "Implementing Total Quality in Schools" and the stakeholder analysis in volume Two, chapter Nineteen, entitled, "Preparing School Improvement Plans."

REFERENCES

Chapter One: Understanding the Requirements for Transformational Leadership

Lewis, James, Jr., *Re-creating Our Schools for the 21st Century - Managing American Schools with Distinction* (Westbury, NY: J.L. Wilkerson Publishing Company, Ltd., 1987, pp. 160-178.

Chapter Two: Changing the Role of the Principal to Effect The Transformation

Lewis, James, Jr., *Re-creating Our Schools for the 21st Century - Managing American Schools with Distinction* (Westbury, NY: J.L. Wilkerson Publishing Company, Ltd., 1987, pp. 160-178).

Chapter Three: Identifying Change Management Skills to Transform Schools

Zaltman, Gerald, David Florio, and Linda Sikorski, *Dynamic Educational Change, Models, Strategies, Tactics, and Management* (New York, NY: The Free Press, 1977, pp.51-90; pp. 91-121).

Murray M. Dalzeil, et. al., *Changing Ways—A Practical Tool for Implementing Change Within Organizations* (New York, NY: Amacom, pp. 25-40, 133-148, 151-158.

Chapter Four: Understanding the New Role of Principal as Social Architect

Lewis, James, Jr., *Recreating Our Schools for the 21st Century* (Westbury, NY: J.L. Wilkerson Publishing Company, Ltd., 1989, pp. 142-159)

Chapter Five: Developing the School Mission

Lewis, James, Jr., *Implementing School-Based Management...by Empowering Teachers* (Westbury, NY: J.L Wilkerson Publishing Company, Ltd., 1989, pp. 41-49).

Chapter Six: Creating a School Vision

Block, Peter, *The Empowered Manager* (San Francisco, CA: Jossey-Bass, 1988, pp. 99-129).

Lewis, James, Jr., *Creating Excellence in Our Schools...by Taking Lessons From America's Best-Run Companies* (Westbury, NY: J.L. Wilkerson Publishing Company, Ltd., 1986, pp. 163-174).

Chapter Seven: Identifying the Shared Values of the School

Lewis, James, Jr., *Implementing School-Based Management...by Empowering Teachers* (Westbury, NY: J.L Wilkerson Publishing Company, Ltd., 1989, pp. 41-49).

Chapter Eight: *Building a Strong and Healthy School Culture*

Lewis, James, Jr., *Excellent Organizations* (Westbury, NY: J.L. Wilkerson Publishing Company, 1989, pp. 119-140).

Lewis, James, Jr., *Achieving Excellence in Our Schools...by Taking Lessons from America's Best-Run Companies*, (Westbury, NY: J.L Wilkerson Publishing Company, Ltd., 1989, pp. 31-45).

Chapter Nine: Empowering Teachers in Schools

Lewis, James, Jr., *Re-creating Our Schools for the 21st Century - Managing American Schools with Distinction* (Westbury, NY: J.L. Wilkerson Publishing Company, Ltd., 1987, pp. 58-84)

Vogt, Judith, F., *Empowerment in Organizations - How to Spark Exceptional Performance* (San Diego, CA: University Associates, 1990, pp. 1-156).

Chapter Ten: *Managing by Walking Around*

Lewis, James, Jr., *Creating Excellence in Our Schools...by Taking Lessons From America's Best-Run Companies* (Westbury, NY: J.L. Wilkerson Publishing Company, Ltd., 1986, pp. 163-174).

Chapter Eleven: Practicing Egalitarianism in the Schools

Lewis, James, Jr., *Re-creating Our Schools for the 21st Century - Managing American Schools with Distinction* (Westbury, NY: J.L. Wilkerson Publishing Company, Ltd., 1987, pp. 128-141)

Chapter Twelve: Arriving at a Consensus

Avery, Michael, Brian Auvine, Barbara Streibel, and Lonnie Weiss, *Building United Judgment: A Handbook for Consensus Decision Making*. (Madison, Wisconsin: The Center for Conflict Resolution, 1981).

Bartov, Glen, *Decision by Consensus* (Chicago: Progressive Publisher, 1978).

Chapter Thirteen: Transforming Schools Through Success Emulation

Camp, C. Robert, *Benchmarking the Search for Industry Practices That Lead to Superior Performance* (Milwaukee, Wisconsin: Quality Press, 1989, pp. 1-236).

Detoro, Irving, J., *Strategic Panning for Quality at Xerox* (Quality Progress No. 4, 1987, 16-20).

Chapter Fourteen: Transforming Schools Through Participative Management

Lewis, James, Jr., *Re-creating Our Schools for the 21st Century - Managing American Schools with Distinction* (Westbury, NY: J.L. Wilkerson Publishing Company, Ltd., 1987, pp. 37-57).

Chapter Fifteen: Implementing Total Quality in Schools

Lewis, James, Jr., *Implementing Total Quality in Education to Produce Great Schools, Transforming the American School System* (Westbury, NY: The National Center to Save Our Schools, 1993, pp. 63-102).

Chapter Sixteen: Installing School-Based Management

Lewis, James, Jr., *Implementing School-Based Management...by Empowering Teachers* (Westbury, NY: J.L. Wilkerson Publishing Company, 1989, pp. 1-301).

Chapter Seventeen: Inculcating Total Quality in the Classroom

Lewis, James, Jr., *Implementing Total Quality in Education to Produce Great Schools, Transforming the American School System* (Westbury, NY: The National Center to Save Our Schools, 1993, pp. 229-254).

Chapter Eighteen: Implementing Outcomes-Based Education

Mamary, Albert, "14 Principals of Outcomes-Based Education," *Principal*, Vol. 73 #3, January, 1994.

O'Neil, John, "Aiming for New Outcomes: The Promise and the Reality," *Educational Leadership*, March, 1994.

Boschee, Floyd, et. al., "OBE: Some Answers for the Uninitiated," ER, Vol. 67, No. 4.

Johnson City School District Materials were used to enable districts to emulate the process with or without the assistance of Johnson City staff.

Other References

I wish to acknowledge the many authors and agencies whose materials I referred to help illustrate the thoughts, ideas and research contained in the volume. Without their assistance, I could not have undertaken this project. The authors and agencies are listed in alphabetical order.

Adams County School District #12, Northglenn, Colorado. Assorted Materials.

Alberta School District, Alberta, Canada. Assorted Materials

Avery, Michael, Brian Auvine, Barbara Streibel, Lonnie Weiss, Building United Judgment: A Handbook for Consensus

Decision-Making (Madison, Wisconsin: The Center for Conflict Resolution, 1989).

Block, Peter The Empowered Manager (San Francisco, CA: Jossey-Bass, 1988).

Bradford, Leland P., Making Meetings Work (San Diego, CA: University Associates, 1976).

California State Department of Education, Program Evaluation Guide, Office of Program Evaluation and Research, 1977.

Dade County School District, Miami, Florida. Assorted Materials.

Daniels, William R., Group Power: A Manager's Guide to Using Meetings (San Diego, CA: University Associates, 1986).

Dimock, Hedley G., Groups: Leadership and Group Development (San Diego, CA: University Associates, 1989).

Doyle, Michael and David Straus, How To Make Meetings Work (New York: Playboy Paperbacks- 1976)

Greenhalgh, John School-Site Budgeting (Lanham, M.D.: University Press of America, 1984).

Hammond School District, Hammond, Indiana. Assorted Materials.

Lewis, James Jr., Implementing School-Based Management...by Empowering Teachers (Westbury, New York: J.L. Wilkerson Publishing Company, 1989).

Lewis, James Jr., Long-Range and Short-Range Planning for Educational Leaders (Boston, MA: Allyn and Bacon) 1983.

Lewis, James Jr., Re-creating Our Schools for the 21st Century (Westbury, N.Y.: J.L. Wilkerson Publishing Company, 1988).

Manning, George and Kent Curtis Group Strength (Cincinnatti, OH: South-Western Publishing Company, 1988).

Marburger, Carl L., One School At A Time (Columbia, MD: The National Committee for Citizens in Education, 1988).

Mink, Oscar G., James M. Shultz, Barbara r., Mink 1z (, doping and Making Open Organizations (Austin, 1X: Learning Concepts, 1979).

Peters, Tom Thriving on Chaos (New York: Random House, 1988).

Reddy, W. Brendan with Kaleel Jamison, Team-Building (San Francisco, CA: University Associates, 1988).

This, Leslie E., The Small Meeting Planner, (Houston, TX: Gulf Publishing Company, 1972).

Zaltman, Gerald, David Floreo and Linda Sikorski Dynamic Educational Change (New York: The Free Press, 1977).

Bibliography

"Annual School-Based Program Budget," 1982-1983 *Planning and Budgeting for Educational Management*, Duval County Schools, Jacksonville, Florida: 1982.

AFT Position Paper. Subject: *School Based Budgeting*, Albuquerque Federation of Teachers.

Auvine, Brian, Betsy Densmore, Mary Extron, Scott Paole, and Michel Shanklin. *A Manual for Group Facilitators* (Madison, Wisconsin: The Center for Conflict Resolution, 1978).

Avery, Michael, Brian Auvtne, Barbara Steibel, and Connie Weiss, *Building United Judgment: A Handbook for Consensus Decision Making.* (Madison, Wisconsin: The Center for Conflict Resolution 1981).

Barron, Melanie, acting Project Director for Superintendent's Work Group on School Based Management. *School Based Management; Recommendations to: Robert R. Spillane, Superintendent, Boston Public Schools.* 17 May, 1982.

Barth, Roland. *Run School Run*. Cambridge, Ma.: Harvard University Press, 1980.

Bartov, Glen, *Decisions by Consensus* (Chicago: Progressive Publisher, 1978).

Block, Peter, *The Empowered Manager* (San Francisco, CA: Jossey-Bass, 1988).

Bradford, Leland P., *Making Meetings Work* (San Diego, CA: University Associates, 1976).

Burack, E.H., and F. Torda. *The Manager's Guide to Change.* Lake Forest, Illinois: Brace-Park Press, 1979.

Burleson, Clyde W., *Effective Meetings*, (New York, N.T.: John Wiley & Sons Co., 1990).

Burton, Nancy, et al. *School-Based Planning Manual*. Seattle Public Schools, Department of Planning, Research and Evaluation. Seattle, Washington: 1982.

Caldwell, Brian J. *Implementation of Decentralized School Budgeting*. Bethesda, Md.: ERIC Document Reproduction Services, ED 161 148, 1978.

Caldwell, Brian J., and Jim M. Spinks, *The Self-Managing School*. Falmer Press, New York: 1988.

California State Department of Education, *Program Evaluation Guide*, (Office of Program Evaluation and Research, 1977). Campbell, Patricia 8. School-Based Management Project: School Site Council Assessment Report. Unpublished report to the Boston School Department by Campell-Kibler Associates, Groton, MA, 1985.

Caputo, Edward M. *Principal or Wizard: Brains + Heart + Courage = Five Principles of School Based Management*. Bethesda, Md.: ERIC Document Reproduction Service, ED 188 344, 1980.

Carnegie Forum on Education and the Economy. *A Nation Prepared: Teachers for the 21st Century*. The Report of the Task Force on Teaching as a Profession. New York: Carnegie Corporation, 1986.

Casner-Lotto, Jill. "Expanding the Teacher's Role: Hammond's School Improvement Process," *American Educator*, January 1988, pp. 349-353.

Clark, Terry. *Introducing School Site Management: A Framework for Citizen Involvement*. Schoolwatch, Inc. Trenton, New Jersey: 1979.

Clear, Delbert K. "Decentralization: Issues and Cornments." *The Clearing House 44* (January, 1970): 259-267.

Clune, William H., and Paula White "School-Based Management: Institutional Variation, Implementation, and Issues for Further Research." Report of the Center for Policy Research in Education, Rutgers, The State University of New Jersey, New Brunswick, New Jersey: 1988.

Collegiality, Participative Decision-Making, and The Collaborative School. ERIC Clearinghouse on Educational Management,

University of Oregon Eugene, Oregon: 1988.

Cowsill, Janice. *School-Based Management*: An Overview. Paper commissioned by Rhode Island Educational Leader ship Academy, Cranston, Rhode Island: 1987.

Cross, Ray. 'The Administrative Team or Decentralization?" *National Elementary Principal* 54 (December 1974) 8S82.

Cunningham, Paul H. *Decentralized Budget Making the Management Team Work*. Bethesda, MD.: ERIC Document Reproduction Service, ED 154499, 1978.

Cunningham, Paul H. *Decentralized Budgeting Making the Management Team Work*. Paper presented at the annual meeting of the National School Boards Association, Anaheim, California: 1978.

Cummings, T.G. "Self-Regulating Workgroups: A Socio-Technical Synthesis." *Academy of Management* Review, 1978,3, 625-633.

Dade County Public Schools. *School-Based Management/Shared Decision-Making A Historical Perspective*, October 1987, Miami, Florida.

Daniels, William R., *Group Power: A Manager's Guide to Using Meetings* (San Diego, CA: University Associates, 1986).

David, Jane L and Susan M. Peterson. "Can Schools Reform Themselves?" *A Study of School-Based Improvement Programs* Mimeographed, Bay Area Research Group, Palo Alto, Calif., 1984.

Deane, Edward. "Toward School-Based Management: A Case Study." *Kappa Delta Pi Record* 12 (December 1975) 52-54.

Decker, Erwin A. and others. *Site Management. An Analysis of the Concepts and Fundamental Operational Components Associated with the Delegation of Decision-Making Authority andControl of Resources to the School-Site Level in the California Public School System*. Bethesda, Md.: ERIC Document Reproduction Service, ED 150 736, 1977.

Deal, Terrence E. and Allan A. Kennedy, *Corporate Cultures:The Rites and Rituals of Corporate Life* (Reading, Mass.: Addison-Wesley Publishing Co., 1982).

Delbecq, Andre L., Andrew Van de Ven, and David H. Gustafson, Group Techniques for Program Planing: *A Guide to Nominal Group and Delphi Processes*, (Glenview, Il.: Scott Foresman and Co., 1975).

Dimock, Hedley G., *Groups: Leadership and Group Development* (San Diego, CA: University Associates, 1989).

Doherty, Victor W. *Framework of Organization and Policy for Evaluation in a Decentralized School District*. Bethesda, Md.: ERIC Document Reproduction Service, ED 109 243, 1975.

Duncan, D.J. and J.W. Peach, J.W. "School-BasedBudgeting Implications for the Principal." *Education Canada*-17 (Fall 1977): 39-41.

Doyle, Michael and David Straus, *How To Make Meetings Work* (New York: Playboy Paperbacks, 1976).

Fischer, Nicholas. *School-Based Management*. Monroe County Superintendent's Office, Key West, Florida, 1982.

Foster, Badi, Nicholas A. Fischer and Karen K. Fischer. *Summary Report: School Site Lump Sum Budgeting*. N.I.E. Contract 400-76 0058. Monroe County, Florida, 1978.

Fowler, Charles W. "School-Site Budgeting and Why it Could Be The Answer to Your Problems." *Executive Educator*. Preniier Issue (October 1978): 37~39.

Greenhalgh, John. *School Site Budgeting: Decentralized School Management*. University Press of America, Lanham, Maryland: 1984.

Guthrie, James W. Creating Efficient Schools: flee Wonder Is They Work At All," in *The Financing of Quality Education*, Urban League of Rochester, New York: 1977.

Guthrie, James W. 'School-Based Management. The Next Needed Education Reform." *Phi Delta Kappa*, December 1986: 305-309.

Hansen, Barbara J., and Carl L. Marburger, *School Based Improvement: A Manual for District Leaders* (National Committee for Citizens in Education, Columbia, Maryland: 1988).

Hansen, Barbara J. *School Transformation. A Trust Process*. Unpublished dissertation, International College, 1983.

Henriquez, Armando J. School-Based Management." Monroe County Superintendent's Office, Key West, Florida, 1978.

Honeyman, David S. and Rich Jensen School-Site Budgeting," *School Business Affairs*, February, 1988, pp. 12-14.

Ingram, Ruben L. "The Principal: Instructional Leader, Site Manager." *Educational Executive* 8 (May 1979): 23-25.

Ishikawa, Kaoru, *Guide to Quality Control*, (Asian Productivity Organization, 1980).

Bibliography

Ivory, Charles M. and James H. Mundy *School Site Councils: A Forum for Educational Leadership*. Unpublished paper, undated.

Kanter, Rosabeth. *The Change Master - Innovation and Entrepreneurship in the American Corporation*. New York: Knowles, Malcolm and Hulda. Introduction to Group Dynamics. Chicago: Association Press, 1972.

Keene, T. Wayne. School-Based Management Missing Link in Accountability?" *Education* 101 (Fall 198Q2:32-37.

Kennedy, Catherine A. "Converting to School-by-School Budgeting," *School Business Affairs*. October, 1984, pp. 4445.

Koeppe, Richard P. "A Report on Site-Based Management for the Cherry Creek Public Schools," (unpublished paper) Cherry Creek Colorado Public Schools, Cherry Creek Colorado: 1986.

Kirkpatrick, Donald L., *How to Plan and Conduct Productive Business Meetings*, (New York, N.Y.: AMACQM, 19872-

Knowles, Malcolm and Hulda, *Introduction to Group Dynamics* (Chicago: Association Press, 1972).

Levin, Henry M. *Finance and Governance Implications of School-Based Decisions*. Draft version prepared for the Work in America Institute, Inc., Scarsdale, New York: 1987.

Lewis, James Jr., *Implementing School-Based Management...by Empowering Teachers* (Westbury, New York: J.L. Wilkerson Publishing Company, 1989).

Lewis, James Jr., *Long-Range and Short-Range Planning for Educational Leaders* (Boston, MA: Allyn and Bacon) 1983.

Lewis, James Jr., *excellent Organizations* (Westbury, New York: J.L. Wilkerson Publishing Company, 1989).

Lewis, James Jr., *Achieving Excellence in Our Schools...by Taking Lessons from America's Best-Run Companies*, (Westbury, New York: J.L. Wilkerson Publishing Company, 1989).

Lewis, James Jr., *The Master Guide - Training and Certifying School-Based Management Facilitators*, (Westbury, New York: J.L. Wilkerson Publishing Company, 1989).

Lindelow, John. "School-Based Management." In Smith, Stuart C., JoAnn Mazzarella, Philip K. Piele, Eds. *School Leadership: Handbook for Survival*. Eugene, Oregon: University of Oregon, ERIC Clearinghouse on Educational Management, 1981.

Longstreth, James. *School-Based Management and Budgeting Systems: A Guide for Effective Implementation*. National Urban Coalition, Washington, DC: 1979.

Malen, Betty and Rodney T. Ogawa. *The Implementation of the Salt Lake City School District's Shared Governance Policy: A Study of School-Site Councils*. EDRS: 1985.

Marburger, Carl L., *One School At A Time* (The National Committee For Citizens in Education, Columbia, Maryland: 1985).

Marburger, Carl. *What is School Based Management?* National Committee for Citizens in Education. Columbia, Maryland: 1981.

Nash, Miebail, *Making People Productive*, (San Francisco, CA.,: Jossey-Bass Publishers, 1985).

Nichols, J. Brian. 'The Budget Process: A Practical Guide for Its Development," *Catalyst for Change*. Fall 1983, pp. 11-13.

Obermeyer, Gary, "A Report on the Status of School-Based Decision-Making," Draft version prepared for the National Education Association, Mastery-In-Learning Project, Washington, D.C., 1987.

Parker, Barbara. "School-Based Management: Improve Education by Giving Parents, Principals More Control of Your Schools." *American School Board Journal* 166 (July 1979): 2S21,24.

Peters, Tom, *Thriving on Chaos* (New York: Random House, 19881.

Pierce, Lawrence C. *School-Based Management*. Eugene: Oregon School Study Council Bulletin 23, 1980.

Pierce, Lawrence C School Based Management. Unpublished paper prepared for the National Committee for Citizens in Education, July 1978.

Pierce, Lawrence C. "School Site Management." Occasional Paper of the Aspen Institute for Humanistic Studies Program in Education for a Changing Society, Cambridge, Massachusetts: 1977.

"Restructuring Schools Through School-Site Management," in *To Improve Education in Rhode Island By The Year 1991: Recommendations of Governor Edward D. DiPrete's 1991 Task Force*. State of Rhode Island and Providence Plantations, Providence, Rhode Island: August, 1987, pp. 12-13.

Reddy, W. Brendan with Kaleel Jamison, *Team-Building* (San Francisco, CA: University Associates, 1988).

Schneider, Gail Thierbach. "Teacher Involvement in Decision-Making: Zones of Acceptance, Decision Conditions, and Job Satisfaction. *Journal of Research and Development in Education* Volume 18, Number 1, Fall, 1984.

School-Based Management and Budgeting Systems: A Guide for Effective Implementation. National Urban Coalition, Washington, DC: 1979.

"School-Based Management Briefing Papers," (unpublished papers) Fairfax County Public Schools Office of Research and Evaluation, Fairfax County Public Schools, Virginia: September, 1986.

South, Oron. *Outline of Presentation for Broward County.* Monroe County Superintendent's Office, Key West, Florida, August 1978.

Stanton, Jim and Ross Zerchykov *Overcoming Barriers to School Council Effectiveness.* Institute for Responsive Education, Boston University, Boston, MA: 1979.

This, Leslie E., *She Small Meeting Planner*, Houston, IX: Gulf Publishing Company, 1972).

Thomas, Donald. *Decentralization as a Management Tool.* Bethesda, Md.: ERIC Document Reproduction Service, ED 057 482, 1971.

Weischadle, David E. "School-Based Management and the Principal." *The Clearing House* 54 (October 1980): 53-55.

INDEX

Absenteeism, 37, 63, 149, 210-211, 234
Action stations instead of offices, 165
Actualized spirit, 143
Adaptation stage, 38, 49
Administration, central, 40, 61, 86, 98-100, 102, 108, 202, 208-209, 211, 236, 311
Albrecht, Karl, 246-247
American Association for Supervision and Curriculum Development (ASCD), 314
Analysis: causes-andeffect, ix, 242, 291; force-field, ix, 33, 95-96, 212, 263, 275, 290-291
Arguing, 159
Art of Japanese Management, 56
Assessment of total quality, 239
Audio-visual aids, 86, 122, 242-243, 263, 277

Bellman, Geoffrey M., 45
Benchmark design for emulation, 205, 214
Benchmarking for Quality Improvement, 214
Block, Peter, 82
Blocking a consensus, 175, 180, 190
Bloom, Benjamin, 314
Board of education, 61, 89, 220, 236, 306
Brainstorming, ix, 82-83, 104, 107, 199, 212, 223, 263, 275, 280, 290-292

Budgets, 46, 48, 61, 122-123, 212-213, 222, 226, 235, 246, 254, 259-260, 264

Carlzon, Jan, 248
Cause-and-effect diagram (fish bone diagram), 263, 271-272, 275, 290, 292
Champions in schools, 21, 33, 115, 118, 131, 145, 149, 282
Changing times and schools, 3-5, 9, 15, 19-20, 22, 31-50, 51, 53-54, 57, 118, 231, 302, 309. *See also* Resistance to change
Classroom practices, 310
Coaching in skills, 35
Commitment to learning, 6-7, 11-12
Communication, 36, 40-45, 49, 54, 58-60, 62, 75, 80, 99, 109, 127, 133, 140, 143, 146-147, 209, 215, 230, 239, 242-244, 251, 265, 273, 294, 306, 309, 316; nonverbal, 158
Communities, viii, 16, 32, 36, 46-47, 69-70, 72, 78, 82, 85-88, 102, 107, 127, 202, 206, 240, 259, 262, 281, 306-307, 310, 314-315
Comparison of egalitarian and inegalitarian schools, 169-170
Competition, 276-277
Compromise, 175
Conference, annual, 266
Conflict resolution, ix, 37, 59, 175, 226

Connectedness (love and belonging), 304
Connecting (meeting), 156-157, 161
Consensus, ix, 19, 21, 46-47, 59, 73, 75, 99, 101, 103-104, 133, 146, 163, 168, 173-193, 200, 209, 215, 225, 231, 234, 263, 273, 278-279; by committee, 187-188, 191; decisions with an exception, 187-188, 190-191; process, 177-180, 221, 226; definition, 174, 190, 305
Constitution (purposes and shared values of the school district), 25
Consultants, 29, 39, 60, 73, 101, 123, 127, 144, 160, 186, 203-204, 212, 235, 239, 257, 261, 263, 267
Continuity and progress of school, 120, 196, 215, 234, 236, 298
Control charts, 242
Cooperation, 174, 176, 190, 271, 276-277, 294
Corporate Culture, 56
Cost of emulation, 200-201, 210
Covey, Steven, 35
Creating Excellence, 79
Creativity, 12, 19, 47, 69, 125, 146, 198, 218, 231, 306
Criticism of ideas in consensus, 190
Crosby, Philip B., 270-271, 279
Curriculum, 81, 83; development, 61, 74; guide, 221
Custodian, 219
Customer-provider interface, 235
Cycles of service, 233, 238, 240, 251

Dade County School District, Florida, 257

Decision-making, ix, 42, 47, 55, 70, 74, 87, 93, 98-99, 117, 133, 136, 146, 163, 165-166, 185, 218, 220-221, 231-232, 241, 256, 259, 267
Delphi technique, 263
Deming, W. Edwards, 4, 270-271, 279, 281-282; Triangle of Interaction, 269, 289-290, 293-294
Denial stage in change, 37, 49
Design teams, ix, 38-39, 50, 74, 82, 90-91, 94, 196, 204, 208-209, 212-215, 239-240, 251, 258, 311- 313, 315
Discussion in consensus, 177
Drucker, Peter, 85

Eating lunch, 23-24, 165. *See also* Socializing
Education process analysis, 244
Egalitarianism, definition, 164-165
Empathy of principals, 41, 49, 158
Empowerment. *See* Teachers, empowerment of
Empowerment interventions, 145-148
Equality: for equal distribution to teachers, 167-168, 170; for teachers' meaningful work, 167, 170; for teachers to satisfy basic needs, 166-167, 170; of power for teachers, 168, 170; of treatment of teachers, 165, 170; of opportunity of teachers, 166, 170
Evaluation, 84; of performance, 127; of principals, 10-14, 29; of program, 265-266; of student learning, 277; of teachers, 22, 46, 63, 84; of the empowerment program, 145

Volume 1—Index

Excellence in education, 54, 58

Facilitation descriptions of teachers' serious concerns, 159, 161
Facilities for teachers, 167
Favoritism, 17
Fear, 238, 240, 271, 275, 291, 294; of loss of power or status, 34, 41, 45-46, 146. *See also* Lack of trust
Feedback, 42, 63, 95, 122, 147, 209, 246, 278
Filley's consensus model, 181-182, 190
Flexibility, 6, 12, 45, 52, 58, 69, 147
Flip chart, 105, 273, 292
Florl, David, 39
Flow chart, lx, 242, 244, 288, 292
Follow-through on teachers' concerns, 159, 161
Freedom with structure in participative management, 227, 231
Funds, shortage of, 36

Gant chart, 212-213
Gaps in emulation, 205, 215
Garfield High School, Los Angeles, 201, 208
Glasser, William, 301, 304
Goals and objectives, 127, 209-210, 215, 219-220, 222, 231, 238, 242, 251, 256, 304. *See also* Monitoring the attainment of objectives
Gordon, 144
Governments in which schools operate, 72
Grades (rankings), 271, 294
Grants, 48

Havelock, 36

Hay Report: The State of Human Resources In American Industry, 169
Heroes. *See* Champions
Hewlett-Packard, 156
Hickman, Craig R., 79
Hicks, Theresa May, 271
Hiring: more minority and women teachers, 166; new teachers, 61, 109, 247, 250
Histograms, 242, 278, 291
Homework, 250, 291
Human resource department, x, 128

Ideological incompatibility, 27
Imagery of vision, 7, 13, 92, 95; definition, 92
Impartiality with teachers, 166
In Search of Excellence, 56, 89
Incubation period of consensus, 175
Individual competition hampering consensus, 186, 190
Information, 42, 60, 81, 139, 146, 178, 180, 222, 225, 248; precise, 36; toteachers, 141. *See also* Sharing information
Instructional program, 70, 81, 309
Instructional strategies, 61
Interdependence, 140, 146, 148

Job description, 52, 146; security, 46-47
Johnson City Central School District, Johnson City, New York, 114, 297-298, 301-303, 305, 311, 314
Juran, Joseph M., 270-271, 279

Key visionary areas, 82-85
Kotter, 33

Lack of trust, 34, 49
Leadership, 3-4, 7, 10, 12, 42, 45, 54, 86, 127, 142, 230, 237
Leavitt, Howard J., 89
Lee, 144
Librarians, 88, 202
Lippitt, 144
Listening: to parents, 104; to teachers, 34, 49, 55, 147, 157, 161

Maccoby, Michael, 16
Malcolm Baldrige National Quality Award, 236, 239, 243-244, 276, 280, 282
Management, people-sensitive, 27-28; visible (by wandering around), ix, 21, 23-24, 29, 46, 55, 60, 86, 155-162
Management Model, 306,309
Manipulation, 19, 29
Meetings and workshops on school vision, 80
Mentoring/Supporting, 142
Mission statement, 273, 291. *See also* School mission
Mistakes used as learning opportunities, 6, 12, 21, 146
Moments of truth, 233, 238, 247-249, 251; definition, 248
Monitoring the attainment of objectives, 220
Morale, 116

Network, cultural, 115, 131, 146
Networking, 310
Newsletters, 86, 109, 119, 278, 381
Nominal group process, ix, 82-83, 102, 104, 107, 182, 223, 263, 290, 292
Nonperformance work, 37

Open-door policy, 24, 109, 146

Optimization: definition, 283
Orientation, 149, 166
Ouchi, William, 221
Outcomes-based education, 297-316; definition, 298-299
Outcomes-Driven Development Model, The 302
Overseeing, 18-19, 29

PTA, 58, 87
Panel consensus, 181-183, 190
Parades, 86
Parents, 47-48, 54, 69, 74, 86, 104, 110-111, 118, 131, 210-211, 235, 240, 270, 274, 276-277, 279-282, 288, 291,314-315
Pareto charts, 242, 275, 291
Parking spaces, not reserved, 165
Participation: consultative, 221; direct, 221
Participative management, 38, 42, 49, 93, 163, 217-232, 234; definition, 218-219
Pedometer, 162
Peer relationship, 127, 140, 149
People-sensitive orientation, 5-6, 11, 108
Performance standards, 42, 220, 230
Pert chart, 212-213
Peters, Tom, 89
Philosophy awareness questionnaire, 128-130
Pilot studies, 46, 254, 257, 262
Planning, 17-18, 29, 38, 41-42, 49-50, 55, 68, 78, 90, 94, 96, 106, 127-128, 156, 201, 211-213, 215, 220, 237-238, 253-254, 260
Power, 136-139, 184-187, 190, 231, 256
Prerogatives of management, 16, 29

Principal: as change agent, 8, 13, 20, 40, 77-80, 99, 113-116; as expert, 144; as responsible administrator, 114-118, 121-125, 127, 131, 138, 223, 226, 237; as social architect, 1, 5, 51-61; as strategic actor, 53, 57-59, 61-62, 78, 90, 94

Principal personal guarantee statement, 31, 46-49

Principals: authority-oriented, 28, 218; relations with students, 79, 280; relations with teachers, 5, 15-16, 19-20, 34, 41-43, 49, 52, 55, 59, 79, 100, 105, 107, 116, 155-161, 165-167, 171, 177-181, 226, 229, 231; traditional, 9, 15, 21-23, 28, 34, 51, 57, 136, 221, 230; transformational, viii, 3-10, 12, 15, 21-23, 25, 28, 42, 45-46, 49, 51-63, 67, 85, 97-98, 100-101, 142-144, 147, 152, 155-156, 163-164, 166-170, 195-198, 207, 218-219, 221, 226-228, 230-231, 254, 258-262, 266, 268, 269-270, 272, 275, 282-283, 288, 293, 293, 297-298, 305, 309, 311-313

Principals and teachers' union, 27. *See also* Unions of teachers

Proactive (long-range) administration, 17-18, 29, 150-151

Problem-solving, ix, 8, 13-14, 17, 20-21, 27, 59, 117, 137, 165-167, 220-222, 231, 256, 309

Problem-Solving Model, 306

Process observer, 47

Professional associations, 201-202

Profound Theory of Knowledge, 269, 271, 276, 279, 282-287, 293-294

Program strategy, 83-85; definition, 84

Promotion of teachers, 53

Providing (resources to teachers), 142

Psychological base, 309

Publicity, 37, 40, 85, 131, 266, 281

Quaker consensus model, 181, 190

Quality control circles, 228

Quality service measurement system, 244, 247, 251

Rambling, 160-161

Reactive (short-range) administration, 16-17. *See also* Proactive administration

Real-life situations taught, 299, 301-302

Recognition and rewards, 7, 11, 21, 24, 36, 43, 48-49, 60, 89, 109, 119, 139, 145-147, 167, 243, 246, 251, 256, 271, 281, 294

Research literature, 202, 308

Resistance to change, 31, 33-37, 43, 45, 49, 276

Resources, more available, 14S

Rites and rituals, 115, 131

Rogers, Carl, 158

Role modeling, 6, 11, 25, 49, 57, 79, 108-109, 119, 128, 131, 142-143, 146-147, 160

Rubin, 140

Run chart, ix, 207, 424, 291

Sabotage of change, 37

Scatter diagrams, 242

Schlesinger, 33

School administration, hard and soft sides, 51-53, 63

School administrators (other than principals), ix, 26, 69

School-based management, 253-268; annual report on, 266-267; coordinator for, 254-255, 257-268; council, 47-48, 84-85, 89, 258, 261-265; model for, 257-258
School culture, 52-53, 55-58, 61, 65, 68, 100, 108, 113-132, 146, 148; definition of, 56, 114
School district's culture, 116
School environment, egalitarian, ix, 114, 120, 131, 146, 148, 163-171, 230. *See also* Comparison of egalitarian and inegalitarian schools; Egalitarianism, defined
School mission, 67-75, 308; statement, 69-75, 94, 101
School philosophy, 21, 24-25, 65-75, 101, 114-114, 119-130, 132, 160, 218, 222, 231, 259, 308
School visitation, 203, 208, 264
Screening prospective teachers, 119-120
Security needs, 49; definition of, 46
Semantic differential voting consessus, 187-188, 190
Sensation needs, 49; definition of, 46
Service quality, 246-247
Shared values statement, approaches to writing, 102-108, 110-111, 115, 122, 127, 273-275, 294
Sharing information, 8, 13, 17, 21, 27-28, 34, 146, 149-151, 183-185, 198
Shewhart/Deming Plan-Do-Check-Act Cycle, 269, 271, 279, 281, 287-289, 291, 293-294
Sikorski, Linda, 39

Silva, Michael A., 79
Skills, thinking, 87-88
Slow-down, 37
Socializing, 5, 11, 24
Staff Development Model, A, 306
Stakeholders, 72, 116, 127, 160, 307, 310, 314-315; definition, 115
Steering committee for school-based management, 254-260, 262, 265-268
Storytelling about school vision, 91, 95
Stress workshops, 93
Structuring of schools, inner, 142
Student exit behaviors (desirable), 308
Students, 16, 36-37, 39, 47-48, 54, 56, 69-73, 78, 81-83, 86-89, 91-92, 95, 102, 105-108, 115, 118, 202, 204, 206, 208, 210-211, 233-235, 240, 247, 250, 256, 269-294, 298, 302, 207-308, 316; failures, 81
Stump speeches, 86-88
Success emulation, ix, 195-215, 241, 241, 244, 251, 301; definition, 196-197
Succession plan, 22, 52; for teachers, 167
Sufficient consensus, 187-188, 190
Superficial and second-level conversation, 158
Superintendents, x, 24-25, 27, 61, 80, 89, 94, 99-100, 136, 144, 155, 174, 208-209, 220, 226, 230, 237, 240, 254, 257, 260, 262, 265, 306, 310.
Sport staff, 202, 219 258
Symbols of school vision, 91, 95
Superintendents, x, 24-25, 27, 61, 80, 89, 94, 99-100, 136, 144, 155, 174, 208-209, 220, 226,

Volume 1—Index

230, 237, 240, 254, 257, 260, 262, 265, 306, 310
Support staff, 202, 219, 258
Symbols of school vision, 91, 95
System of Profound Theory of Knowledge, 269, 271, 276, 279, 282-287, 293-294

Tannenbaum, 143
Teachers, 16, 61, 84, 102, 107, 113-127, 131, 201-202, 219, 224-225, 235-236, 247, 251, 255-256, 260-261. *See also* Principals
Teachers' duty schedule, 137, 150
Teachers, empowerment of, ix-x, 9, 11, 17-18, 22, 33, 42-43, 52-53, 60-62, 69, 72, 93, 95, 100, 127-128, 133-154, 163-164, 168, 223-224, 237, 256j
Teachers, participation in transformation, vii-viii, 4, 19, 21-23, 32, 35, 39, 43-44, 47, 56, 58, 73-74, 88, 93, 98-99, 153, 228-229, 267, 269-273, 275, 278-282, 288-291, 293-295, 298, 306-307, 311-313
Teachers' personal and school goals, 23, 26, 28, 36, 44, 55, 137, 167
Team dynamics, ix, 19-20, 22, 33-36, 38-39, 52-53, 57, 59-60, 62-63, 70, 83-84, 86, 90-91, 93-95, 101, 106, 110, 117-119, 124-127, 138, 145, 150, 152, 174, 180, 182, 188, 207, 220, 223, 225-227, 230-231, 234, 239-241, 259, 273, 277-279, 281, 288, 292, 295. *See also* Design team
Theory: of systems, 282-283; of variation, 283-285; of knowledge, 285; of psychology, 286-287

Total Quality education, 38-39, 146, 173, 199, 233-252, 269-295, 298; models, 239, 251
Training and development, 6-7, 11, 20, 24-25, 35, 38-39, 46-48, 57, 59, 61, 84, 102, 105, 107, 109, 119, 121-126, 128, 132, 145-146, 166-167, 174, 204, 206, 210, 212-213, 220, 226, 231, 237-238, 251, 254, 257, 259, 262-264, 267, 279-280, 294, 301, 303, 309, 311-312, 316
"Training for Change Agents," 36
Traveling to see best-run schools, 7, 12, 29, 257, 264. *See also* School visitation
Tribus, Myron, 285
Trust, 27, 69, 146, 150, 153, 185-186, 190, 228-229, 231, 247, 256, 307. *See also* Lack of trust

Unanimity in consensus, 175
Unions of teachers, 25-27, 40, 69, 116, 231-232, 255-256, 259-261

Values, core, 6-7, 11-12, 16, 25, 40, 42, 44-46, 52-53, 55-58, 79, 81, 83, 89, 91, 94, 97-111, 120, 127, 131, 143, 146, 237, 251; definition of values and of shared values, 98
Vision, 7-8, 12-13, 25, 32, 42-43, 46, 49, 52, 62, 68, 77-96, 108, 118, 122, 146, 148, 150-151, 164, 237, 251, 273; definition of, 53; statement, 273-274, 294

WIIFM(What's In It For Me?), 36
Wages and benefits, 166, 169

Waterman, Robert, 89
Win-win basis for consensus,
    176, 184, 189-190, 292-293

Zalenik, Abraham, 79
Zaltman, Gerald, 39